T0282920

Advance Praise for *Passion Struck*

"It's easier than ever to become complacent or stuck, but John Miles reminds us that we can lead and contribute with intention if we choose."

—Seth Godin, *New York Times* bestselling
author of *The Song of Significance*

"This book will ignite a fire in your belly! If you're looking to overcome life's obstacles, embrace your passion, and cultivate a profound sense of purpose in your everyday life—there's no better teacher than John."

—Kris Carr, *New York Times* bestselling author,
wellness activist, and cancer thriver

"Passion Struck is a transformative book that empowers individuals to unlock their purpose, find fulfillment, and create the life they've always desired. John R. Miles creates the ultimate guide that combines self-discovery, understanding psychology, and taking responsibility for personal growth. Drawing on his own experiences and insights from prominent authorities, John inspires readers to embark on their unique journey of becoming their greatest selves. *Passion Struck* is a must-read for anyone seeking to unleash their potential and live a life filled with passion, purpose, and authenticity."

—Dr. Marshall Goldsmith, Thinkers50 #1
executive coach and *New York Times* bestselling
author of *The Earned Life*, *Triggers*, and *What
Got You Here Won't Get You There*

"In this pioneering book, John R. Miles shows anyone striving to succeed—be it parents, students, educators, athletes, or business people—that the secret to living life to its fullest is not dictated by talent but a special blend of passion, resilience, and intentionality that he calls 'Passion Struck.'"

–Captain Christopher "Chris" Cassidy, retired NASA astronaut, and United States Navy SEAL; president and CEO of the National Medal of Honor Museum Foundation

"In a time when depression, hopelessness, and loneliness are prevalent, becoming Passion Struck is an even more crucial goal. John R. Miles seamlessly integrates over seven years of research, demonstrating that you can get closer to your self-realization by choosing growth through genuine intentionality."

–Scott Barry Kaufman, Ph.D., bestselling author of *Transcend* and *Choose Growth*, host of *The Psychology Podcast*

"When it comes to being passion struck, John Miles leads from the front. He understands that passion fuels all great success—and this outstanding book will help you find your passion and align with it to fulfill your most audacious dreams. With his formula, you will be unbeatable!"

–Mark Divine, *New York Times* bestselling author, retired Navy SEAL, host of *The Mark Divine Show*, speaker, and entrepreneur

"Living a life that aligns with your values is a precious gift. But whether it's our work or our relationships, so many of us are on cruise control...fuzzy on our values, unsure of our purpose, dismissive of our talents. That's why I love what John's done in *Passion Struck*: these pages meet you exactly where you're at, with heartfelt motivation and clear, concrete steps to actualize your purpose."

–Dr. Emily Morse, host of *Sex with Emily*
and bestselling author of *Smart Sex*

"We desperately need leaders with passion, resilience, intentionality, and moral character to tackle the complex global problems requiring systems change. In his groundbreaking book, John R. Miles lays out a framework for self-realization and the path to creating a new generation of creative catalysts that can collectively impact the world for the better."

–Jeffrey C. Walker, author of *The Generosity
Network*, former vice chairman of JPMorgan
Chase, managing partner of JPMorgan
Partners, and chairman of New Profit

"In an age focused on materialism and self-obsession, Miles boldly addresses the path to unlocking our deepest, most unanswered needs: purpose, passion, perspective, resilience, meaning, and self-realization. Passion Struck is a must-read for anyone striving to live life to the fullest and with no regrets."

–Dawna Stone, bestselling author, winner
of NBC's *The Apprentice: Martha Stewart*,
health coach, speaker, and entrepreneur

"We are living in the most unprecedented time of modern history where there is so much nihilism, fear, distrust and anger. John's dedication and passion to addressing this existential crisis in our society is a key elixir in finding our purpose in the midst of so much suffering."

–Dr. Jay Lombard, D.O., neurologist
and author of *The Mind of God*

"John Miles shines a bright, exquisitely researched light on the mindset required to break free of perceived limitations and take a life-changing leap forward. On top of that, he'll show you how keep that winning momentum going—no matter what gets in your way. *Passion Struck* is a tour-de-force of practical, groundbreaking guidance for unlocking your true potential."

–Steven Konkoly, *Wall Street Journal* and #1 Amazon bestselling author of more than twenty books including *Deep Sleep, The Jakarta Pandemic, Hot Zone, The Rescue*, and *Fractured State*

"If you want to reach your full potential and intentionally create the life of your dreams, read this book. It will take you there."

–Dara Kurtz, bestselling author of *I Am My Mother's Daughter* and creator of crazyperfectlife.com

"John R. Miles has gifted humanity with an evidenced-based framework to IGNITE passion, AMPLIFY Performance, and UNLEASH Creativity to create and to be the difference we want to see in the world. Let this masterpiece serve as a blueprint to support you on your unique and beautiful path."

–Andrew Marr, bestselling author of *Tales From the Blast Factory*, chairman of Warrior Angels Foundation, and retired Green Beret

"In these fast-moving, often tumultuous times, wise and effective leadership is critical. John R. Miles's *Passion Struck* provides a clear view into how legendary leaders achieve overwhelming success. This is required reading for today's leaders looking to achieve elite performance and future leaders entering the arena who are looking at the foundational steps to take."

–Nir Bashan, author of *The Creator Mindset*

"A practical guide to overcoming apathy and discontentment, John R. Miles has distilled the important lessons of how to live intentionally and dance through life with no regrets."

–Hilary Billings, CEO and cofounder of Attentioneers, Miss Nevada United States 2013

PASSION STRUCK

TWELVE POWERFUL PRINCIPLES TO UNLOCK YOUR PURPOSE AND IGNITE YOUR MOST INTENTIONAL LIFE

JOHN R. MILES

A POST HILL PRESS BOOK
ISBN: 979-8-88845-140-3
ISBN (eBook): 979-8-88845-141-0

Passion Struck:
Twelve Powerful Principles to Unlock Your Purpose
and Ignite Your Most Intentional Life
© 2024 by John R. Miles
All Rights Reserved

Cover design by Farrukh Bala

Post Hill Press
New York • Nashville
posthillpress.com

Published in the United States of America
1 2 3 4 5 6 7 8 9 10

CONTENTS

**Part 3: The Most Important Piece of the
Puzzle—The Psychology of Progress**

MESSAGE FROM THE
AUTHOR + DEDICATION

For Josh and Olivia.

I am eternally grateful that this book is in your hands. This book's words culminate a significant portion of my life and career experience. I hope it serves you and others who read it by helping you to express your unique talents, grit, and gifts and to transform your creativity and service to the world in a way that brings you fulfillment.

Passion Struck is based on concepts and methods that I've discovered, implemented, and taught with extraordinary success for more than thirty years. I wrote it to train the next generation of leaders how to deploy their passion and achieve peak performance regardless of their pursuit.

I've given my all to writing this book for you. And I greatly thank all the people worldwide who have inspired me over the course of my career, including the passion-struck leaders who allowed me to interview them during the book's creation.

And, so, with a whole heart, I humbly dedicate this book to you, my two children, and the reader. The world needs more trailblazers who find their calling, pursue it passionately, and have a positive impact on the world. Why wait when you have it in you to make a choice, work hard every day, step into your sharp edges, and do something every day that scares you and promotes self-realization? I hope you choose to start today.

With love + respect,

John R. Miles

A NOTE TO THE READER

Passion Struck is a framework for changing your life, and within the pages of this book, you hold the power to embark on a remarkable transformation. Trust in the process, embrace your unique journey, and let *Passion Struck* be your trusted companion as you unlock the extraordinary potential within you. Together, let us unleash your purpose, ignite your passion, and create an intentional life that truly fulfills you.

To support you on this exhilarating path, I invite you to explore my blog at www.johnrmiles.com or https://medium.com/@JohnRMiles. There, you'll find thought-provoking posts filled with insights tailored to help you navigate the challenges and triumphs of intentional living. For more tools and resources to perfect your passion struck journey, visit https://passionstruck.com/.

Additionally, don't miss my weekly top-rated podcast, *Passion Struck with John R. Miles*, where I delve deeper into the principles and practices that will empower you on your quest. Throughout this journey, you'll encounter QR codes highlighting key insights and sharing additional resources to enrich your experience.

In this book, we go beyond universal principles and academic studies—we tap into the immense wisdom found in personal experiences. I'll share inspiring stories from remarkable individuals who have embraced the passion-struck life, serving as beacons of inspiration to guide you as you chart your own unique path toward fulfillment.

No matter when you read this or where you stand in your life, know that you are in the right place to make a profound choice—to be passion struck. You have every right to shine, and with *Passion Struck* as your guide, you'll unleash the brilliance within you.

FOREWORD

Imagine a world where most people wake up each day driven, grounded in their values, and content with their careers, relationships, and well-being. Sadly, that's not the reality we face. Right now, our world grapples with an existential crisis as countless individuals worldwide question the very meaning and significance of their lives.

Many of us tie our self-worth to our achievements; you might be familiar with this struggle. I certainly am. Escaping the comfort zone of mediocrity is a monumental challenge. I've heard from people who seem to have it all—thriving careers, stable incomes, loving families—yet they can't shake that sense of disappointment or emptiness. They ache for something more—a profound meaning that's eluding them.

Can you relate? Let me be clear—the good life isn't bad. Many would trade places in a heartbeat. But here's the question: Is this the life you truly want? Is this the story you want to tell your future self?

These are the tough questions high achievers ask, and if you're one of them, I want you in on this conversation. Perhaps you're already chasing your dreams, living large. You've cultivated a deliberate mindset, but you know there's no "peak." You crave that extra edge, exploring ways to magnify the impact of your choices.

Whether you're stuck, struggling, feeling unfulfilled despite the "good" life, or poised to surpass your current level, you're in the right place. All it takes is the intentional choice to change.

Change tends to scare us instinctively. I often say that the fear of success and failure are two facets of the same underlying fear—the fear of change itself. To truly embrace transformation, you must embrace the discomfort and take every necessary step to make that change happen.

But what awaits on the other side? A life brimming with fulfillment, serving humanity, and achieving your truest potential. Yet, this journey is incredibly challenging. When we think of change, we often focus on the sacrifices, not the gains. We must envision the potential beyond that crossroads.

The images we craft in our minds wield tremendous power. It wasn't my first encounter with the show when I stepped onto Shark Tank as a guest shark. I had already visualized myself as a shark for years before it manifested in reality.

I've consistently advocated pushing forward with a bold vision, steadfast commitment, confident courage, and unwavering honesty. So, when John shared his aspiration to help people create the most intentional life possible, I was hooked.

This book is centered on discovering your core purpose and passion and then taking intentional action toward achieving them. In my life, I steer by the principle of "Burn the Boats," a magnetic force guiding me through life's intricate paths. I intentionally gravitate towards those who share these principles, surrounding myself with kindred spirits. When I met John and delved into his book, I immediately sensed that we were united in our mission of empowering individuals to seize their fullest potential, radiating positive transformation throughout the world.

Every day, I see people achieving remarkable feats. What sets them apart? Their courage to chase their dreams and change lives. Through John's book, you'll learn how to apply this mindset to build a life and career driven by purpose, resilience, and deliberate action rather than fear.

This isn't just about behavior change. It's about self-realization. Choosing the unknown. Finding meaning. Becoming your best self, intentionally.

While many books explore finding your purpose or passion, few guide you in turning it into action. This gap matters because acting on your passion is the most crucial part of becoming Passion Struck.

Being brave is tough. Fear stalls us. Imagine acting despite it. What change could that bring?

The good news is that intentionality is like a muscle that grows stronger the more you use it. *Passion Struck* not only teaches you how to exercise intentionality, but it also provides guidance on taking small, boundary-pushing actions to expand your zone of optimal anxiety. With each action, you'll feel less fear and more confidence.

John reminds us that the greatest antidote to many of life's problems isn't achievement. It's taking action. If you desire a limitless life but don't know how to take "extraordinary" action or the steps to lead you there, this book is for you.

And that's an idea worth sharing.

Be Passion Struck, and inspire on!

Matt Higgins

PREFACE

PREFACE

Are you happy with your life? In other words, are you living what you would describe as a fulfilling and satisfactory existence?

This is a simple question that often receives an instinctive answer: "Yes!"

But I urge you to dig a little deeper and be honest with yourself.

I lived what I once thought was a great life, and it most certainly was great on the surface. By all societal standards, I had enjoyed an incredibly successful career. I had achieved my professional goals of becoming a multi-industry CEO, making it to the Fortune 500 C-Suite, a practice leader in a Big Four consulting firm, and a decorated Naval officer. I had earned many awards and recognitions that most would die to have on their resume. And yet, something was missing.

As much as it seemed that things were perfect, I was, in fact, living life on autopilot. I was like a pinball and directionless. I didn't love what I was doing. I felt like I was living someone else's life instead of the one that God had intended for me.

I had taken the path of what I look back on as a portfolio career, where I was doing multiple things and rising the professional ladder, in jobs that really didn't inspire me and weren't my calling. I hid behind the mask of pretense, afraid to confront the stuck points that engulfed my self-identity and restricted my true potential. I was making great money and had all the tangible things life could offer, but I felt lonely, hopeless, bored, indifferent, and lost.

Why? Because I valued the material and vain things of life, which include money, prestige, and recognition that society gravitates towards, above the crucial aspects that genuinely matter: family, relationships, passion, convictions, values, health, love, and legacy. I was contributing to the fulfillment of other people's goals but wasn't pursuing my own dreams. For decades, I had gotten so captured in what I believed I had to do that I stopped listening to my heart.

And I am not alone.

As Henry David Thoreau famously said, "The mass of men lead lives of quiet desperation." He is right. Too many of us are willing to settle instead of intentionally pursuing our dreams.

Do you ever feel like you are not you?

We lose ourselves, ultimately relinquish the joy in our lives, and become unhappy because of the hopelessness brought on by unintentional living. This lack of intentionality causes us to spend so much time faking our lives that we forget who we really are. It leads to burnout, fatigue, lassitude, and emotional exhaustion—all the things that I was feeling.

We define our self-identity by the vehicle we drive, the size of our house, the weight of our purse, our social circle, the media influencers we follow, and the clothing we wear. This revised materialistic version of the "dream life" is causing many to wear the shroud that I wore. It attempts to mask the reality of who we are and causes us to pursue self-centered ambitions instead of people-centered ones to help others.

Today, fewer people are taking the leap of faith to pursue their dreams. Individuals from the millennial and Generation Z cohorts, who should be leading the charge into a new era of entrepreneurship, are increasingly shunning the idea. The high levels of student and personal debt are often cited as lowering an individual's propensity to start a business. (Experts have pointed to the spiraling $1.5 trillion student debt[1] in the U.S. alone as a major factor.)

However, I believe that the true underlying issues lie elsewhere: indifference, insecurity, self-doubt, conformity, and entitlement that stem from the systemic exploitation of social norms. Too many of us today are wearing a mask each day and expending significant energy in an attempt to conform to someone else's expectations of who we should be and what we should strive for. Consequently, our society is increasingly plagued by apathy, complacency, despair, and egotism brought on by the selfish desires for money, comfort, and power.

This book holds a profound purpose—to break free from the constraints of this flawed system and empower you to build a life and career with unwavering intention. It's a rallying cry, guiding you towards self-actualization and significance. Within its pages, a movement is sparked—a declaration that a meaningful life is not only possible but well within your reach. Together, let's ignite this journey towards a purposeful and fulfilled existence.

Why Should You Listen to Me?

Over the past seven years, I've researched juggernauts from the worlds of technology, sports, government, entertainment, academia, arts, and business to understand their steps to unlocking their full potential. I interviewed many of them on the *Passion Struck* podcast. These studies and interviews revealed commonalities in how these luminaries approach decision-making, problem-solving, adversity, innovation, behavior change, adaptation, anxiety, and leadership. I combined these findings in each chapter with the personal lessons that I learned over the course of my career, from my failures and my successes.

Ultimately, the principles that I describe in this book apply to all of our lives. It doesn't matter where you grew up, where you went to school, or what you have accomplished to this point. Past failures are simply that: in the past. The only way to feel genuinely fulfilled and passionate is to stop hiding who you are. Stop pretending and start showing the world the real you by intentionally choosing to love and cherish *yourself* and by taking the intentional daily actions to make your dreams a reality.

I purposefully embrace the word "intentional" to convey a profound truth. To truly live—to transcend mere existence—demands a deliberate commitment to embracing your authentic self and unearthing your deepest desires. It is this unwavering intentionality that propels you towards the fulfillment of your purpose, infusing your being with the tenacity to pursue it relentlessly. Embrace this resolute path, for within it lies the power to unlock the extraordinary and seize the life that beckons you with unwavering allure.

For many years, psychologists, scientists, and existential philosophers have debated whether we are free to choose the conditions of our existence and discover our true purpose. At the heart of their deliberations lies a fundamental question: Are we bestowed with the freedom to shape the very essence of our existence and unearth our true purpose?

Though certain attributes may be immutable and circumstances may impose limitations, I hold steadfast in my conviction that our intentional pursuits possess the power to bridge the chasm between reality and aspiration. It is through the unwavering intentionality we infuse into our endeavors that we inch ever closer to the realms of our dreams and aspirations. The pursuit of our passions, the unwavering commitment to our goals, serves as the compass guiding us toward the destiny we ardently seek.

Being Apathetic Is a Choice; Being Intentional Is a Choice

Our belief system defines our present and our future. We must recognize that our mindset, feelings, thoughts, and opinions become habitual. What we contemplate today, we risk perpetuating tomorrow, unless we consciously and intentionally embark on a transformative journey, seeking new insights and forging a different path for our thoughts. That is what I hope to provide in this book: information that you can use to chart a new life, based on lessons learned by some of the most inspirational people on the planet. It is my fervent hope that this reservoir of knowledge will illuminate your path, guiding you towards a life defined by purpose, passion, fulfillment, and significance.

As President Theodore Roosevelt said,

> The credit belongs to the man who is actually in the arena, whose face is marred by dust and sweat and blood; who strives valiantly; who errs, who comes short again and again, because there is no effort without error and shortcoming; but who does actually strive to do the deeds; who knows great enthusiasms, the great devotions; who spends himself in a worthy cause; who at the best knows, in the end, the triumph of high achievement, and who at the worst, if he fails, at least fails while daring greatly.

Unlocking your purpose and having the intentional willpower to become your best self will allow you to fight your fight and claim your space in the arena of life.

I hope you dare greatly.

CHAPTER 1

THE POWER OF PASSION, PERSEVERANCE, AND INTENTIONALITY

People who exercise their embryonic freedom,
day after day, little by little, expand that freedom.
People who do not will find that it withers until
they are literally "being lived." They are acting out
scripts written by parents, associates, and society
—Stephen Covey

I want to lead you through a short thought experiment.

In your mind—or better yet, on a piece of paper—take a moment to write down one or two of your biggest life goals. Take the seat belt off for this one, and really think of which dream, desire, passion, or goal has always been sitting patiently in the back of your heart, longing for its chance to break free and burst into reality.

Have it written down? Now, flip it over, and write down the answer to the following questions: What is the biggest fear that keeps you from realizing that dream?

Why do so few of us pursue our dreams?

Why do we cower from committing to work on something about which we are genuinely passionate?

Why do so many people, regardless of profession, settle for less?

Think about it. Jim Collins, author of *Good to Great: Why Some Companies Make the Leap...and Others Don't*, discovered in his prominent research that there are very few great businesses and even fewer genuinely inspirational leaders. Carol Dweck, author of *Mindset: The New Psychology of Success*, explored why so many of us live with a fixed mindset. And Katy Milkman, author of *How to Change: The Science of Getting from Where You Are to Where You Want to Be*, uncovered that it's easier to settle for a life that is good enough than it is to make deliberate behavior changes attached to living an intentional one.

Why? We all know people who are happy with "good enough." What do I mean by that? The truth is that some people are satisfied with the ordinary.

For the vast majority, passing through life looks something like this:

Birth
Graduate elementary school
Graduate middle school
Graduate high school
Attend college or trade school
Get a stable job
Buy a house
Raise a family
Pay off the mortgage
Retire
Death

While this overly crude simplification doesn't do justice to any number of achievements occurring during the span of someone's actual life, this well-trodden path neatly illustrates the point I'm trying to make: not pursuing our dreams is far from an isolated case.

The Social Cycle Theory[2] argues "that events and stages of society and history are generally repeating themselves in cycles." And I believe that we are in the midst of a new cycle—just as reeducation was necessary to endure and succeed in the Industrial Age, the same holds for the Information Age. The only difference is that the system stayed the same when this shift happened. According to a 2016 report on economic mobility,[3] "Since the 1970s, income inequality has again soared to levels not seen since early in the 20th century. While the economy more than doubled over these four decades, the rising tide did not lift all boats." There are many reasons for this (greed, money, power, political divide, shareholders). Still, the result of all of this means that once again, people can no longer rely on what's worked in the past to provide what they need in the future.

The once-pulsating vitality and indomitable spirit of entrepreneurship, which propelled the United States to the zenith of admiration worldwide, now languishes in a steady, three-decade decline. Numerous studies,[4] employing diverse methodologies to gauge the rise of high-growth firms and measure entrepreneurial growth, converge upon a disquieting consensus: the quintessential American dream, once an aspiration that resonated across the globe, teeters precariously at a tipping point.[5] It has evolved into an elusive aspiration, becoming something that fewer people can attain, much less hope for. I believe that we are amidst a global emergency for much of society.

Let's look at this through the lens of the Kauffman Foundation,[6] a non-profit fostering entrepreneurship, which publishes its Kauffman Startup Activity Index that measures startup density. Its 2021 report[7] shows that in 2013, the Startup Activity Index was at its lowest point in the past twenty years, and "in the first year of the pandemic, the opportunity share of new entrepreneurs plummeted. It decreased from 86.9 percent in 2019 to 69.8 percent in 2020, representing the largest drop over the past 25 years and perhaps much longer." The rate of new entrepreneurs from the entire population starting a new business was only 0.36 percent in 2021. The 2015 Kauffman density graph (see Figure 1) illustrates how the decline in startup density actually started more than thirty years ago.

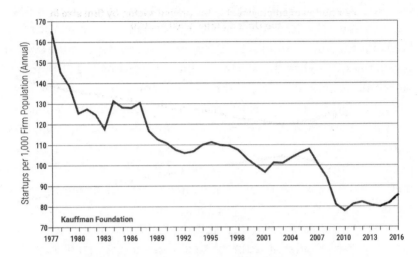

FIGURE 1: The Kauffman Index graph[8] of startup density,[9] or the number of startups per 1,000 firms, doesn't look like the hockey stick that we might expect to see. Startup density has been decreasing since the Kauffman Foundation started measuring it in 1977.

A profound revelation emerged from a comprehensive study[10] conducted by the Brookings Institution. The findings reverberate with a resounding truth: the startup rate, a barometer measuring the emergence of new organizations as a proportion of the entire business landscape, has plummeted by nearly half since the year 1978. This distressing decline, vividly illustrated in Figure 2 of the Bureau of Labor Statistics' chart, showcases a stark juxtaposition. The once-vibrant realm of nascent small businesses, the lifeblood of innovation and economic growth, has been engulfed in a precipitous descent since 2005. Conversely, large enterprises, boasting more than 250 employees, surge forth with an inverse and relentless ascent. This stark divergence paints a vivid portrait of an economic landscape besieged by ominous tides of change, as the very foundation of vibrant, agile entrepreneurship crumbles before our eyes. These staggering visuals encapsulate the urgent need to confront this unsettling reality and reignite the spirit of innovation, creativity, and risk-taking that once set our world ablaze.

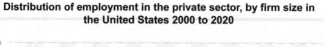

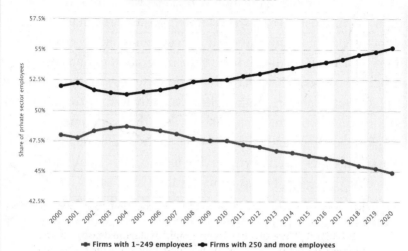

Firms with 1–249 employees   Firms with 250 and more employees

FIGURE 2: This chart from the Bureau of Labor Statistics[11] shows the distribution of employment in the private sector by firm size from 2000 to 2020 in the United States. For this statistic, firm size is calculated by the firm's number of employees. In 2020, firms with more than 250 employees employed 55.12 percent of the private-sector workforce in the United States.

"A global emergency" may sound pretty stark, but it's an accurate description all the same. We are witnessing daily evidence of this as deep social, economic, political, and geographical rifts; economic immobility[12] and income inequality[13] are causing people to reject or shift traditional values and beliefs. Other key indicators of this global emergency can be observed in the growing decline of work engagement. The Gallup "State of the Global Workplace: 2022 Report" found that only 21 percent of the world's full-time workers are engaged in and love what they do, costing employers $7.8 trillion in lost productivity.[14] And, as a group, only 29 percent of millennials are engaged at work.[15] Said another way, nearly 80 percent of the world's full-time employees loathe their jobs.

Every day of sitting in the cubicle is another day checked off before the weekend, the end of the month, the next vacation, and, before you know it, retirement. The paycheck provides just enough motivation to get out of bed in the morning but not enough to put in extraordinary effort. Nor is it low enough to give the inspiration to find another job or start a business. So, we have a situation whereby many of us do just enough, nothing more, nothing less, patiently waiting for a chance to do something we actually care about when the time comes.

However, that time rarely comes, and we reach a point where our efforts no longer mean anything. We feel hopeless in our attempts to overcome these negative situations for the better. So, we sit idle in our current conditions because this perceived lack of control becomes a trained behavior. What we believe is what we become, and when that sets in, we cannot experience joy or optimism in our life.

Here's what many people don't understand: The opposite of joy is not unhappiness. The opposite of joy is the lack of intentionality in our lives, leading to chronic hopelessness. This state of meaninglessness, akin to nihilism, is a dire condition where the very essence of existence loses all significance. It creeps into every aspect of life, work, and society, leaving behind an abyss devoid of purpose.

The impact of this insidious affliction is far-reaching. It fosters stagnation, indifference, loneliness, and resignation, eroding the belief in life's purpose and fading memories of brighter days. This profound metamorphosis traps you in a mere existence, falling tragically short of the life you desire. It's a surrender to hopelessness, and apathy takes hold of your surroundings, severing ties to work, relationships, and the very core of your being. How do you change this narrative? How can you wake up each morning genuinely excited to tackle the challenges that lie ahead?

The most pressing gap we face today is the skillset gap. Large institutions and governments failed to adapt to the Information Age, leaving millions of people to grapple with the harsh reality of jobs being replaced by outsourcing, automation, robotics, and artificial intelligence (AI). And unfortunately, this trend is only going to intensify.

These millions of individuals urgently need an alternative way to acquire the essential skillsets and education required to thrive in this new system. It's time to recognize that we, as humans, are the ultimate adaptation machines, designed to learn and evolve. In essence, each one of us is a new textbook, capable of embracing change and seizing opportunities to make our mark in this rapidly evolving world.

What Does It Mean to Actually Give a F*ck?

My apologies for the expletive-laden heading, but I've deliberately chosen it for a reason. Many leading authors, most notably Mark Manson,[16] continue to espouse that "negativity is the path to positivity" and urge their readers to "ignore every step-by-step system for success." In both of his books, *The Subtle Art of Not Giving a F*ck* and *Everything is F*cked*, as well as in his articles,[17] Manson argues that we should f*ck "finding the positives in life" and instead focus on the tolerance and acceptance of the negative experiences. Manson believes that "success is just something everyone has made up, and it is not even real."[18]

I agree with Manson that:

- "We should be comfortable being different,"
- "Care about something more important than adversity,"
- "What matters are a person's intentions,"
- "Showing unconditionality by being unconditional yourself," and
- "Constantly choose where to put our f*cks."

But I couldn't *disagree* more on a significant element: passion and purpose should *drive* your life and your work.

You should want to live your dreams and strive to develop your abilities and talents fully. If you don't get passionate about what you're doing, you'll never undertake your calling. You'll become yet another slave to the "do just enough until the weekend" mantra that is trapping so many of the world's current employees.

When I think of trying to relate the importance of giving a f*ck, I often find myself thinking of the famous Steve Jobs quotation: "Your work is going to fill a large part of your life, and the only way to be truly satisfied is to do what you believe is great work. And the only way to do great work is to love what you do."

Jobs's critical message here is often overlooked. It's in the first sentence: "Your work is going to fill a large part of your life…" This realization cannot be understated. As part of one of the biggest studies of occupational health,[19] the World Health Organization unveiled that we spend a third of our entire lives at work. Let that sink in for a moment. Apart from sleeping, there is no other activity you will spend more of your life undertaking. What has been the point if you've spent that time wishing away each day between weekends?

Steve Jobs realized this fact early, as have many other passion-struck leaders I've had the pleasure of meeting, researching, and interviewing. We'll delve deeper into what defines a passion-struck leader because there are many valuable lessons that can help to shift our perspective on work and life in general.

In analyzing the data and insights provided by those I've studied over the past seven years, I have developed several key concepts from my interviews, research, and observations. During my lengthy investigation, I also found that several factors I'd expected to influence my results or to be common trends were less significant than I would have thought. Surprisingly, some of these dynamics that did *not* affect a passion-struck transition included heritability, wealth, IQ, school grades, aptitude, and birth zip code.

Suppose those factors didn't influence that transition from run-of-the-mill to unstoppable juggernauts of their respective industries. What *are* the secrets behind their rise to prominence and becoming passion struck?

What Defines Those Who Become Passion Struck?

In her groundbreaking book *Grit: The Power of Passion and Perseverance*, Angela Duckworth concluded that grit (the combination of passion and perseverance) matters more than talent.

Her theory is that "when you consider individuals in identical circumstances, what each achieves depends on just two things, talent and effort. Talent—how fast we improve skill—absolutely matters. But effort factors into the calculations twice, not once. Effort builds skill. At the very same time, effort makes skill productive."

She illustrates this through the formula

talent x effort = skill and skill x effort = achievement.

Her study of grit started at the United States Military Academy, examining why some cadets graduated and others failed to do so. She concluded after years of research that it was because of grit. And, I won't argue that grit plays a significant part in determining that outcome. However, I can speak to and observe this through a different lens: one of first-hand experience.

I graduated from a similar institution to West Point—the U.S. Naval Academy. And, I had the perspective of being a member of the Brigade Honor Staff, overseeing the largest cheating scandal[20] in the institution's history. That experience taught me a fundamental lesson: It is not the mega-events in our life that define us. Instead, it is the infinite tiny moments, those critical micro choices that occur daily and how they alter our mindset and behavior, that matter the most.

The Naval Academy's purpose is "to develop Midshipmen morally, mentally, and physically and to imbue them with the highest ideals of duty, honor, and loyalty." Like the West Point cadets, the Midshipmen learn to consider the choices they make carefully because once they graduate, their lives and the lives of those they lead depend on them.

When I started to think about this experience through the lens of everyday life and to research visionaries, creators, athletes, founders, and game-changers, a light bulb went off. As I examined Duckworth's formula, I found that an essential input was consistently missing: intentionality.

In other words, if we know what our ultimate goal is (graduating from the Naval Academy or West Point and becoming an officer), then we need to pursue the daily actions to get there and identify the impediments in the way of that goal and eradicate them. And the only way to do that is by being intentional. You can have all the grit in the world, but if you are not deliberate in deploying it, you will never reach your full capabilities. Also, suppose you are not intentional with your core values. In that case, you will cheat yourself, as hundreds of Midshipmen of the Class of 1994 did on the Electrical Engineering final exam.[21]

In writing, a transition is a word or phrase that connects one idea to another. This connection can occur in a paragraph or between paragraphs. These transitions are used to show how different subject matter is linked to other subject matter that you're relating to the reader and how the reader relates to the overall theme of the blog post, paper, or book you're writing.

Like these transition points in writing, we have transition points connecting important life events that are intrinsically tied to our intentions. Whether it's evil, good, desire, meaning, worry, doubt, achievement, frustration, or the direction of our lives, all of it is decided in daily micro choices to which we pay little attention.

Yes, Duckworth is correct in her observation that grit is one of the core attributes possessed by those cadets who graduate. Still, they also had something equally important, if not more critical: intentionality.

Being intentional helps you to comprehend the importance of what you aim for in life and directs your behaviors and actions to help you achieve it. Just as essential, it enables you to understand what you're *not* aiming for. Intentionality gives you greater clarity around your aspirations and takes the guesswork out of where to invest your focus and time. This intentionality makes the difference between someone achieving self-realization versus achievement alone.

During the *Passion Struck* podcast interview with Katy Milkman,[22] who co-founded the Behavior Change for Good Initiative with Angela Duckworth, I stated: "I can have all the grit in the world. However, I will not reach my end goal if I don't know how to drive it intentionally." I then asked Milkman about her view of the statement, how she thought that Duckworth would respond, and about her opinion on the importance of intentionality in behavior change. Milkman explained:

> Hanging around Angela [Duckworth], I don't think she would say grit is the only ingredient. It's just one ingredient that seems important to success and that she's studied. And she's done a lot of work on situation modification with James Gross, Ph.D., a brilliant psychologist at Stanford University. And I think she also thinks that's a very important component of success. Situation modification basically means intentionality—having a recognition that if my situation isn't going to support my goals, then I need to change it.

Milkman continued:

> I think, in that sense, she [Duckworth] would certainly agree that it's intentionality—having an understanding of your purpose and how to best approach it is going to be another important ingredient to success. I certainly agree with it. And it's part of the reason I wrote the book *How to Change*. I felt like science had given us a lot of insights into what we could do if we had an intention and a goal that weren't clearly enough articulated to a wide audience and best use case limitations, and so on. So, I think both Angela [Duckworth] and I would agree with your premise.

This experience and observation led me to define a theory on why some achieve the realized self while others do not. I wrote volumes of diagrams and comparisons and reviewed data that test this theory, thinking about it, sometimes alone and often bouncing it off colleagues and family. The result is two simple equations that build on Duckworth's work and add a crucial element. Here they are:

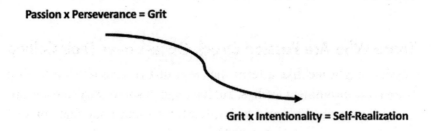

Passion x Perseverance = Grit

Grit x Intentionality = Self-Realization

FIGURE 3: The Theory of the Psychology of Self-Realization.

The theory of the psychology of self-realization says that self-realization depends on passion, perseverance, and intentionality when considering people in identical situations. Grit, the strength of character—absolutely is essential. But it is not the only factor in the calculation. The Second Law of Thermodynamics is one of the most fundamental laws of nature. It says that as energy is transformed or transferred, more and more of it is wasted. The Second Law of Thermodynamics also states that in any closed system, that system will move towards entropy unless you inject energy.[23] Another way to think about this is that if you have a goal, you have to put energy into the inputs during the micro choices in life to achieve the outcome you want, or you will encounter inertia. That is what it means to have intentionality—to direct our mindset, beliefs, and actions in alignment with our character, goals, and core values.

And that is what it means to be passion struck. Becoming passion struck isn't a destination. It is the never-ending pursuit of harnessing all that you are in the service of realizing your best self, so you can help to elevate the bar for the rest of humanity. It is the journey to self-realization through passion, perseverance, and intentionality.

Essentially, those who are passion struck are so fervent about their calling that they have the grit and intentionality to pursue it to the ends of the earth and fulfill their purpose—even if that means potential financial, reputation, and career peril. Those who are passion struck address the novel problems impacting society. They intentionally align their values with what best brings them bliss.

Those Who Are Passion Struck Obsess over Their Calling

Passion might feel like a term that wouldn't receive much attention from many prominent leaders, but having met some of the most influential leaders in the world today, trust me when I say that couldn't be any further from the truth. These leaders obsess about what they do; more precisely, their lives are intentionally fixated on the problem they are trying to solve. It keeps them up at night, dominates every conversation, and drives them to achieve their aspirations no matter the obstacle or the number of times they fail.

During one encounter with Salesforce founder Marc Benioff in 2010, I began to finally pierce the veil guarding the barrier to becoming passion struck. I was fortunate to spend a great deal of time with Marc over a few years as we toured cities across the globe to promote the power of cloud computing. During one of our conversations, I asked him what gave him the impetus to launch what would become the world's most prominent customer relationship management (CRM) software and cloud-computing company. I was intrigued by his answer:

> I had it pretty good before starting Salesforce. I interned for Steve Jobs during college, and after graduating, I joined Oracle. Over the next four to five years, I got my head down and worked my way through various corporate roles on the sales, marketing, and

product development side. At 23, they named me
Oracle Rookie of the Year. By the time I was 25, they
had made me a millionaire. A year later, they made
me a vice president.

Stunned by what was apparently such an abundance of success at
Oracle, I asked the obvious follow-up question, "So what happened?
Why leave?" Marc paused for a few seconds to stew over the matter
before answering with astonishing brevity: "I didn't feel fervent about
what I was doing, and I knew I wouldn't be happy and fulfilled unless
I pursued my passion."

When pressed further, he explained:

After 13 years at Oracle, I still felt unfulfilled and was
itching to try something else; I just didn't know what.
So I asked Larry Ellison, the founder and CEO of
Oracle, if I could have his blessing to take a sabbatical.
I then spent the majority of the next year traveling.
I spent a great deal of time in Hawaii in particular,
where I studied meditation in depth.

I wanted to harness the power of meditation to try
and discover an idea that would inspire my genuine
passion. Hour after hour, I sat there, contemplating
problems within the software industry. After taking
a swim with a pod of dolphins, it suddenly came to
me. Why do software companies force their products
onto clients' servers? What if they could access appli-
cations on a centralized cloud-based server, literally
whenever or wherever they want, just by using their
browser? In other words, what if a company could sell
software as a service rather than a product?

And that was it. Benioff had found the key to what I was searching for.

It turned out to be a difference-maker for Marc Benioff to pursue his passionate obsession. After much time spent on reflection, he now had a problem (in his case, pursuing cloud computing) that became his life's calling. Countless setbacks (such as the dot-com bubble), numerous battles (including with his old boss Ellison), and innumerable sacrifices later, he had created the world's most prominent software-as-a-service (SaaS) company in the world.

How? He became passion struck.

This example perfectly illustrates the power of passion and perhaps why those who are genuinely intentional in life leave others behind. If we followed Mark Manson's mantra of not building a career about which we are passionate, we would have far fewer innovators in our time. The Marc Benioffs of this world wouldn't exist. They would have simply stuck with their well-paid, agreeable jobs and done nothing to threaten the security of their corporate cubicle existence.

Marc Benioff took a leap of faith based on his purpose with passion, perseverance, and intentionality. It's a decision that's been paying dividends ever since. But not everyone makes that decision.

Do You Have What It Takes to Become Passion Struck?

In a word, yes.

You might wrongly assume that you shouldn't be passionate about something because you feel uncomfortable about potentially hitting the dizzying heights that the likes of Richard Branson, Oprah Winfrey, and Steve Jobs experienced. But in my view, passion should not be viewed in that paradigm. You don't have to be a famous billionaire to be passion struck. That's not what the term exclusively predicates.

If you feel that you are ready to listen to your inner voice and take the first step on the journey toward becoming a growth-seeker of tomorrow and "expanding your freedom," below is a framework you can use as a roadmap to your success. I created it using a combination of my seven years of research on peak performers and the lessons I learned over my thirty-year career on how to achieve personal fulfillment.

The twelve-step framework applies six distinct mindset shifts and six fundamental behavior shifts (in your character and beliefs) that you'll need to embrace to reach your goals. Some will have to be tackled early in your journey, while others will act as epiphanies late in your development. There is an order to these steps, and some can occur concurrently. These steps underpin a personal journey. The same one that the leaders before you undertook to unlock an intentional life.

The Passion Struck Framework: The Twelve Steps to Unlocking an Intentional Life

FIGURE 4: The passion-struck framework is the twelve steps of unlocking an intentional life.

In Part One, I outline the key mindset shifts, which consist of six steps:

1. Mission Angler
2. Brand Reinventor
3. Mosquito Auditor
4. Fear Confronter
5. Perspective Harnesser
6. Action Creator

In Part Two, I detail essential intentional behavior changes for aspiring passion struck individuals:

1. Anxiety Optimizer
2. Originality Embracer
3. Boundary Magnifier
4. Outward Inspirer
5. Gardner Leader
6. Conscious Engager

Subsequent chapters explore deploying these shifts in your life using the "psychology of progress."

We will start by analyzing billionaire Jim McKelvey. Although McKelvey may not be a familiar name, he is a modern entrepreneur and artist who co-founded the financial-services platform Square and the non-profit LaunchCode. He is now working on a new venture called Invisibly, where his passion-struck obsession is disrupting the current publishing industry paradigm.

It is important to recognize that each individual possesses the innate potential to achieve extraordinary feats. However, it is crucial to acknowledge that the path to becoming passion-struck is not for the faint-hearted; it necessitates unwavering dedication to self-improvement and a resolute pursuit of your own aspirations. Not everyone is suited for the journey of becoming passion struck, as it demands a high level of commitment and unwavering personal agency.

The likes of Marc Benioff are few and far between for a reason. Nevertheless, by embracing the principles contained in this book, you gain a methodology for making informed decisions that can propel your personal or business accomplishments to unprecedented heights. Embrace the power to reshape your narrative by cultivating and relentlessly pursuing your passion with unwavering determination and intentionality. Allow it to serve as the unyielding force that propels you forward every single day, infusing your life with a sense of purpose and fulfillment. Embrace your passion, wield it as a compass in the pursuit of your dreams, and let its radiant light guide you towards a future brimming with purpose, accomplishment, and self-actualization. Like the leaders profiled in this book, I have succeeded and experienced personal breakthroughs, as well as had significant setbacks on other occasions. In the end, the measure of our lives is determined by the choices we make. They are intrinsic to our ability to face the future and stay steadfast in our resolve to recognize our *why* and live intentionally.

As I've said before, when all is said and done, your life's work leaves an indelible mark on your legacy.

It's up to you to decide how much you care.

My resolute motto is simple yet powerful: Make a choice, make it happen, and work every day intentionally towards whatever that goal is. Step into the sharp edges, do something that scares you, don't pull away, and don't overthink.

Imagine what our world would look like without leaders willing to make decisions, step forward into the unknown, and intentionally decide that fear wouldn't stop them. It is through the visionary actions and transformative mindset of our world's greatest thinkers and industry trailblazers that momentous movements and inspirations have been birthed. How did they achieve such awe-inspiring feats? By orchestrating a profound shift in both their mindset and behavior. Will fear arise with sharpened blades ready to attack? Absolutely. While it is normal to be afraid even when we feel ready, when we face our fears with passion, perseverance, and intentionality, we will see that there really wasn't much to fear.

At the beginning of this chapter, I asked you to write down the most significant fear(s) that keep you from realizing your dream. Now I ask you: Will you allow your fears to stop you, or will you face and overcome them?

Remember, the greatest gifts we have to offer are our chosen impacts on the world, loved ones, and ourselves, and we must not allow anything to stop us from giving them.

PART 1

MINDSET SHIFTS— HOW SELF-REALIZERS NEED TO THINK

CHAPTER 2

MISSION ANGLER—MUSTER THE POWER TO DO SOMETHING GREAT

*Passion is energy. Feel the power that comes
from focusing on what excites you.*
—Oprah Winfrey

Apathy is the enemy of passion.

As humans, we often shy away from making waves, falling victim to the herd mentality. It is similar to an angler who gets the lucky drop when he sees a shoal of fish gather. Similar to these fish, many individuals drift through life without daring to challenge their status quo. They hit their modest targets, create a comfortable life, but deep down, they know there's more to achieve.

We daydream about success, admiring business titans, athletes, and entrepreneurs, but we fail to realize that they are not fundamentally different from us. They simply mustered the courage to do something different. They found purpose and pursued passion, making their visions a reality.

Like you, they craved a sense of purpose; they yearned for a passion-filled life. And yet, while so many sit idly as years and decades pass by, they overcame their fear of failure and the unknown and took the first step along their journey to becoming passion struck. What empowers these individuals to go to such lengths is a deep, underlying sense of purpose. They set out to solve a novel problem. They make the problem personal and aren't satisfied until they turn their vision into reality.

Several years ago, I held a prominent position in the C-suite of a large corporation. I found myself surrounded by exceptional individuals, masters of their craft. The experience was undeniably enriching, yet a gnawing restlessness began to stir within me. The work had lost its vibrancy, its spark, and I yearned for something more—a realm of boundless growth and self-discovery. In the depths of introspection, I pondered what the truly ambitious would do in my shoes, and it was then that the notion of seeking guidance from a career coach took root.

Little did I know that this decision would become one of the best decisions I've made. In this hour of soul-searching, my coach unveiled a priceless metaphor. He encouraged me to become a life crafter and to envision my life as a stool—a structure supported by multiple legs. But herein lay the revelation: my stool only had one substantial leg—the relentless grind. While it met my material and lifestyle needs, it failed to nourish me holistically, leading to burnout and a loss of passion. I had become disengaged, apathetic, and hopeless.

The coach then asked me to consider adding another support leg to my "life stool." "In fact," he said, "think about adding multiple new legs!" I didn't know what to say. I'd never really thought about things from that perspective. It was an entirely novel way of perceiving my life. By life crafting the way I wanted my life to be, I could infuse passion into all areas of my life rather than sporadically seeking it outside of work. Inspired by this insight, I proceeded to create five legs on the stool, symbolizing different facets of my life: emotional health, physical health, mental health, spiritual health, and relationship health. The choice of these five legs can vary for each individual, but viewing it in this manner showed me that I needed to dig deep to identify areas in my life where I felt stuck.

This shift in perspective allowed me to recognize that I had the power to craft my life differently. It was a call to dig deep, identify areas in my life where I yearned for growth, and muster the determination to make a change. The notion of becoming a mission angler in all aspects of my life took hold, propelling me towards a new sense of purpose and fulfillment. The power to do something different lies within each of us, waiting to be unlocked and harnessed to create a life of purpose, joy, and meaningful impact. Let's now examine the science of life crafting.

Unleashing the Science of Life Crafting: Unlocking a Purpose-Driven Life

Life crafting, akin to the mission angler, is an active process that entails reflecting on your present and future life, setting goals in crucial areas like relationships, career, and well-being, and taking concrete steps to shape your life according to your values and aspirations. It serves as a dynamic framework that empowers individuals to explore and align with their life's purpose.

The profound research[24] conducted by psychologist William Damon emphasizes the crucial role of purpose development in shaping a fulfilling life. Damon's extensive work reveals that purpose arises through a blend of introspection, exploration, and whole-hearted dedication to pursuing goals that resonate with one's core values and passions. By embracing the principles of life crafting, individuals gain the tools to intentionally design a life that reflects their deepest values and brings them true fulfillment.

On the Passion Struck podcast, I discussed life crafting with Hal Hershfield, a renowned behavior scientist and expert in the science of the future self at UCLA Anderson School of Management. During our conversation, I delved into the impact of a lack of purpose on our future selves and how we can transition from fearing our future to fulfilling it.

As Hershfield explained,[25] these questions ultimately revolve around our "big why"—the driving force behind our aspirations and actions. Without a clear sense of purpose, it becomes challenging to envision where we want our future selves to be. It's akin to desiring more money in the future without a clear understanding of how we intend to use it.

Hershfield describes it in this way, "On some implicit level, having that bigger-picture purpose in mind may be really helpful when it comes to envisioning what my future self will be doing. And thinking more deeply about how the things I'm doing right now will impact that person."

Having a broader purpose in mind helps us envision our future selves more vividly and contemplate how our present choices shape that person. By embracing a deeper understanding of our purpose and considering how our current actions contribute to our future selves, we can embark on a transformative journey towards fulfillment and create a more intentional and meaningful future.

Furthermore, research in positive psychology, led by scholars such as Martin Seligman and Carol Dweck, supports the idea that intentional life design plays a vital role in enhancing well-being and fulfillment. Seligman's concept of "positive psychology" emphasizes the importance of engaging in activities that leverage personal strengths and promote a sense of meaning and accomplishment. Dweck's groundbreaking work on mindset[26] highlights the significance of adopting a growth mindset, where individuals believe in their capacity to develop and grow, enabling them to embrace challenges and persevere in the pursuit of their life's purpose.

Through this intentional exploration and goal-setting process, life crafters align their actions and decisions with their values, passions, and purpose. They make deliberate choices that steer them towards a life that is congruent with their authentic selves. This intentional approach enables individuals to prioritize what truly matters to them, rather than being swept along by external pressures or societal expectations.

Life crafting also involves making concrete plans and taking actionable steps towards desired outcomes. Individuals identify the necessary resources, skills, and support systems required to manifest their vision. By actively pursuing their goals, life crafters cultivate a sense of agency and ownership over their lives, embracing responsibility for their own happiness and fulfillment. Let us delve into the connection between life crafting and the power to enact change and do something different.

The Power to Do Something Different

Today's digital world is more competitive than ever,[27] yet large and small businesses alike find it easier to stick with familiar ideas, procedures, and ways of doing business. Inertia kicks in. Following unwritten rules or guidelines in an industry or sector because "that is the way that things have always been done" seems like the path of least resistance. A recent study released by McKinsey Global Institute reports that roughly one-fifth of the global workforce will be affected by the adoption of AI and automation, with the most significant impact in developed nations, such as the U.K., Germany, and the U.S. In 2022, 50 percent of companies in developed nations believed that automation will decrease their full-time staff, and by 2030, robots are expected to replace 800 million workers worldwide.[28]

In the face of impending societal and work environment changes, cultivating a relentless thirst for personal and professional advancement becomes paramount. Embracing a learning mindset that eagerly embraces new knowledge, hones fresh skills, and readily adapts to ever-evolving circumstances is the key to becoming a mission angler and flourishing amidst the transformative tides of change. Thriving in this era demands unyielding commitment to the continual development of one's abilities, leaving no room for complacency. That is, a passion for continually learning new skills and adapting to new environments. Allow me to make this abundantly clear as we embark on your journey: Succumbing to the allure of familiarity and complacency is simply not an option for those who are passion struck. Embracing the status quo is fundamentally incompatible with crafting a life brimming with purpose and ignited by unbridled passion. While some individuals may find solace in coasting through the current climate, those who are truly driven by passion yearn for something greater. They refuse to settle for mediocrity and tirelessly strive to exceed their own expectations, pushing the boundaries of what is possible.

Fortunately, a significant number of individuals refuse to settle for mere mediocrity. They yearn for crafting their life with a profound sense of purpose that drives them each morning, propelling them relentlessly towards their life's ultimate goal. These individuals challenge conventional norms, shatter the shackles of apathy, and cannot rest until they have realized their hidden potential. Instead, they embrace the razor's edge, fearlessly confronting their deepest anxieties with an unwavering determination to achieve greatness. But how do they accomplish this remarkable feat? They craft a mission that is truly worth pursuing.

The glossy images of celebrated business icons gracing magazine covers inspire us to contemplate what it would be like to embody their level of success. However, the psychological pressures we face cannot be vanquished overnight, and if we're not cautious, we risk remaining trapped in our old habits, where the yearning to become a true game-changer is overshadowed by fear of failure or fear of the unknown.

Do you want to look back on your life and lament:

> "I wish I had taken that risk," or "Wouldn't it have been cool if we actually executed that crazy idea?"

No. Of course not!

Ultimately, it's about harnessing the power to do something different. That's the true game-changer. Even though the road to different may be full of hidden obstacles or what feel like overpowering fears, *different* is what is necessary to get where we want to go. There's no better person to talk to about mustering this power of doing something different[29] than Jim McKelvey,[30] the co-founder of Square. Though Jim McKelvey may not be a household name, he stands as a testament to the extraordinary achievements that can be attained by embodying the spirit of a mission angler.

Naturally, I wanted to hear what he had to say about how we could tap into that same kind of power.

An Extremely Impressive Entrepreneur

Ever since he was a child, Jim was interested in entrepreneurship and technology. In his earlier days, he wrote and published a handbook on UCSD Pascal and Apple Pascal.[31] Along with his technological interests, Jim's various jobs early on in his career included glassblowing, contracting for IBM, and founding a CD-cabinet manufacturing company called Disconcepts.

Jim was an essential force behind several different startups that he still owns.[32] Arguably, the most notable startup is Square. Along with Twitter co-founder Jack Dorsey, Jim created this game-changing startup that powers countless numbers of small businesses. While Jack designed the software for Square, Jim designed the hardware,[33] including Square's famous credit card reader. The hardware was so impressive that not only has Square grown to be a $17.5 billion company,[34] but the design of Square's credit card reader has been inducted into the Museum of Modern Art in New York City.[35]

We might all agree that co-founding one multibillion-dollar company would be enough for any one career. Yet Jim has been an essential force in a number of different startups. Before Square, Jim was a co-founder of Third Degree Glass Factory,[36] a glass-art education center and studio in St. Louis. In 2012, he and several St. Louis-based entrepreneurs founded Cultivation Capital,[37] a venture capital firm that focuses on early-stage companies in life sciences, software, and agricultural technology. His nonprofit LaunchCode,[38] whose mission is to foster new talent and create pathways for employment and on-the-job training, was next. Last (but not least), Jim went on to found Invisibly,[39] which provides users with the tools and power to choose how they want to experience the digital world.

It's hard to imagine how one man could do more, but Jim is also a director for MoneyOnMobile, Inc.,[40] which helps Indian citizens and residents to pay for goods and services through their smartphones, and was appointed as an independent director of the St. Louis Federal Reserve.

What sets McKelvey apart is his ability to see beyond the conventional and envision a better future. He embodies the qualities of a true mission angler—a visionary who recognizes that true greatness lies in determination, taking risks, and pursuing a purpose that is larger than oneself. McKelvey's journey serves as an inspiration, reminding us of the power we possess to make a meaningful impact when we wholeheartedly commit to our mission.

Transformational Leadership and a Sense of Purpose: Insights and Advice

Jim's resume is certainly impressive. He has been the leading force behind startups that we take for granted today. Whether you purchase coffee at your favorite coffee shop or a new pair of jeans from a local boutique, you're likely using a product that Jim created. His impact extends far beyond mere financial success. McKelvey's ventures have had a profound influence on industries and communities, creating opportunities, jobs, and transformative solutions.

How did Jim find the power to do something different?

Well, there's some good news—and some bad news. We'll start with the bad. There is no defining playbook or guide that can help everyone. If there *were* such a manual to invoke us all to muster the courage to do something different, we'd all be doing it. And then, how different would it be? If you found a trading or investing edge that worked every time and was accessible to everyone, your edge would no longer be an edge. It would simply disappear.

On the other hand, the good news is that Jim's journey offers some key principles and strategies that we *can* all include and leverage in our lives and careers to drastically increase the chances that we find the power to do something different.

Relying on an Overarching Sense of Purpose

During my discussions with Jim, I was struck by how often he talked about his "sense of purpose." The goal of doing something that has never been done before. Of taking a vague idea, one that may even have surfaced in the minds of others, and bringing it to fruition. It's the drive behind the idea that exemplifies what makes someone passion struck. Whether it's finding a solution to an identified problem in life, or one identified in the marketplace, with the problem and sense of purpose at hand, these leaders find the courage to try things that have never been tried before.

In essence, the passion-struck individual possesses an unwavering commitment to problem-solving. They are driven to disrupt and challenge the status quo, using their energy and determination to bring about meaningful and substantial change in the world, even in uncharted territories. What fuels these individuals to go to such extraordinary lengths is their profound sense of purpose. They internalize the problem, making it deeply personal, and remain unsatisfied until they transform their vision into tangible reality. Their relentless pursuit of their mission sets them apart, propelling them to take bold actions and create a lasting impact.

That is precisely what Jim McKelvey did when he and Jack Dorsey created Square. The origin story of Square is well-known.[41] Jim and Jack came together after Jim lost a sale for his hand-blown glass art because he had no way of accepting credit cards. While most other entrepreneurs would have simply thrown up their hands and kept on with the way they were doing things, the experience gave Jim and Jack pause. They weren't satisfied with the status quo. How could they implement a way for small business owners and entrepreneurs to accept credit card payments? And how could they do it in a way that was seamless and easy to use?

Their clear purpose fueled the creation of Square, as they wholeheartedly focused on finding solutions and navigating significant obstacles, shaping Square into what it is today. Similarly, Invisibly aspires to revolutionize the online experience for readers, offering greater personalization and engagement, while also empowering publishers with improved monetization strategies.

McKelvey explains his distinctive approach[42] this way:

> For unsolved problems, we don't have experts, we don't have something that we can copy, and because we can't copy it, we are left to discover new solutions. The problem with those new solutions is that they tend to create new problems. So what happens—in

these companies especially, but also just in general—is that you kind of solve the problem and then you create another problem, and that problem then requires the process to be repeated.

Nothing stops transformational leaders with a sense of drive and purpose. And change can reach societal levels as well, helping to make the world a better place.

Look no further than the remarkable example set by Gary Vaynerchuk, a true titan in the entrepreneurial realm, who, much like the illustrious Jim McKelvey, has personified the essence of unyielding purpose throughout his awe-inspiring journey. Driven by a deep-rooted passion for business and innovation, Vaynerchuk's sense of purpose became evident when he took charge of his family's wine business. With an acute ability to perceive future trends, he recognized the transformative potential of e-commerce and digital marketing. Guided by his purpose to revolutionize the industry, he fearlessly ventured into the online landscape, propelling the wine business to unprecedented heights.

But Vaynerchuk's purpose-driven mindset didn't stop there. Driven by his relentless desire to create meaningful change, Vaynerchuk founded Vayner Media, a trailblazing digital marketing agency. His visionary instincts led him to foresee the power of social media and content marketing, empowering brands to navigate the digital revolution.

Vaynerchuk's profound understanding of his purpose and unwavering commitment set him apart. He constantly adapts and evolves, inspiring and empowering others to pursue their dreams in the ever-changing digital landscape. Through his books, speeches, and online presence, Vaynerchuk shares his purpose, igniting a fire within countless individuals to embrace change and seize opportunities.

As a mission angler, Vaynerchuk exemplifies the transformative power of purpose. His dedication and foresight have made him a purpose-driven entrepreneur and thought leader, creating a lasting impact on the world. In Vaynerchuk's story, we find a powerful reminder that a strong sense of purpose can lead to personal success and a positive influence on the world.

A Willingness to Act without Knowing What's Ahead

McKelvey clearly has a determined and overarching sense of purpose. But beyond that, I discovered that his success stemmed as much from purpose as from being willing to act even when there are no clear examples to follow. He explains that "it all starts with a problem that does not have a known solution, which is really profound because most of the problems that we have in our lives have been solved by other people."

Let's face it. Why would you take a chance on some crazy idea that has never been tried before? When the people around you are telling you it's a crazy idea that'll probably never work? When the implicit boundaries on what is possible and not possible normally limit our dreams and make it easy to back down and settle?

Because it's worth it.

McKelvey knew that. He knew that his ability to keep achieving, to take the initiative even when there were no obvious models for what he was trying to accomplish at hand. When Jim and Jack were throwing around the idea for Square, there was nothing like it in existence. The mobile-payments industry was in its infancy. There was no well-defined playbook that could launch their idea and achieve early product-market fit. There was no comfort in copying market share leaders or relying on competitors to set an example. They had to start from scratch, to design both the hardware and software *they* wanted to see in the real world. They had a novel problem that they were striving to solve.

Were there trials and tribulations along the way? Of course. But that's where passion-struck leaders jump in. They see the trials and tribulations as opportunities and incentives to do more, solve more, and be more. Square is just one example of Jim's propensity for a bias for action even when there is no clear path to success. For recognizing the opportunity in what seems like failure. To take that opportunity to design a product or service from first principles.[43]

Indeed, venturing into the unknown without a clear example to follow can be incredibly daunting. The absence of a well-defined path can evoke fear and uncertainty. However, it is precisely this fear that can serve as a powerful catalyst, propelling you toward your desired destination.

Embracing the unknown and taking courageous action in the absence of a clear example is a driving force behind your journey. It is the impetus that fuels your determination to forge your own path, to chart new territory, and to break free from the constraints of conventional thinking. By embracing this fear head-on, you open yourself up to infinite possibilities and discover untapped reservoirs of strength within.

While it may be uncomfortable to step into uncharted territory, it is within these unexplored realms that true growth and transformation occur. It is in these moments of uncertainty that you have the opportunity to shape your own narrative, to redefine success on your own terms, and to leave an indelible mark on the world.

So, despite the initial trepidation, recognize that the absence of a clear example is not a hindrance but a gift. It grants you the freedom to forge your own unique path, to unleash your creativity, and to pioneer new frontiers. Embrace the fear, harness its energy, and let it propel you toward the extraordinary. For it is through daring to venture into the unknown that you will discover the boundless potential that lies within you.

Going Along with the Crowd

The capacity to resist herding is another powerful way to help you rise to the top of the pack. To do that, you need to do the unthinkable: open yourself up to criticism, ridicule, and embarrassment. Does this seem as difficult for you as it does for me? If it does, I wouldn't be surprised. As humans, we are inherently biased towards *not* making waves. That's what makes us so susceptible to the herding mentality.[44] Even when we face no physical danger as a result of stepping away from the crowd, we are psychologically biased toward sticking with it out of a misguided belief that it's the safer route to take. Regardless of experience level or intelligence, every passion-struck leader out there was willing to step away from the herd to bring his or her idea to the world.

What's interesting is that those who become passion struck recognize these psychological pressures, yet choose to put them to the side to reach their goals. They are willing to accept that failure is part of the process. As McKelvey reminded me, temporary failure is inevitable when passion-struck leaders try to do more. It's their laser focus on making a world-centric difference that differentiates them from the crowd.

McKelvey agreed every single day to put himself out there and open himself up to criticism, even the doubt expressed by his friends, family, and colleagues. It took fortitude to resist the herd mentality, the idea of safety. The idea behind Square was a daunting one. The payments industry is notoriously tricky, and McKelvey and Dorsey's company centered on the burgeoning concept of mobile payments. Regardless, they were willing to risk public ridicule to do it differently. They mustered the power to do it differently—and to succeed.

Essentially, this idea of mustering the power of doing something different requires you to separate yourself from the crowd. The power lies in the word *different*. It can be quite scary and lonely sometimes. Jim and other entrepreneurial leaders have faced doubts and criticism over their careers. Yet the bottom line is that this is the price of admission for accomplishing true change in the world.

Doing It for Ourselves

Undoubtedly, it is unrealistic to expect that we can replicate the precise levels of success achieved by individuals like McKelvey, Vaynerchuk, or Benioff, for we each possess our unique set of advantages and challenges. We harbor our own distinct ideas and sources of motivation that propel us forward. It is these factors that hold utmost significance in our personal journeys. That's what matters. Still, emulation of what's worked and who it's worked for is a good place to start:

First, identify a cause, problem, or project that encompasses your overall sense of purpose.

For McKelvey, starting Square appealed to his purpose because he was working to solve a pressing problem that he was *personally* experiencing. He loved his glassblowing work but found himself sacrificing sales because he couldn't accept credit card payments.

There are no limits to your sense of purpose. It can be anything! You might feel driven to make life easier for your community by delivering the best customer experience possible in your sector. Whatever it is, make sure that that drive is present in the work that you're doing. It's what inspires out-of-the-box thinking and allows you to develop solutions that the competition has never considered.

Now let's look at *finding the courage to act without clear examples.* MeKelvey's many ventures underscore his ability for courage, so do seemingly superhuman entrepreneurs like Gary Vaynerchuk. What about you?

It's the Mental Game That Matters

It's my long-held belief that it's all about the mental game. Focusing inward to press forward regardless of any prevalent thinking to the contrary. Action rules everything in this case, so taking small steps makes a big difference. Constantly focus on your strengths and double down on them. McKelvey and Dorsey didn't have everything figured out on day one when they created Square, but they were brave enough to launch experiments that would bring them closer to their goals. You have to do the same thing when you are trying to determine your future vision.

Does it surprise you that the mental game may be more difficult to navigate than the physical game? I learned this at the Naval Academy. You can learn it in the business world. Either way, it's about moving past fear into impassioned action.

And, finally, there is your *ability to resist herding*. This is your time to shine. To have the courage to act without walking in the shoes of anyone ahead of you. To avoid succumbing to any counterpressure and expectations from others.

It *can* be done.

> Are you comfortable with the fact that you may be drastically wrong in your thesis?
> Are you willing to withstand the puzzled looks and judgments of others?
> Are you willing to stand alone, apart from the herd?

If you answered *yes*, congratulations. The more you are willing to be wrong, step into courage, withstand judgment, stand apart from the herd, and resist the herd, the easier it is to continue resisting the impulse to capitulate. You become inoculated to others' opinions that invite you to stop pursuing your goals. Granted, feedback isn't worthless. Opinions on your project, company, or leadership qualities can provide just the stimulus you need to propel necessary change. But no opinion should prevent you from pursuing an "unconventional idea" based on the herd's rejection. While non-conformists may not always be right, the payoff is nothing short of massive when they are.

Doing Leadership Differently

Yes, passion-struck leaders like Jim do things differently, including how they place a high priority on inspiring their team. But they don't stop there. They recognize their duty and obligation to use their resources to influence positive change in the world. Passion-struck leaders are willing to take a stand in the boardroom and the world, whether they're creating new hardware to help small business owners or having the courage to donate a percentage of total sales to certain activist groups. No matter the naysayers, criticism, or even temporary failures, they keep going, making success virtually inevitable.

You could be sitting on a game-changing idea as you're reading this. But if it remains in the confines of your brain, you'll never know what that vague idea or a better iteration of an existing solution to a problem could achieve. That's why the first step on your transformational journey is to become a "mission angler"—harnessing the power to do something novel.

Scan this QR code for additional insights and bonus material.

Chapter Exercises: Unleashing Your Mission Angler Potential

- Seeking Purpose: Reflect on your life and experiences to uncover moments when you felt a deep sense of purpose or fulfillment. Write a personal narrative highlighting these instances and identify common themes or values that resonate with you. Use this reflection to craft a mission statement that encapsulates your purpose and drives you forward.

- Embracing Courage: Identify an area in your life where you've been holding back or playing it safe due to fear or uncertainty. Write down the potential risks and rewards of stepping outside your comfort zone in this area. Develop an action plan to courageously pursue a new direction, acknowledging that embracing discomfort often leads to personal growth and expanded possibilities.

- Navigating the Uncertain Path: Select a goal or aspiration that is currently uncertain or challenging. Break it down into smaller, manageable steps and create a roadmap with specific milestones. Visualize potential obstacles and develop contingency plans to overcome them. Take one brave step forward and document your progress along the way, celebrating each milestone reached.

- Cultivating Authenticity: Reflect on areas of your life where you've been influenced by societal expectations or the opinions of others. Identify one area where you can break away from the crowd and express your true self authentically. Write a personal manifesto or declaration embracing your unique qualities and values. Share it with a trusted friend or mentor for support and accountability.

- Finding Inspiration: Seek out individuals, books, podcasts, or documentaries that embody the mission angler spirit. Engage with their stories and insights, extracting lessons that resonate with your own journey. Create a vision board or collage incorporating images and quotes that inspire and remind you of the path you are forging.

Remember, these exercises are designed to help you discover your purpose, tap into your untapped potential, and navigate the uncharted territory with courage. Embrace the transformative power of authenticity and the rewards that come from charting your own course, separate from the crowd. Your mission angler journey awaits—take the first step with confidence and conviction.

CHAPTER 3

BRAND REINVENTOR—NEVER BEING AFRAID TO REINVENT YOURSELF

If you wait for the fear to go away, the opportunity will go away too.
—Leslie Biodgett

Comfort is the enemy of adaptability.

We all become comfortable at some point in our lives. We feel a great sense of undeniable safety and belonging by waking up each day to go to work, carrying out a series of familiar tasks during the day, and returning to our families for dinner and TV before bed. For many of you, the idea of continued reinvention (trading the comfortable for the unknown), is an idea close to your worst nightmare. But it shouldn't be.

In the immediate aftermath of realizing that you'll have to leave comfort behind, you might also understand that you might have to fundamentally change what got you to this point in your career in order to achieve your overall ambitions. That was definitely the case for my own passion-struck journey.

However, the issue today is that many people do not have a firm understanding of their self-identity. We tend to imagine ourselves as someone who is a bit more successful than we really are. This perception is mostly shaped by external factors: our upbringing, religion, friends, social media, and other external influences. Yet, to truly reinvent ourselves requires us to analyze who we really are and accept our strengths and weaknesses. This analysis is one of the most important steps in the journey and one that is often most overlooked.

Why? Because it can be an uncomfortable process.

For some, this realization is more paralyzing than the fear of failure. Leaving the safety net of waking up each day to go to work, carrying out a series of familiar tasks during the day, and returning to our families for dinner and TV before bed is too much to bear. But reinvention must become second nature to those desiring to be passion struck. It extends beyond just our careers and permeates all aspects of life, empowering us to constantly evolve and seize new opportunities.

Throughout my studies of passionate and successful leaders, a common thread emerges: they possess a deep understanding that personal growth thrives within the realm of continuous self-reinvention. These exceptional individuals willingly set aside the comforts of their social circles, familiar routines, established careers, work colleagues, and personal hobbies, all in the pursuit of their goals. They wholeheartedly immerse themselves in their endeavors, constantly seeking new connections and industry contacts. Moreover, they exhibit a remarkable ability to adapt and transform their very essence, aligning themselves with the person they need to become in order to achieve success. But, none of this happens without first understanding our self-identity—our goals, values, beliefs, and a whole set of associated self-representations and self-evaluations.

Dan Schawbel,[45] a partner and research director at Future Workplace, interviewed more than 1,200 remarkable individuals. These interviewees ranged from CEOs and celebrities to authors, politicians, and even an astronaut. Throughout his conversations, Schawbel keenly observed a prevailing characteristic shared among them all: the consistent pursuit of reinvention.

Regardless of their respective fields or backgrounds, these individuals understood that reinvention was not just a luxury but a necessity. They recognized that in a world of constant change and evolving dynamics, embracing the idea of reinvention was a powerful tool for personal growth, professional advancement, and staying ahead of the curve.

Whether it was a CEO seeking to transform their company's business model, a celebrity exploring new creative ventures, an author pushing the boundaries of their writing style, or a politician adapting to the changing needs of their constituents, each person acknowledged the value of reinventing themselves to achieve their goals.

Through his interviews, Schawbel discovered that the act of reinvention was not a one-time event but an ongoing process. It required self-reflection, a deep understanding of one's strengths and weaknesses, and the courage to embark on new ventures.

As Eleanor Roosevelt eloquently put it:

> Do one thing every day that scares you. You gain strength, courage, and confidence by every experience in which you really stop to look fear in the face. You are able to say to yourself, "I lived through this horror. I can take the next thing that comes along." You must do the thing you think you cannot do.[46]

Embracing Change: The Path to Continuous Adaptation

In our quest to embrace change, Aidan McCullen, the author of *Undisruptable: A Mindset of Permanent Reinvention for Individuals,*

Organizations and Life, offers a thought-provoking Zen proverb that encapsulates a profound insight:

"Knowledge is learning something new every day. Wisdom is letting go of something every day."

This simple yet powerful statement reminds us that true wisdom extends beyond accumulating knowledge. While learning and acquiring new information are important, it is equally vital to cultivate the ability to let go of outdated beliefs, perspectives, and habits. Wisdom emerges from the deliberate process of shedding what no longer serves us, creating space for personal growth and transformation.

McCullen astutely observes that while many aspire to change the world, few daydream about transforming themselves. The human brain tends to perceive new ideas as abnormal and instinctively resists them. This natural inclination poses a formidable barrier to embracing transformational change on a continuous basis. To overcome this resistance, individuals must actively shed outdated information, making room for new insights and approaches.

Just look at Marc Benioff, Gary Vaynerchuk, and Jim McKelvey from the previous chapters. Do you think Benioff wasn't scared to throw away his over-achieving career at Oracle in pursuit of a new opportunity (Salesforce), no matter how "right" it felt to do so? Or that Jim McKelvey wasn't apprehensive about transitioning from a glassblower at Third Degree Glass Factory to become the co-founder of Square? And what about Gary Vaynerchuk? Was he not nervous about leaving his prosperous job in the wine industry to embark on establishing Vayner Media? Of course, they were. But by confronting that fear of reinventing themselves face on, they managed to overcome obstacle after obstacle and create three of the largest and most successful companies in the world.

I, myself, have had to reinvent who I was on many occasions, sometimes by choice, other times as a result of the circumstances unfolding around me. Each time I went through the holistic alterations to reinvent myself, I became a better person for it. At the conclusion of my time in the military, I examined my next life chapter and applied to the CIA, National Security Agency (NSA), FBI, and Drug Enforcement Agency (DEA). I ended up accepting the offer to join the FBI as a special agent. However, just a week before my Quantico class, I received a call from my detailer to say that there was a funding shortfall, and my class was put on hold indefinitely.

Instead of taking on a menial job and waiting for the class to be reinstated, I took action. I researched where I could apply my skill set in cybersecurity, leadership, and operations from the military and learn business acumen. The answer became clear to me that management consulting offered both. After contacting a variety of firms, I eventually landed a role with Booz Allen as an associate, before leaving after a few years to become a senior manager at Arthur Anderson, leading its cybersecurity practice for the Southwest.

But then, the Enron scandal struck, and my entire book of business evaporated in a matter of weeks. Suddenly, I found myself once again at a crossroads, facing the daunting task of reinventing myself.

The emotional and financial toll of witnessing my long-term aspirations crumble was profound. It was a pivotal moment that forced me to reassess my trajectory and embrace change. Determined to explore new horizons and gain global experience, I delved into the world of technology-driven transformation, with the ambition of becoming a successful CIO. Through perseverance and hard work, I spent nine years honing my skills within multiple Fortune 100 companies, eventually achieving the esteemed position of a CIO at Dell.

However, as time passed, I felt an insistent call to change course and follow my true passion. Over the past decade alone, I have undergone multiple reinventions, each marked by a significant personal rebranding and an unwavering commitment to confronting the fear of the unknown. From stepping into the role of COO to taking the reins as CEO, and eventually embracing the path of an entrepreneur, author, speaker, and podcaster, each transformation demanded a deep introspection and a willingness to embrace uncertainty.

These reinventions were not merely superficial changes; they were profound shifts that reshaped my identity and propelled me towards a life aligned with my true calling. Each time, I faced the fear of venturing into uncharted territories, willingly leaving behind the comfort of familiarity for the promise of personal and professional growth. It was in these moments of self-reinvention that I discovered the immense power of embracing change, fully realizing that the unknown held infinite possibilities waiting to be explored.

The journey of reinvention is not without its challenges. It demands resilience, adaptability, and an unwavering belief in one's own potential. It requires us to shed old beliefs, redefine our purpose, and fearlessly pursue our passions. But through these transformations, we find the courage to redefine our path and create a life that aligns with our deepest desires.

As I reflect on my own journey of continuous reinvention, I am reminded that the fear of the unknown should never hinder our pursuit of growth and fulfillment. It is through embracing change, confronting our fears, and carving new paths that we unlock our true potential and leave an indelible mark on the world.

So, let us not shy away from reinventing ourselves time and time again. Let us embrace the profound transformations that beckon us, for it is in these moments that we unlock our greatest potential and discover the extraordinary possibilities that await us.

From Linebacker to Hollywood's Leading Man

When it comes to athletes, the contrast is stark between those who reinvent themselves and prosper and those who stand still and suffer the consequences. I think one of the best examples of an athlete constantly reimagining himself and how he defines himself is Dwayne "The Rock" Johnson. His story underscores the power of continual reinvention to become one of the highest-paid actors in Hollywood today.[47]

While many of you will know Dwayne Johnson as one of the most bankable Hollywood stars around, not that long ago, his hopes and aspirations were far different from those of today. For one, he had a troubled childhood, which involved bouncing around homes and schools across the country as his dad toured the wrestling circuits of the World Wrestling Federation (WWF), now World Wrestling Entertainment (WWE). Even though his father was a professional wrestler, the Johnsons were anything but financially secure. Johnson and his mother were evicted from their Honolulu home when he was just fourteen, and he turned to pickpocketing tourists to survive. While in police custody as a result of his activities, he realized that he had to change: he had to reinvent himself.

He assessed those around him in his life and realized that the most successful around him were guys who worked on and looked after their bodies. So, he set about working out as much as possible, hoping that he could somehow transform physical attributes into better opportunities in life. That work paid off. After a chance encounter with a high school football coach, in a bathroom reserved for faculty members, he was asked to play for the school team. After becoming a standout defensive football player in his high school days, Johnson went on to be recruited by the University of Miami Hurricanes on a full scholarship. Even though his role at college was much more limited (thanks to the emergence of the previously mentioned Warren Sapp),[48] he still managed thirty-nine appearances, seventy-seven tackles, and formed a part of the 1991 National Championship-winning team.

Undeterred by a lack of interest from the NFL upon graduation, he signed with the Calgary Stampeders to prove doubters wrong and earn his right to a spot in the Canadian Football League (CFL). Two months later, he was cut from the team, and his dream to play professional football was in tatters. He moved back in with his parents, and he's often publicly recalled how he unearthed his wallet on the 4 a.m. drive back from Miami to Tampa,[49] and counted a five-dollar bill, a one-dollar bill, and some change. After everything he had been through, he had barely seven dollars to his name. Once again, he found himself at rock bottom (no pun intended), needing to reinvent himself to survive.

This time, he looked within his family and secured a tryout at one of the WWF's minor league events. While his wrestling lineage may have helped him to secure an audition, his progression through the system became anything but expedited. He spent months on end touring with minor wrestling events before landing his TV debut in 1996 on the *Survivor* series. His initial reception was lukewarm as best, and he had a hard time holding on to his spot on the weekly wrestling show *Monday Night Raw*. After spending some time on the sidelines nursing a knee injury, he refused to try to win back the adoration of the crowd upon his return. Instead, he teamed up with fellow wrestlers Faarooq, D'Lo Brown, and Kama to form the Nation of Domination. By embracing the villainous "heel" role required in wrestling, Johnson was able to make the transition from Rocky Mavia (his original wrestling name) to the persona known as The Rock. And he would continuously refer to himself in the third person with phrases like "The Rock says," and "Do you smell what The Rock is cookin'?"

His performances in this new role piqued the interest of Vince McMahon at the WWF. He soon realized that The Rock would be much better suited to a solo role within the organization. A storyline was scripted to disband the Nation of Domination, and Johnson burst out of his shackles to subsequently dominate the WWE as it is now known for the next decade. Once he reached the top, Johnson decided he was going to try his hand at acting, even though he was at the peak of his wrestling career. Despite landing $5.5 million for his first leading role in the movie *The Mummy Returns*, many of his subsequent films were box office flops, and he began to question his latest reinvention. However, he trusted his gut and redoubled his work effort, putting out several movies per year until he landed transformative roles in franchises such as *G.I. Joe* and the *Fast and Furious* movies. The rest, as they say, is history.

Johnson's story underlines why reinvention, no matter how scary, rarely ends in disaster. It takes a particular type of person to leave an industry while on top (as was the case with wrestling), but it was a decision that has continued to pay dividends ever since. Just as with my experience, some reinventions were forced upon him, whereas the transition from wrestler to actor was a decision he made himself. When everyone was calling him crazy for "throwing away" his wrestling career, he knew, as did I, that once you've wholly reinvented yourself once, you lose the fear surrounding doing so again.

In the realm of personal reinvention, athletes often come to mind as individuals who undergo profound transformations. Yet, the journey of veterans transitioning from their time in the military to the business world, especially those without the same physical advantages, presents a unique and inspiring challenge. Amongst the myriad stories of reinvention, there is one that stands out above the rest: the remarkable tale of the special operators behind American Freedom Distillery.[50]

These exceptional individuals, driven by an unwavering sense of purpose, embarked on an intentional path of reinvention. They embraced the power of resilience, adaptability, and relentless determination to forge a new chapter in their lives. Transitioning from the demanding world of special operations to the nuanced terrain of entrepreneurship required them to navigate uncharted waters, utilizing their exceptional skills and unwavering commitment to excellence.

From Elite Warriors to Elite Bourbon-Makers

The incredible tale of Horse Soldier Bourbon is a testament to the extraordinary journey of its founders, John Koko, Mark Nutsch, and Scott Neil, and their reinvention. In the wake of the devastating 9/11 attacks, while the nation watched in shock and horror, a team of twelve Green Berets sprang into action. Unbeknownst to them until just forty-eight hours before their insertion, their mission, named Task Force Dagger, required them to navigate the treacherous Afghan landscape on horseback. With little time for preparation, they faced a series of daunting challenges that they had to overcome on the fly.

Cut off from regular communications and facing overwhelming odds with a forty-to-one disadvantage, these brave men, known as the Horse Soldiers, fought alongside local allies in intense battles. Their unwavering determination and strategic prowess resulted in the capture of Mazar-i-Sharif, a crucial Taliban stronghold. The remarkable saga of the Horse Soldiers became the inspiration for a book, a movie,[51] and a monument at the 9/11 Memorial in New York,[52] immortalizing their heroic actions.

Almost two decades later, the retired special operators, including Scott Neil, Rob Schaefer, Mark Nutsch, Bob Pennington, Tyler Garner, and John Koko, alongside Elizabeth Pritchard-Koko, embarked on a new mission to continue their legacy. It was during this remarkable journey that their shared love for whiskey deepened, and the allure of bourbon-making captured their hearts. This led them to found American Freedom Distillery, driven by a shared purpose and a desire to make their mark. At the core of their all-American company is their prized creation, the award-winning Horse Soldier Bourbon. Each bottle proudly features molds crafted from steel salvaged from the site where the Twin Towers once stood, serving as a powerful symbol of resilience and remembrance.

Reflecting on their journey, Neil shared with me a pivotal moment during a horseback trip out west with Koko and Pritchard-Koko. While exploring the possibilities for the next phase of their lives, they stumbled upon the Grand Teton Distillery in Driggs, Idaho. The couple who owned the distillery allowed them behind the scenes, sparking an "aha!" moment. Inspired by this experience, they spent the following weeks visiting craft distilleries across the country, solidifying their passion for the industry. It was during this remarkable journey that their shared love for whiskey deepened, and the allure of bourbon-making captured their hearts. They resolved to establish a brand that would epitomize their values and redefine their purpose.

Their quest for knowledge led them to Scotland, where they trained at Wolfburn Distillery with a friend who was a Royal Marine. From there, they traveled to Ireland to learn from one of the oldest distilling families in the world. Immersed in the craft, they delved into the intricacies of bourbon-making, even attending a distilling school in Kentucky. The distilling community embraced them, generously sharing information and expertise. They were committed to launching their product only when it met the high standards they set for themselves.

The men transformed themselves from elite warriors to elite bourbon-makers. They devoted themselves to mastering the intricate art of distilling, blending, and aging, relentlessly pursuing perfection in every sip. Through countless trials and tribulations, they painstakingly crafted a bourbon that would captivate the palates of connoisseurs, a testament to their unwavering commitment to quality and craftsmanship.

But their vision extended far beyond the creation of exceptional bourbon. They aspired to leave a lasting legacy, one that would honor the heritage of bourbon-making. They dreamt of establishing a distillery in the heartland of Kentucky, a place renowned for its rich history and passion for whiskey. This decision embodied their deep respect for the craft and their desire to contribute to the tapestry of the industry they had come to love.

The journey of reinvention embarked upon by Koko, Neil, Schaefer, Nutsch, Pennington, Garner, and Pritchard-Koko is a testament to their unwavering determination, resilience, and the pursuit of their passions. They transformed themselves from elite warriors into master distillers, channeling their expertise, discipline, and unwavering spirit into the creation of Horse Soldier Bourbon. It stands today as a symbol of their unwavering commitment to excellence, their willingness to embrace change, and their indomitable spirit of reinvention.

There's no doubt that Johnson's, and the Horse Soldiers' reinvention stories are inspirational, but how can you apply their experiences to your life?

Why Reinvent Yourself?

I was recently watching separate interviews with famed guitarist Eddie Van Halen and singer-songwriter David Gray. Both of them discussed the need for reinvention during their musical careers. Van Halen explained how he initially was a pianist, then a drummer, and then when he realized that his brother Alex was better than he was, he switched to playing guitar. We know the rest of the story. And, even though he ended up altering how the guitar is played, he continually had to take it up a notch and invent something new. Staying stagnant was never an option. After the phenomenal success over a decade of releasing chart-topping hits, Gray realized that he was at an inflection point and needed to reinvent his style. He got out of his comfort zone and created an edgier[53] sound featured on the album *Draw the Line*. Although it resulted in his poorest performing album release, the reinvention allowed him to pivot into what he calls his second phase.

Through all these examples, it is essential to understand that passion-struck leaders do not reinvent themselves at a moment's notice. As mentioned, Marc Benioff already had a career that would have been the envy of millions,[54] but it didn't fulfill him. He was willing to put it all on the line to reinvent himself as an entrepreneur, and it paid off in a way even he could never have imagined. He struggled at first, and it took him many years of working out of his garage, and then house, to do it.

There's no doubt that the process of reinvention, no matter your age, can feel like a huge risk. You're putting your degrees, industry experience, and earning power at risk for the pursuit of something you're genuinely passionate about, with no guarantees of success. Nonetheless, if you've emotionally checked out of your career, then the thought should be as exhilarating as it is terrifying.

Whether you desire the ability to travel more, return to study, become passionate about what you do for a living, or earn an income not possible in your current industry or position, reinvention is a process that is different for everyone. For most, it is a development that takes place over several years or even decades. It certainly doesn't happen overnight. Remember, this is a process whereby you are both changing how you view yourself and altering the perceptions of those around you. That is going to take time. So don't become disheartened if your transformation takes longer than you'd anticipated.

With regards to specific lessons that you can learn from successful reinvention stories, I have found through my research that, no matter the particulars of a journey, reinvention stories boil down to four critical takeaways. You'll need to grasp and master them all to genuinely reinvent yourself, as passion-struck individuals have done before you.

1. Ditch Comfort

The biggest obstacle to any reimagination or reinvention of who you are is comfort. As mentioned in the opening of this chapter, comfort is the enemy of adaptability. In all the examples I have described, comfort was available. I could have continued in my role as a CIO at Dell, Dwayne Johnson could have wrestled to his heart's content, and the Horse Soldiers could have gone into civil service or defense and security contracting.

And yet, none of us did. Why? Because comfort wasn't an option for us. If you're comfortable in your current situation, it's likely that you're standing in the way of your potential. Reinventing yourself is frightening; and yes, there is a chance of failure lurking in the shadows, but let me tell you this: every triumphant leader, fueled by unwavering passion, has tasted the bitterness of failure along their arduous journey. It is through these failures that they have discovered their true strength. But here's the harsh reality: if you shy away from taking that audacious leap and fail to learn from your stumbles, you will forever dwell in a realm of uncertainty, ignorant of the remarkable feats you were destined to achieve. The prospect may be intimidating, but the price of complacency far outweighs the risks of reinvention.

Take a step in the right direction by challenging yourself to break free from the comfort of a familiar routine. Instead of following the same daily pattern, try incorporating a new activity or hobby into your schedule. It could be something as simple as taking a different route to work, trying a new recipe, or exploring a genre of music or literature that you've never experienced before. By venturing outside your comfort zone in these small ways, you open yourself up to new perspectives and possibilities. This subtle shift in routine not only stimulates your mind but also fosters adaptability and a willingness to embrace change. By exposing yourself to the inherent fear of change, you will become more adaptable to new situations. The more you become used to this type of adaptation, the better you will become at reinventing yourself when the time comes.

2. Create a Vision for Your Future Self by Measuring Your Gains

"If you can dream it, you can achieve it," so the saying goes. There's no point merely saying you want to reinvent yourself; you need a purpose attached to it. Otherwise, you'll never follow it through. When I left Dell, I realized after a conversation with Tony Robbins that while I enjoyed the CIO role, I came to the harsh realization that it was not my ultimate calling and it left little room for anything else. I used my reinvention first to become a successful CEO, and then to create the necessary space in my life to carry out the speaking, writing, and consulting about which I felt passionate. In doing so, I had to examine where I was in life, compared to my past self, and where I eventually wanted to go (my ideal), and face the reality between the gap and the gain, something that Benjamin Hardy refers to in his book that he co-wrote with Dan Sullivan, *The Gap and the Gain: The High Achievers' Guide to Happiness, Confidence, and Success.*[55] In my interview with Hardy from the *Passion Struck* podcast, he explained the concept:

> *The Gap and the Gain* is a model by which you measure your own experience, and you measure yourself and you measure other people. And really, we're all measuring ourselves and our experiences in certain ways. And in society, we've been trained to do it in a way that leads to what Dan would call the gap,

which is where we're measuring ourselves, our progress, our experiences against an ideal. And I see this
all the time in myself. And usually, if you're feeling
bad about yourself, it's because you're in the gap.
It's because you're measuring where you are against
where you thought you should be or where you could
be or what you wish had happened.

The gain is a totally opposite way to live life. And
it leads to more intrinsic motivation, it leads to getting
a lot more connected with your core self, and leaving
the gap alone, not that none of us are ever perfect. We
all go into the gap regularly, where we're measuring
ourselves or some other situation against an ideal, but
the gain is really very simple. It's about just measuring
yourself backward against where you were before.[56]

For Dwayne Johnson, the picture of his gain was very different.
He went from a professional football player in the CFL to a wrestler
over time to put food on the table for his family and move out of his
parents' apartment. His motivation was to provide an income and not
let them down, which drove him on through the monotony of the
minor league wrestling events spread across the country.

For the Horse Soldiers, their fascination with a shared commitment to "excellence" drove them forward towards reinvention. In
envisioning our future selves, we must confront a pressing issue that
plagues many: a lack of firm understanding of our true identity. We
often find ourselves creating an idealized version of who we are, a
projection of success that surpasses our current reality. However, to
embark on a genuine reinvention, we must summon the courage to
delve into the depths of our being and unravel the intricate tapestry
of our true selves. It necessitates a profound analysis, an honest con-
frontation with our strengths and weaknesses. Yet, it is precisely this
pivotal step that tends to be overlooked and underestimated in our
journey of transformation.

The process of self-analysis demands vulnerability and a willingness to face uncomfortable truths. It requires us to peel back the layers of societal expectations, shed the masks we wear, and bravely confront the essence of our being. Only by understanding who we truly are can we lay the foundation for a meaningful reinvention—a reinvention that aligns with our authentic selves.

Let us not underestimate the power of self-reflection as we navigate this transformative journey. Through self-analysis, we unlock the doors to our passions, unveil untapped potential, and embrace the unique qualities that set us apart. It is within this exploration that we discover the raw materials from which we can shape our future self—a self grounded in self-awareness, self-acceptance, and self-love.

As you engage in this process, consider an example: Imagine you are an individual seeking to transition from a corporate career to entrepreneurship. Perform a deep self-analysis to identify the reasons behind this desire for reinvention. Perhaps you yearn for greater autonomy, the opportunity to pursue your passions, or a desire to make a meaningful impact on the world. These fundamental principles serve as your "why"—the bedrock of your reinvention journey. By holding steadfast to your "why," you navigate the twists and turns of your journey, embracing the transformative power of self-reinvention. With each obstacle you overcome, you emerge stronger, more resilient, and closer to the person you aspire to become.

3. The Significance of Fresh Starts

As humans, we possess an inherent inclination to structure our lives around significant events, marking the transition from one chapter to the next. It is during these moments of reinvention that we find ourselves fueled by a unique motivation—an opportunity to leave behind the old and embrace the new. With a clean slate before us, we are unburdened by past limitations, enabling us to embark on transformative journeys. This liberating concept holds tremendous power in shaping our behavior and catalyzing personal growth.

Research conducted by University of Pennsylvania behavior scientist Katy Milkman and her colleagues[57] sheds light on the importance of recognizing and highlighting these opportunities for fresh starts, no matter how small they may seem. Even the simple act of entering a new week, with Monday as a prominent symbol of renewal, can spark profound changes in our actions and choices. This phenomenon stems from the psychological shift we experience when we perceive ourselves as transitioning from the old version of who we were to an empowered "new me."

The power of fresh starts lies in their frequency and accessibility. They are not confined to major life events; instead, they present themselves in various forms throughout our lives. Each Monday, for instance, holds the potential to inspire us to pursue healthy habits and set new goals. By consciously acknowledging and leveraging these moments of renewal, we can harness their transformative energy to fuel positive change.

Milkman writes in her book *How to Change*, "We're more likely to pursue change on dates that feel like new beginnings because these moments help us overcome a common obstacle to goal initiation: the sense that we've failed before and will, thus, fail again."

Consider the profound impact of simply flagging an upcoming birthday. This subtle reminder can motivate individuals to reevaluate their financial habits and start saving more for retirement. It exemplifies the power of fresh starts in instigating behavioral shifts and encouraging us to take proactive steps towards our desired outcomes.

4. Rebrand Yourself

Perhaps the most challenging step of the procedure is rebranding yourself. As we mature, we begin to develop a specific self-image, and that self-image can be incredibly difficult to let go and replace. From the age of a young teenager, all that Dwayne Johnson wanted was to be a professional football player. A few months after graduation and his dreams lay shattered on the ground, leading to depression.[58]

After working through his mental health battles, he realized quickly that his football career was over and that he had to close off that part of his life to move on. That's why his first move after moping around his parents' apartment for two weeks wasn't to contact the WWF. Instead, it was to put in a phone call to Calgary Stampeders coach Wally Buono to say he wasn't going to try out next season and was going to focus on other projects instead. That move was significant because it marked a personal rebranding—Johnson no longer identified with the sport of football; he had severed that tie forever.

With that in mind, look to redefine yourself as part of the process. Practice saying and believing new things about yourself, and really mean them. All transitions are tough, but by cutting ties to what you once held dear, you can begin to reshape who you are as both a person and a professional. For instance, let's say you're an attorney reinventing yourself to become a business owner. When it comes time to take just another legal case, you need to cut off that safety net and go all-in on your new identity.

"Why?" Is the Most Important Question for Reinvention

It holds the key to unlocking our true motivations, aspirations, and meaning. By understanding our deeper motivations and aligning our reinvention efforts with our true purpose, we can embark on a transformative journey that leads to greater fulfillment, success, and a life that is true to who we are. Both my personal story and those detailed within this chapter perfectly illustrate that reinvention is possible for anyone. In fact, it's frequently thrown at us rather than being a conscious choice. However, at least in the cases of McKelvey, Johnson, and myself, once that reinvention was forced on us, we all reinvented ourselves of our own volition.

Why?

Because we recognized its power. We learned from our earlier reinventions that they have the ability to change our lives for the better. Although they are frequently accompanied by trials and tribulations, whatever has awaited us on the other side has always proven worth the journey.

That's why you need to trust me when I say that you can reinvent yourself. You, too, can reap the rewards of making a fundamental change to your life. It's a distinct path for all of us. Some will endure more hardship than others. Some will struggle with loneliness, while others will be wracked with self-doubt and fear when things don't initially go as planned.

But as the old adage goes: true courage isn't about not feeling fear; it's about feeling fear and acting anyway.

Therefore, I urge you to choose the courage of reinvention, rather than letting the fear of change choose your future for you. Unfortunately, if you lack the conviction to reinvent yourself to match the required skills, values, and beliefs of each step of your journey, you won't make it to your end destination.

By becoming a "brand reinventor" you can become an unstoppable force. Once you realize that comfort and the fear of change are your real enemies, you'll be able to do what is necessary to make your dreams into a reality, no matter what it takes. This stage isn't easy and overlaps with both the previous and the next principle of this framework—weeding out the mosquitoes in your life.

Scan this QR code for additional insights and bonus material.

Chapter Exercises: Learn the Power of Reinvention

- Vision Board: Create a visual representation of your desired brand identity and future self. Compile images, words, and symbols that resonate with your aspirations and values. Arrange them on a board or create a digital collage as a constant reminder of the brand you aim to become.
- Define Your Values: Reflect on your core values and principles. Clarify what you stand for and what drives your actions and decisions. Articulate your values, as they will serve as guiding principles in shaping your brand identity.
- Personal Brand Audit: Conduct a thorough evaluation of your current brand image. Assess your online presence, social media profiles, resume, and professional networks. Identify areas where your brand may need improvement or realignment with your reinvention goals.
- Personal Brand Story: Craft a compelling narrative that communicates your brand's unique journey, strengths, and aspirations. Write your personal brand story, highlighting key experiences, accomplishments, and lessons learned. Practice sharing this story in a concise and impactful manner.
- Personal Branding Statement: Develop a clear and concise personal branding statement that encapsulates your unique value proposition, expertise, and passions. Craft it in a way that resonates with your target audience and differentiates you from competitors.

Remember, reinvention is a transformative process. Embrace these exercises as opportunities for self-discovery, growth, and transformation. With determination, exploration, and a commitment to reinvent, you will unlock the power to create an authentic brand that reflects your true self and paves the way for a successful future.

CHAPTER 4

MOSQUITO AUDITOR — AVOID THE MOST DANGEROUS ANIMAL ON THE PLANET

*Without doubt, the most common weakness of all
human beings is the habit of leaving their minds
open to the negative influence of other people.*
—Napoleon Hill

Toxicity is the enemy of world-class success.

As I was listening to the radio on my daily commute, the talk show host posed a question to the audience: "What's the deadliest animal on the planet?" A series of educated guesses ran through my head. The Mojave rattlesnake? The great white shark? The Australian box jellyfish? Perhaps the crocodile or a tiger?

As it turns out, I wasn't even remotely close. These predators don't even make a dent on the numbers of human deaths racked up by the world's deadliest animal—the mosquito.[59] The predators I once considered formidable hardly make a mark when compared to the studding toll inflicted by the world's most lethal creature—the mosquito.[60] Astonishingly, these tiny insects claim more human lives annually than sharks do in an entire century. While sharks account for fewer than a dozen human fatalities per year worldwide, the mosquitoes' devastating impact translates to a staggering 50,000 times that number.[61] What makes a mosquito so dangerous?

Why Mosquitoes Are the Most Dangerous Animal on the Planet

Mosquitoes claim so many lives because they can carry and infect humans with a range of potentially deadly diseases. Unfortunately, if you thought it was just malaria, you're significantly wide of the mark. Zika, West Nile, Chikungunya, dengue, yellow fever, Japanese encephalitis, and malaria are all mosquito-borne diseases.

All told, these tiny flying insects kill more than one million people every year and account for 17 percent of the estimated global burden of infectious diseases.[62] Worse, they can pass these diseases on to other parasites, increasing the risk to us humans further still. The most concerning species is the Anopheles mosquito, which is responsible for the deaths of 400,000 people (mainly children) through malaria transmission.

And yet these insects seem so unassuming and benign. You wouldn't think twice about swatting one away that was bothering you—which got me thinking. There are numerous examples in the business and personal world whereby people spend so much time and energy staying out of their perceived predators' clutches that they miss the invisible mosquitoes sucking the blood from them right before their very eyes.

Confused? Let me explain.

The Sharks and the Mosquitoes— Learn to Distinguish Which Is Which

While many of my colleagues have dedicated their careers to fretting over the predators that lurk (let's call them sharks) in their lives, I have come to realize the immense significance of differentiating them from the minuscule yet formidable mosquitoes. Mastering this discernment holds the key to expediting the attainment of your goals and aspirations.

The Helpful Sharks

The presence of a mentor embodying the qualities of a shark can wield remarkable benefits for both personal and professional growth. In this context, the term "sharks" alludes to seasoned and accomplished individuals who gracefully assume the role of guides, providing invaluable direction, unwavering support, and profound wisdom to those less experienced. These mentors possess the ability to share their own vast experiences and knowledge, acting as beacons of guidance, steering their protégés away from common pitfalls, imparting new skills, and illuminating the intricate nuances of the respective industries. In a business setting, a shark is usually defined as someone above you in the corporate food chain, most likely your boss, or a mentor of higher rank that has a direct influence on your future career trajectory. In a personal setting, it could be a life coach, friend, your mother or father-in-law who may hold you to a higher standard than that of your parents, or indeed your spouse or significant other.

However, the truth is, no matter the setting, and regardless of how scary the shark may be, they are the catalysts that propel us forward, compelling us to reinvent ourselves, summon untapped reservoirs of strength, and forge resolutely ahead in our life journeys. They serve as the driving force behind our relentless pursuit of growth and trans-formation, pushing us to reach unparalleled heights of achievement and self-realization. An example that highlights the significance of having a shark mentor is my friend Matt Higgins, who is the CEO of RISE Ventures and served as vice chairman for the Miami Dolphins, executive vice president for the Jets, and was a guest "shark" on the Emmy-award-winning TV show *Shark Tank* during seasons 10 and 11. In a *Passion Struck* podcast interview with me, Matt shared his experience with the Jets and Dolphins and emphasized the impor-tance of having an owner who acted like a shark to the organization:

> Sports teams are no different than any other business that people look to for leadership at the top; they look for somebody who sets the tone in organizations that have enduring values, where people can orient them-selves to tend to perform better. So I think you need visible owners, you need active owners, you need owners who really care and you need to understand communication, because back to the point of insecu-rity, I don't think people perform well when they're very insecure and they don't know where they stand. When people don't know where they stand, they fill in the blanks and assume they're standing on quick-sand. I think when you have an owner who occupies the role and communicates at least to the coaches and GMs and understands where they stand, [that] is a strong mentor. And when they don't, they create a vacuum where everyone's vying for power.[63]

Additionally, sharks can introduce their mentees to people in their network, help them to navigate challenges, provide emotional sup-port, and hold them accountable for their goals. Ultimately, having a shark mentor can provide guidance, support, and motivation to help individuals to achieve their goals and reach their full potential.

Whether it's the fear of getting on the wrong side of your boss or avoiding the shame of letting a personal mentor down, the result is the same. They give you the motivation to develop, grow, and progress in life. In other words, sharks are helpful to you in life. They give you an impetus and edge over your peers. By contrast, mosquitoes are so deadly they'll drain the life out of you before you've even had the chance to notice.

Navigating the Presence of The Deadly Mosquitoes

Human mosquitoes are nowhere near as easy to distinguish as human sharks and cleverly disguise themselves as colleagues, mentors, family members, or friends while draining our energy and impeding our progress. They come in differing guises too, making their identification and avoidance all the more challenging.

During a thought-provoking interview with Robin Sharma, a renowned leadership expert, bestselling author, humanitarian, and motivational speaker, we delved into the pivotal role that relationships play in translating our grandest aspirations into meaningful, intentional results in our daily lives.

Sharma shares a valuable insight, stating, "I think you can change the world or be around negative people; you can't do both. And there's a lot of great science on emotional contagion[64] that confirms that we pick up the dominant emotions of the people we spend most of our time with. So doing an audit where you ask yourself, 'Who are the people in my life that elevate my joy?' And 'Who are the people in my life that steal my joy every time I come up with a new idea?' or they say, 'You know what? I watched or listened to *Passion Struck*. I'm going to do this. I'm going to run a marathon, start a business, or repair that relationship.' And that person says that that'll never work. Those are the people that are keeping you from world-class in so many ways."

66

Sharma's insightful revelation underscores the pivotal choice between charting our desired path in life or allowing negative influences to permeate our surroundings, shining a light on the potent force of emotional contagion and our inclination to internalize the prevailing emotions of those we share significant time with.

By identifying the individuals who inspire and elevate us, we can actively cultivate relationships that fuel our drive and propel us towards our goals. Simultaneously, recognizing and minimizing the impact of those who diminish our confidence and hinder our progress empowers us to create an environment conducive to achieving world-class success in all endeavors.

In the following sections, we will explore the three types of deadly mosquitoes we may encounter, beginning with those who employ flattery, sing our praises, and exploit our connections for personal gain.

Type 1: The Bloodsucker

In our relentless quest for personal growth and transformation, complacency stands as a formidable adversary. Those who yearn for change understand that settling is not an option; they constantly seek discomfort, challenge the status quo, and question established norms. Yet, lurking in the shadows, a stealthy and pernicious force threatens to derail our progress—the metaphorical bloodsucking mosquito.

In an intriguing conversation with Terri Cole, a distinguished psychotherapist, relationship expert, and author of the enlightening book *Boundary Boss*, we explored the bloodsucking mosquito, also known as what she refers to as a "boundary destroyer." This elusive yet potent force challenges our personal boundaries and obstructs our path to growth.

Cole explained, "The boundary destroyers are people that fall into their own category, so much so that I had to do a whole chapter on them [in *Boundary Boss*]. These are emotionally manipulative people who want what they want from you, no matter how you feel about it, no matter what your situation is."

The bloodsucking mosquito represents those who habitually dismiss and violate the boundaries of others. Their repertoire consists of emotionally manipulative tactics as they doggedly pursue their own objectives. Whether encountered in personal, familial, or professional relationships, these individuals undermine the boundaries we endeavor to establish, leaving us feeling disrespected, drained, and emotionally manipulated.

Gaslighting, love bombing, and emotional coercion are their weapons of choice used to assert control and override the boundaries we set. Their actions have profound and far-reaching consequences, leading to stagnation in our professional trajectory and personal fulfillment. Succumbing to the incessant onslaught of these bloodsucking mosquitoes confines us to a plateau where growth is stifled, and our true potential remains unrealized.

To illustrate the detrimental influence of these mosquitoes, imagine a scenario in a corporate setting where an ambitious and talented professional, whom I will refer to as Sarah, finds herself facing the challenges of working with a boundary destroyer. Sarah has always been known for her innovative ideas, exceptional work ethic, and ability to think outside the box. Her dedication to pushing boundaries and seeking growth has propelled her career forward.

However, Sarah encounters a colleague within her team, whom I call Emily, who exhibits the characteristics of a boundary destroyer. Emily constantly undermines Sarah's contributions, dismisses her ideas, and attempts to diminish her achievements. She utilizes subtle manipulation tactics, such as taking credit for Sarah's work or downplaying her successes during team meetings.

Whenever Sarah proposes a new approach or challenges the status quo, Emily responds with dismissive comments, attempts to belittle her, or even tries to sabotage her projects behind the scenes. Emily's actions are driven by deep-seated insecurity and a desire to maintain control and prominence within the team.

Despite Sarah's relentless efforts to establish clear boundaries and assert her ideas, Emily consistently violates these boundaries, leaving Sarah feeling disrespected and drained of her creative energy. The toxic dynamic fostered by Emily's behavior profoundly impacts Sarah's professional growth and seeps into her personal life, fostering self-doubt and eroding her overall confidence.

Drawing from personal experience, I, too, have crossed paths with an array of these bloodsucking mosquitoes, much like Sarah, both professionally and personally. In such situations, it became abundantly clear that succumbing to their manipulative tactics would only perpetuate a toxic environment and compromise my growth and well-being. To counteract their influence, I recognized the need to assert myself, protect my achievements, and refuse to be a pawn in their self-serving games.

These bloodsucking mosquitoes possess an arsenal of strategies designed to dismantle the boundaries we meticulously construct. They challenge our self-worth, question our intentions, and exploit our vulnerabilities. Their actions erode our confidence, hinder our personal growth, and confine us within the suffocating walls of stagnation.

We must first recognize their presence and the havoc they wreak to overcome the insidious influence of bloodsucking mosquitoes. Armed with self-awareness and an understanding of their manipulative tactics, we can reclaim our personal power and establish firm boundaries that protect our emotional well-being.

Drawing wisdom from experts like Terri Cole, we can learn to assert our boundaries confidently and unapologetically. By standing firm in the face of manipulation, we preserve our authenticity, maintain our self-worth, and refuse to be ensnared in the web of toxic relationships.

Type 2: The Invisible Suffocator

Among the ranks of deadly mosquitoes, another breed emerges—the "glass half empty" individuals who permeate your inner circle. These elusive creatures pose a considerable challenge, as their presence often goes undetected, making it arduous to extricate them from your life. These are the individuals who cling to the status quo, having achieved a certain level of success in their own careers, and seek to influence those around them to adopt a similar outlook. For example, if you were to gain a promotion, rather than be excited for you and congratulate you, they immediately gravitate toward negativity. "Think of the extra hours you're going to need to put in at work." "How are you going to fit in time with the kids?" "That's a lot of pressure; you might not last long."

While their true nature becomes more apparent from an outsider's perspective, identifying them when they wield immediate influence in your life proves to be a formidable task. If you find yourself mired in a sense of stagnation, be it in your professional endeavors or progress towards personal goals, it is imperative to examine the members of your inner circle and evaluate their impact. Do they occupy a similar level of ambition and drive as you? Do they belittle your efforts to go the extra mile? Do they harbor an aversion to change, clinging desperately to the familiar in your social or professional spheres?

When working with one of my mentors, Tony Robbins, he once said to me: "The quality of a person's life is most often a direct reflection of their peer group's expectations." If those expectations always stay the same, how do you expect to progress as an individual? As I've stated many times before, comfort never leads to breakthrough ideas. You have to embrace change and say *yes* every once in a while, even if it scares you.

As you assess the members of your inner circle, a profound revelation may emerge. The pernicious impact of these "glass half empty" individuals becomes glaringly apparent, acting as a barrier to your personal growth, impeding your relentless pursuit of excellence, and suffocating your aspirations. Their lackluster outlook holds the power to keep you anchored in a world of mediocrity, thwarting your potential for greatness.

Imagine pursuing a long-held dream of starting your own business. You're fueled by passion, determination, and a clear vision of success. However, in the midst of your journey, you encounter an invisible suffocator, let's refer to him as Mark, a close friend who, unfortunately, harbors a deeply pessimistic mindset.

Whenever you share your ambitious plans and aspirations with Mark, he immediately begins highlighting all the potential pitfalls and challenges. He dismisses your ideas as impractical, pointing out all the reasons why they won't work. His constant negativity starts to seep into your psyche, causing doubts to creep in and erode your confidence. You find yourself second-guessing your abilities and questioning whether your dreams are truly attainable.

Mark's pessimism extends beyond mere skepticism. He actively discourages you from taking risks or making bold moves, warning of inevitable failure and the consequences of stepping outside your comfort zone. His constant barrage of negativity weighs heavily on your spirit, casting a shadow over your enthusiasm and dimming the once bright flame of your dreams. As a result, you start hesitating, playing it safe, and settling for mediocrity, all because you've internalized Mark's glass-half-empty perspective.

In this scenario, the glass-half-empty person, Mark, becomes a significant roadblock on your path to fulfilling your dreams. His persistent negativity chips away at your confidence, erodes your motivation, and stifles your willingness to take risks. The dream that once burned brightly within you loses its luster under Mark's influence, and you find yourself settling for a life far from the one you had envisioned.

The impact of an invisible suffocator on your life and career can be profound. Their pessimism and constant negativity have the power to undermine your self-belief, hinder your progress, and stifle your potential. By casting doubt on your aspirations, they create a cloud of uncertainty that hampers your ability to take bold actions and pursue your dreams with conviction. Their influence can lead you down a path of mediocrity and missed opportunities, as you find yourself settling for less and shying away from the risks that could lead to your greatest achievements. It is crucial to take a courageous stance and reevaluate your alliances. Surround yourself with individuals who share your hunger for progress, who fuel your ambition, and who champion your pursuit of positive change.

Type 3: The PITA

In the tapestry of human interactions, there exists a breed of individuals who embody the essence of annoyance, frustration, and sheer exasperation—the dreaded pain-in-the-ass mosquitoes. Though you may not be familiar with the PITA abbreviation, their presence is likely all too familiar in your life. These elusive creatures can be remarkably difficult to detect initially, blending seamlessly into the fabric of everyday life. However, their impact on our well-being and the trajectory of our endeavors is undeniable. Let's delve deeper into the consequences of these insidious creatures at work and in our personal lives, shedding light on their disruptive nature.

To truly understand the PITA's intentions, one must observe their distinctive behavioral patterns. They are the ones who profess one thing to your face while covertly pursuing an entirely different agenda. These are the investors who lure you with the promise of financial support, only to encroach upon your daily operations and devour your precious time with incessant queries. They are the friends, peers, or bosses who seek your advice, only to discard it as inconsequential, only to later resurrect it as their own original thought. These are the demanding clients who expect exclusive attention, disregarding the needs of your other valued customers and stunting the growth of your business. In various contexts, these PITAs can be found, their impact reverberating through our personal and professional spheres.

Unmasking the Impact of a Pain-in-the-Ass Mosquito in the Workplace

In a vibrant and dynamic workplace, where synergy and teamwork are valued, a troubling presence silently takes hold. Picture a team of dedicated professionals, united by a shared vision and a commitment to excellence. However, lurking amidst their unity, a pain-in-the-ass mosquito begins to disrupt the harmony they have worked so hard to cultivate.

Let's call this individual Alex. Initially welcomed with open arms, Alex possesses an impressive skill set and a reputation for getting results. The team is hopeful that Alex's expertise will elevate their collective performance. But soon enough, it becomes evident that his impact is far from positive.

Rather than fostering collaboration, Alex consistently undermines their colleagues' contributions. Dismissing alternative viewpoints as inconsequential, he exerts a domineering presence in meetings, leaving others feeling overshadowed and undervalued. His need for control and constant one-upmanship creates an atmosphere of tension and discord.

In addition to his disruptive behavior, Alex's insatiable hunger for recognition becomes increasingly apparent. He demands attention and validation, often at the expense of their teammates. Interrupting conversations and downplaying others' accomplishments, he monopolizes the spotlight, leaving his colleagues frustrated and demoralized.

Moreover, Alex's lack of transparency and selective sharing of information further strains the team's efforts. Withholding crucial details and vital insights, he impedes progress and hinders collective problem-solving. This lack of cooperation and willingness to collaborate undermines the team's productivity and stifles their ability to innovate.

Despite efforts to address the issue and provide constructive feedback, Alex remains resistant to change. He dismisses others' concerns, unwilling to recognize the negative impact of his actions. This stubbornness erodes team morale, creating divisions and sowing seeds of discontent.

How a Pain-in-the-Ass Mosquito Can
Disrupt Your Personal Harmony

Imagine your personal life filled with joy, fulfillment, and a nurturing support system. You cherish the relationships that empower and uplift you. However, amid this harmonious existence, a pain-in-the-ass mosquito infiltrates your personal sphere, leaving a trail of frustration and disruption in her wake.

Let's refer to this mosquito as Lisa. At first encounter, Lisa may seem innocuous, perhaps even friendly. But as you spend more time together, you realize her presence is far from beneficial. Lisa exhibits a pattern of behavior that consistently drains your energy and hampers your personal growth.

In conversations, Lisa dominates the dialogue, rarely pausing to genuinely listen or show interest in your thoughts and experiences. Instead, she eagerly redirects the conversation back to herself, dismissing your contributions without a second thought. Her self-centeredness becomes increasingly evident, leaving you feeling unheard and devalued.

Furthermore, Lisa possesses an insatiable need for validation and attention, often at your expense. She expects you to cater to her demands, placing her desires above your own well-being. Your time and energy are continuously diverted towards meeting her expectations, leaving little room for self-care and personal development.

In social settings, Lisa consistently seeks the spotlight, overshadowing others and undermining your accomplishments. Her constant need to be the center of attention erodes your self-confidence, leaving you questioning your worth. The toxic presence of this mosquito stifles your personal growth, hindering your ability to flourish and embrace your true potential.

As you attempt to address these issues and establish boundaries, Lisa remains resistant to change. She dismisses your concerns and continues to prioritize her own interests, oblivious to the negative impact she has on your personal life. Her toxic influence erodes your happiness, leaving you drained, frustrated, and questioning the authenticity of your cherished relationships.

These scenarios underscore the detrimental effects of a pain-in-the-ass mosquito on your personal and work life, irrespective of gender. Their ability to mask their true intentions, create disarray within our environments, and resist alternative perspectives is a menace we must confront head-on. By recognizing their impact and safeguarding ourselves against their influence, we fortify our path to success and protect our well-being. As we bid farewell to these disruptive creatures, we embark upon a new chapter, ready to forge meaningful connections, embrace growth, and cultivate a positive environment where our goals can flourish.

Unveiling the Invisible Influence of Mosquitoes

I had the pleasure of interviewing Jonah Berger, author and renowned marketing professor at The Wharton School of the University of Pennsylvania. In his compelling book, *Invisible Influence: The Hidden Forces That Shape Behavior*, Berger delves into the intricate ways in which our actions are molded by others. During our conversation on the Passion Struck podcast, I had the opportunity to dive deeper into the buzzing significance of negative influence.

Berger explains, "The focus of *Invisible Influence* lies in unraveling the intricate psychology of social influence and its profound impact on our behavior. For example, are we more likely to run faster on a treadmill if we're running next to someone else? Why, when we have someone else in the car, is more difficult for us to parallel park? How we want to be unique sometimes, and how we go along with the crowd other times. Influence is a powerful tool. If we understand how to use it, we can make ourselves better off. But we have to see it first."

Much like elusive mosquitoes, these influences often lurk within our subconscious, stealthily manipulating our behaviors. However, their presence is anything but trivial. It's not a simplistic case of conformity or imitation. Rather, it entails a delicate dance between desiring differentiation and seeking connection—a waltz with the bloodsuckers, invisible suffocators, and pains in the ass of influence. We strive to be optimally distinct, preserving our individuality while harmonizing with the collective.

Berger's work sheds a glaring light on the complexity of human behavior, exposing the hidden forces that silently guide our choices. How our behavior is shaped by observing others and the need to strike a balance between fitting in and standing out. It beckons us to be vigilant, embracing our agency in the face of these buzzing influences. By recognizing and harnessing the power of invisible influence, we gain the ability to navigate the social ecosystem with finesse, crafting a more fulfilling life—one that is impervious to the persistent buzzing of mosquitoes.

Those Wanting to Become Passion Struck Need to Avoid Mosquitoes at All Costs

Here's something you need to consider, and it may come as a surprise. Some of the most influential people in your life could well be mosquitoes. That's why they are so dangerous—because even if you do manage to spot peers that are actively harming your progression, it may be too painful or challenging to strip them from your life.

They could be your closest friend from high school or your work-shy co-worker. It doesn't matter who they are. What matters is the impact they can have on your life and career. When you manage to identify a potential mosquito in your life, keep your distance, actively swat it away or eliminate it from your life completely.

Human mosquitoes, like their real-life counterparts, can inflict life-altering damage, which, in many cases, won't become apparent until you're nearing the end of your time here on Earth. So make sure to perform a mosquito audit at your earliest possible convenience. Otherwise, you could be accidentally fraternizing with the most dangerous animal on the planet.

To better illustrate what it's like to get up and conduct a mosquito audit, I want to share the stories of two outstanding passion-struck people. The first is someone I know personally, and the second is one of the best-known female leaders and entrepreneurs in the world: Thaddeus Bullard (also known as Titus O'Neil) and Oprah Winfrey.

Like the other leaders we've discussed, Thaddeus and Oprah have dealt with considerable obstacles in their careers. They have faced doubts and fears. They have dug deep, risen up after failing, taken ongoing action, and, most important, used the mosquito principle to achieve massive success.

Even though we may not achieve their level of success, Thaddeus's and Oprah's attitudes towards emerging from failures and being laser-focused on their goals is an example for all of us. Their insights and life stories can motivate us to overcome our own challenges that block us from achieving our own goals.

Thaddeus Bullard: Overcoming Adversity Both Inside and Outside the Ring

Thaddeus Bullard has an unbelievable life story. I wouldn't be surprised if it is eventually made into a movie. There are so many takeaways from Thaddeus's life. Still, the most obvious to me is his willingness to keep persevering and paying it forward—even if he literally and metaphorically gets punched in the face and started his life with horrible influences.

Just the other evening, I happened to watch the news reporting on how Thaddeus had performed yet another selfless act. A Hispanic immigrant teen spending his last days in hospice was being recognized for achieving his goal of becoming the first in his family to graduate high school. Thaddeus was there beside the grief-stricken family, honoring the teen's accomplishment. Thaddeus paid the teen's medical bills along with the cost of his funeral proceedings. This is not a one-off for my friend; it is how he daily lives life.

From the moment that he was born, Thaddeus faced tough circumstances. When she was eleven years old, Thaddeus's mother was raped by her boyfriend, and gave birth to Thaddeus nine months later in the projects in Florida with no father figure in his life.

Thaddeus's early life was no piece of cake. As he told me, "I was labeled a kid that would be dead or in jail by the time I was sixteen." Thaddeus was surrounded by mosquitoes, bad influences, and self-limiting beliefs. He thought he was destined for failure. How did Thaddeus avoid this fate? What was his saving grace? Attending the Florida Sheriffs Boys Ranch, a renowned organization that takes in at-risk youth and offers them a sense of direction. "People invested in me when they had nothing to gain in return," Thaddeus says.

At twelve, Thaddeus's life veered in a new direction. He recalls that a stranger told him, "I love you, and I believe in you." This positive motivation lit a fire under Thaddeus, convincing him that he did not need to face a tragic fate as a teenager. He made the decision that day to start removing toxic people and influences from his life. It wasn't easy. It took him years to make the changes that ultimately saved his life. Conducting a mosquito audit, as we discussed earlier, is never a simple task.

He then worked hard in school and discovered his talent for football. *USA Today* and *Parade* magazine recognized Thaddeus as an All-American defensive end.[65] He received an athletic scholarship to the University of Florida, where he played in forty-four regular-season games and was elected student body vice president. After graduating from the University of Florida, Thaddeus joined the Arena Football League,[66] playing for teams like the Tampa Bay Storm and the Utah Blaze. When his Arena Football League career ended in 2007, however, Thaddeus had to make a choice. Football had been a significant part of his life for more than ten years, and this stage of his life was coming to an end.

As we've discussed, making such a significant career transition would make anyone nervous. That said, Thaddeus stayed strong. His decisive action propelled him into a similar career that capitalized on his inherent strengths, into the world of professional wrestling. Not everyone is suited for professional wrestling, which requires not only physical talent but commitment. Thaddeus is a passion-struck leader in that he didn't let the inevitable shortcomings get in his way of becoming the professional wrestler he dreamed of being.

It's safe to say that Thaddeus accomplished his goal. Thaddeus adopted the name Titus O'Neil and became a legendary wrestler in the WWE. In 2013, Thaddeus ranked eighty-second of 500 singles wrestlers in the *Pro Wrestling Illustrated* rankings. He's also a former one-time WWE Tag Team Champion and WWE 24/7 Champion. Significantly, along with his wrestling career, Thaddeus gives back through his passionate involvement in charity work with many different nonprofit groups in the Tampa Bay region and beyond.

Thaddeus Bullard exemplifies the concept of the mosquito audit by fearlessly confronting overwhelming setbacks, negative influences, and destructive role models while remaining steadfast in his pursuit. He refuses to be deterred. Through unwavering determination and resilience, Thaddeus embodies the essence of a passion-struck leader who never backs down. His ability to forge ahead and triumph over these challenges defines his remarkable journey.

Oprah Winfrey: The Definition of Resilience

While Thaddeus Bullard may not be a household name, Oprah Winfrey certainly is. No one can deny that the "Queen of All Media" and North America's first African-American multibillionaire has lived an astounding life. I've been blessed to meet Oprah, and her story is an inspirational one.

Just like Thaddeus, Oprah's path to success was not paved with fame and privilege. She didn't enter the world as "Oprah Winfrey, the most influential woman in the world."[67] Instead, she had to navigate a treacherous road of setbacks, negative influences, and challenges that would have deterred many from moving forward. Similar to the relentless bloodsucking mosquitoes, Oprah faced daunting circumstances.

Born to a single teenage mother, Oprah's early life was far from easy. Raised by her strict grandmother, she endured regular physical abuse. Poverty and loneliness were constant companions. Life seemed bleak, and the invisible influence of her environment threatened to keep her trapped.

Conditions remained the same even when she moved to be with her mother in Milwaukee. Her mother worked as a maid, and the long hours meant that Oprah was often alone. When she was nine, Oprah was raped by her nineteen-year-old cousin. She continued to suffer sexual abuse from members of her family until about four years later, when she ran away from home. Even after running away from home, the tragedy didn't stop, as Oprah became pregnant and lost her child soon after birth.

Let's pause here and acknowledge the magnitude of injustice that Oprah faced from a very young age, with regular abuse and nowhere to turn. It's difficult to fathom how anyone could recover from this type of extended trauma and adversity.

Oprah's story could have been one of perpetual pain and sorrow, but fortunately, her resilience prevailed. She credits her father for turning her life around. After the death of her baby, she moved in with her father, who provided a stable home life and prioritized education. This, combined with her mental fortitude to conduct a mosquito audit and move past her prior tragedies, allowed her to pursue her passions.

Ultimately, Oprah turned the tables. She embraced the freedom and possibilities of high school where she studied public speaking and drama. With fire and motivation, Oprah won a state beauty pageant, was elected school president, and took on a part-time job reading the news at a local radio station. Oprah faced unquestionable adversity in those early years but refused to be discouraged. Her passion for communications and broadcasting deepened in college when she landed her first professional job at a Nashville television station. A promotion to co-anchor of the six o'clock news for a Baltimore ABC affiliate made all her hard work pay off.

That's when Oprah hit a significant roadblock and was ultimately demoted from her position as co-anchor. The reasons aren't exactly clear, but there's a good argument to be made[68] that Oprah was set up to fail. Regardless of the catalyst, Oprah was reassigned to a writing and reporting position, where she struggled. Oprah Winfrey was at a crossroads. She has previously stated[69] that she looks back on those years as a failure, at which point she could have taken this extremely discouraging obstacle at face value and backed down. The demotion could have driven Oprah into a dark depression, which could have compounded on itself and made the barrier more intense and more daunting.

But, as we all know, the story has a happy ending. Oprah was pushed down, and she got back up. She again decided to implement the mosquito principle and rid herself of the negative influences that were holding her back. Her setback became the fuel to keep pursuing her television broadcasting career. From the ABC affiliate in Baltimore, Oprah took a "step down"[70] and found a job as a co-host of a local talk show called *People Are Talking*. From there, she parlayed her experience into a television job in Chicago, where she caught her big break.

The rest, as they say, is history. Oprah eventually signed a syndication deal for a show titled *The Oprah Winfrey Show*. *Oprah* was nationally syndicated for twenty-five years and was the highest-rated television show of its kind in history. Along with being the "Queen of All Media," Oprah started her own company (HARPO Productions), obtained a net worth of almost $3 billion, and was awarded the Presidential Medal of Freedom in 2013.

Oprah's journey showcases the indomitable spirit needed to overcome invisible influences and rise above adversity. It serves as a reminder that even in the face of daunting challenges, resilience and a determination to swat away negative influences can propel us toward our dreams. Oprah Winfrey is a shining example of how the power of the human spirit can triumph over even the most persistent mosquitoes of life.

How We Use the Mosquito Audit to Punch Today in the Face

Thaddeus and Oprah are special people who faced countless numbers of tests throughout their careers and lives and persevered. To be frank, many of us aren't going to encounter nearly the same challenges that Thaddeus and Oprah faced. Nonetheless, we can incorporate several lessons from their lives when we get down or discouraged. In doing so, we are on the way to becoming passion struck.

One of the most important things that we can do is to *be decisive*. Throughout this book, I emphasize how passion-struck people take action even amid massive uncertainty and unfathomable setbacks, just as Thaddeus and Oprah did.

Thaddeus wanted to become a professional wrestler, though the path wasn't crystal clear. Oprah wanted to become a television broadcaster even after she was demoted and there was no guarantee that she would get even close to her goal. Thaddeus and Oprah didn't back down from their challenges. They kept at it—they removed the people and influences that were holding them back, even if they didn't know how they would get from point A to point B.

When we face personal or professional setbacks, it's up to us to adopt the same mentality. After getting punched in the face, it's critical to get back up, brush ourselves off, and continue taking action towards our goals and auditing out those things that are holding us back. This is true even if you don't know what your next step should be. In that case, it's helpful to envision your long-term goal and work backward. Chart out the specific actions that you must take to achieve personal or professional nirvana. Breaking out your long-term goal into small steps can help you to find the courage to succeed—even if you've been knocked down.

The bottom line is that action rules everything. Even if you're initially off the mark, experimentation and iteration can get you back on track. So when you receive that metaphorical punch, focus on getting back up and taking action. It sounds simple, but the way you handle yourself goes a long way in making you more resilient, determined, and, yes, passion struck.

From there, I strongly encourage you to *find a mentor (or several mentors)*. They don't even need to be mentors in a professional setting, although that can certainly help. Mentors can provide priceless guidance and inspiration when you face those inevitably dark moments. Most important, find one who will tell you the truth with brutal honesty. You need someone in your life who you can be completely open with about your passions and struggles.

Looking at Thaddeus's and Oprah's lives, we can see that several vital individuals guided them through dark times. For Thaddeus, it was the guidance he received at the Florida Sheriffs Boys Ranch. In Oprah's early days, it was her father, her teachers, and her colleagues at her part-time job at the local radio station.

There are virtually no requirements for mentors in your life. They can be more experienced hands at your job or individuals you respect in your community. Whoever it is, find that mentor and stay in touch with them—in both good times and bad. When you are feeling down or ready to give up, your mentor can be just the person you need to help you to keep pursuing your goals.

Becoming an Expert Mosquito Auditor

Using the mosquito principle is never easy. Often, we find it all too easy to stay on the floor and not take the actions that are necessary for our personal growth.

Nevertheless, staying on the floor is a choice. You can choose to get up and rid yourself of the negative influences in your life. Passion-struck people like Thaddeus and Oprah provide excellent examples of how we can bounce back from adversity and close in on our goals.

The road is not easy, but, ultimately, you are in control of how you react to adversity. Taking ownership of your actions after failures and setbacks shows that you're on your way to becoming passion struck.

If you find yourself stalling early on in your journey, undertake this mosquito audit and remove those who will cause you problems moving forward. Mosquitoes don't have to only be people in your life. They could be activities you are pursuing that distract you from your journey.

Much like tracking your calories for a diet, you will be shocked to discover who and what is defining your self-identity for you each day. When you discover identity sources that don't match your goals, expectations, or convictions, tear them out and ruthlessly throw them away. Only when you do away with those elements that are fighting for control of your identity can you take back control and drive your development.

The invisible suffocators could be the activities you spend doing with your biker group, kickball league, or poker club. Meanwhile, bloodsuckers and PITAs are often the places you spend your time, like happy hours, bars, or binge-watching TV series. These activities may have their time in place in moderation, but if they are sapping your time and energy, they need to be moderated or eliminated.

Once you have cleaned house, start doing the hard work of replacing those identity-killers with people and content that you trust to lead you well in defining your unique self-identity. Collect, analyze, and adopt the concepts and ideas that align with your identity, but don't allow them to define you.

Removing or distancing yourself from these people and distracting activities, influences, and habits can and will be painful, but it's part of the overall process of redefining who you are during your transition to becoming passion struck. Surround yourself with like-minded people and activities that are going to help you grow in your career. When you become a mosquito auditor, you'll notice the difference almost immediately.

Scan this QR code for additional insights and bonus material.

Chapter Exercises: Conduct a Mosquito Audit

- Identify Energy Drains: Make a list of activities, relationships, or situations that consistently drain your energy and leave you feeling depleted. Reflect on why these elements have such an impact on you. Consider whether they align with your values and goals, or if they are holding you back. Develop a plan to minimize or eliminate these energy drains from your life.
- Reflect on Your Inner Circle: Take some time to assess the people in your inner circle, including friends, family, and colleagues. Ask yourself whether they exhibit any mosquito-like traits, such as negativity, constant criticism, or a lack of support.
- Evaluate the Impact: For each person you've identified, analyze how their presence affects your mindset, emotions, and overall well-being. Consider whether they inspire and uplift you or drain your energy and hinder your progress. Write down the specific ways their influence impacts your life.
- Set Boundaries: Determine what boundaries you need to set with the identified individuals to protect yourself from their negative influence. This may involve reducing contact, establishing clear expectations, or creating distance where

necessary. Write down the specific boundaries you want to implement.

- Seek Supportive Relationships: Identify individuals who bring positivity, support, and encouragement into your life. Make a list of people who inspire you, believe in your dreams, and genuinely want to see you succeed. Consider how you can nurture these relationships and create a stronger support network.

Remember, performing a mosquito audit is an ongoing process. Regularly reassess the people in your life and adjust your boundaries and mindset as needed. By surrounding yourself with positive influences, you can create an environment that nurtures your growth, happiness, and success.

CHAPTER 5

FEAR CONFRONTER—REALIZING THAT YOU ARE YOUR BIGGEST COMPETITOR

*Sometimes, it is the people no one imagines anything
of who do the things that no one can imagine.*
—Alan Turing

Hopelessness is the enemy of aspiration.

You are the most challenging critic you will ever face.

Need proof? Let me lead you through a short thought experiment. In your mind—or better yet, on a piece of paper—take a moment to write out a few of the biggest opportunities ever presented to you.

Have it documented? Now, as you think about those opportunities, write down the answer to the following question: Did you pursue the opportunity or let it pass by?

How often are we presented with amazing opportunities only to let some of them go by the wayside? Once you've started taking a look at your life and decisions that altered your trajectory moving forwards, it's time to examine yourself a little more closely. In an earlier section, we analyzed our self-identity, which lays a critical foundation. To build on it, we review the actions keeping us from achieving our passion-struck journey in this stage.

Who Are You?

Identity is found all around you each day. From the scroll of a social media channel to a conversation with a loved one, nearly every medium you engage with is working to develop and define your identity. The key is not knowing how self-identity is being created but who or what influences it.

Your self-identity operates as a guiding compass or North Star—setting parameters and defining expectations for how you will interact and engage with the world around you. Every decision you make and action you take is prepared behind the scenes by your identity. As you can imagine, being passion struck requires a solid and stable self-identity. This is vital to ensuring that your voice has a seat at the table where the world is moving.

Why Our Biggest Competitor Is Ourselves

Every morning, I embark on an early walk with my dog Bentley. While some may view it as a routine activity, this time holds immense value for me. It's a crucial opportunity to set my mindset and focus on the day's essential tasks.

During these walks, I listen to podcasts that spark ideas and inspiration at the break of dawn. One episode of *Impact Theory* featuring actress Hilary Swank left a profound impact on me. She stated, "Our biggest competitor is really ourselves." I couldn't help but pause and reflect on that statement. When was the last time I honestly evaluated myself?

Personal growth requires brutal honesty in self-assessment. Identifying flaws, accepting them, and devising strategies to overcome them are vital steps. Realizing that I am my biggest obstacle empowers me to silence my inner critic and explore innovative concepts. Ask yourself the same question: Have you embraced the transformative power of introspection? Often, we become entangled in others' actions and achievements, neglecting the impact of self-assessment.

This is where change begins. Embrace failure as a stepping stone toward growth and become a "fear confronter." By embarking on this courageous journey, you can shift from limitations to passion and purpose. As a passion-struck trailblazer, mastering the art of self-assessment is crucial. Unaffected by external noise, you'll realize that only you can stand in the way of your success. Challenge the inner voice that whispers, "You can't." Embrace relentless determination and unwavering belief in yourself. Let this journey of self-discovery and personal growth be your guiding light, illuminating the path to a brighter, more empowered future. You may have been cast as the underdog in your own story, but it's time to rewrite that narrative and embrace your potential.

Navigating Chatter and Cultivating Our Inner Voice

On the *Passion Struck* podcast,[71] I interviewed Ethan Kross, a renowned psychologist from the University of Michigan Ross School of Business and the author of "Chatter." We delved into the transformative power of introspection and self-reflection. Ethan eloquently emphasized the incredible tool we possess: language. He highlighted how we silently employ language to contemplate our lives in diverse ways. Kross explains:

An amazing tool we possess is language, and we can silently use language to reflect on our lives, which we do in very different ways. It has various manifestations. We often use language to rehearse what we're going to say during a presentation or before an interview or date. We also use language to motivate ourselves and make sense of our experiences. When we experience adversity, we turn our attention inward to come up with a story. Why did this happen to me? How can I learn from this?

Sometimes our attempts to do that, though, backfire. We turn our attention inward. We introspect, get stuck in a negative thought loop; we start overthinking things well. Oh my god, what am I going to do? Why did this happen? And we just keep spinning. That's what "chatter" refers to—this process of getting stuck in a negative thought loop. It captures phenomena like rumination and worries; rumination tends to be about things that happened in the past and, when we're dwelling on them, concerns about things in the present or future.

As Ethan describes, we can become trapped in a negative thought loop, experiencing what he refers to as "chatter." This phenomenon encapsulates being stuck in a cycle of negative rumination and worry. Rumination fixates on past events, incessantly dwelling on them, while worry revolves around present or future concerns, generating anxious "what-if" scenarios. The key aspect is the lack of progress towards our goals despite investing significant effort, akin to a hamster tirelessly running on an exercise wheel.

Chatter, in its essence, presents a profound challenge that we, as a species, often confront. It hampers our ability to make meaningful strides forward, inhibiting our growth and well-being. Understanding and addressing this issue is crucial for navigating the complexities of our inner worlds and finding a path towards greater clarity, resilience, and fulfillment.

Why Is Self-Reflection Essential?

Self-reflection allows us to delve into the depths of our being, increasing our understanding of who we are, our values, and the motivations behind our thoughts and actions. By engaging in this introspective journey, we gain the insights necessary to align our lives with our aspirations, paving the way for a more fulfilling existence.

In essence, by unraveling the complexities of chatter and embracing self-reflection, we unlock the key to personal growth, well-being, and the realization of our true potential.

By merely pausing and evaluating yourself, you will be surprised by what you uncover. By answering questions, such as, "Why did I act that way in situation X?" "Why do I always hate doing task Y?" and "Why is that my opinion on subject N?" you can begin to understand your inner workings intimately, and adapt and evolve as a human being.

If the concept of self-identity is novel to you, that does not mean that you lack an identity. It is more likely that outside sources have been in the driver's seat to create and define your identity for you.

> *I am not what I think I am, and I am not what you*
> *think I am. I am what I think you think I am.*
> —Charles Horton Cooley

Need proof? Consider your core values, your personal mission, or your goals. When you look over those personal guiding principles, whose voice do you hear in your mind?

While borrowing the insights and leadership qualities of other industry leaders is a great way to grow and develop your leadership skills, allowing another individuals, organizations, or media sources to define your goals and aspirations is a surefire sign that your self-identity is being crafted and curated by someone other than yourself.

It is vital that you take control of your identity and not permit another person or faction to define it for you. This will only limit your potential as a future leader. What the world needs is not another version of a worn-out idea, concept, or scheme.

What will turn the cogs in the wheel of future leaders are the unique experiences, passions, and convictions that define you as an individual. Those whom you lead every day—friends, family, team members, other leaders—are all looking to you to boldly move forward into the unknown with unyielding confidence built on a strong self-identity.

It's about *willingly* taking the step into the unknown, accepting that failure isn't just probable; it's likely. It's about embodying the spirit and boldness of a lion.

Lions face risk day-in, day-out. They are the biggest risk-takers in the animal kingdom. Every morning when they wake up, lions know that if they don't hunt, they will starve. An almost permanent state of discomfort defines their lives. And yet, the lion has rightly been dubbed "the king of the jungle." Why? Because lions do what it takes to survive and subsequently thrive.

When you take your first step to do something different, just remember that the odds facing lions are just as stark as yours. Only one in every eight lions born survives to adulthood.[72] According to data from the Bureau of Labor Statistics,[73] if you're starting a new idea or venture, you face similar odds.

We Spend Our Time Looking Outward Instead of Inward

To help you understand why looking inward is so important, it might be worth framing it in a business context. Most businesses spend the majority of their time looking out of the window rather than in the mirror.

I have been part of the corporate world for more than twenty years, and I have spent a lot of that time obsessing over competitors and competitive advantage. To be honest, it's what most companies do. However, doing so is taking the easy path. It's *easy* to look through the window to assess the competitors across the street, critiquing them and looking for weaknesses to exploit.

What isn't so easy is shunning the window and looking into the mirror placed before you. It's tough to examine yourself or your internal team members, looking for your own weaknesses and your own shortcomings. However, suppose you manage to pull it off. In that case, you can better adapt, develop, and evolve to become a new version of yourself that inherently creates a personal "edge" over your peers or a competitive advantage over rival companies.

Unleashing the Power of Introspection: A Lesson from Lowe's

Allow me to share an illustrative anecdote that underscores the transformative potential of introspection in the pursuit of success. During my tenure at Lowe's, our attention was largely consumed by our competitors—Home Depot, Menards, and independent hardware stores vying for a share of the market. Yet, it was a moment of profound introspection that ignited a spark of innovation within our organization and set us on a path to revolutionize the retail industry.[74]

In that pivotal moment, we dared to ask ourselves tough questions about how we were truly serving our customers. It was through this introspective journey that we envisioned an audacious concept—a fully interconnected store and digital experience that would redefine customer expectations. Little did we know, we were on the cusp of achieving the elusive Holy Grail of retail, a feat that Home Depot is now endeavoring to undertake with their multibillion-dollar "One Home Depot" project.[75]

Imagine a world where your entire customer journey, whether in-store, on a mobile device, or on the retailer's website, seamlessly integrates into a unified and anticipatory experience. Store associates communicate with you promptly, follow up without prompting, and empower you to track the status of your purchase and related services in real-time. This interconnected shopping experience, born out of our introspection, held the potential to reshape the retail landscape.

However, despite our initial momentum, we inadvertently became our own greatest competitor in making this transformative vision a reality. The enormity and complexity of the undertaking proved challenging to comprehend fully. While our initiative garnered some executive support, it failed to secure its position as top priority for Lowe's. In stark contrast, The Home Depot, under the leadership of former CEO Craig Menear, wholeheartedly embraced this concept to make it their number one focus.

The opportunity to achieve a seamlessly interconnected shopping experience slipped through our fingers, overshadowed by competing initiatives, international expansion, and a heavy emphasis on looking outward instead of inward. This enlightening chapter in the history of Lowe's underscores the critical role of introspection in shaping our path to success. It invites us to question, reflect, and challenge our own assumptions and priorities. By embracing the transformative power of introspection, we unlock the potential to transcend limitations and chart a course towards innovation and greatness.

Overcoming Your Personal Obstacles

When you realize that you are your biggest obstacle, you can start to take steps to silence your own inner critic and move toward truly innovative concepts and a growth mindset. A real-life example of a veteran overcoming her inner *I can't* critic is marine-turned-mountain-climber Kristie Ennis.

The morning of June 23, 2012, began as a routine day. Sergeant Ennis was in high spirits. She attended check-flight briefings and then set off on her last mission during her second Afghanistan combat tour. It was on that final flight when her helicopter crashed while performing combat resupplies. Ennis was severely injured.[76] The crash left her with broken bones, burns, a traumatic brain injury, and damage to her spinal cord, jaw, and left leg. Ultimately, she underwent forty surgeries and her doctors were forced to amputate her left leg.

Following extensive time in the hospital, Ennis considered ending her own life as the impacts of her physical and invisible injuries engulfed her. However, at this moment of crisis, she experienced a breakthrough—overcoming the voices telling her that she couldn't rise from the ashes of her traumatic experience and limitations. Ennis decided that just because she was missing a limb, experienced head trauma, and was disabled, she didn't have to give up living a full and fulfilling life:

> Looking at my life, people can see me now climbing Mt. Everest, or receiving an award, or whatever it may be. They see these glorious images and pictures. But, what they don't see are the dark days and the hard days. Like having to put my leg on in the morning and how miserable that can be. Especially at the beginning of my recovery. It was hard to do things for myself. I think that is what makes it hard for people to go through these periods of transition. They think they are all alone.

Ennis decided to wrestle back her life from the edge of despair and set a personal goal to push past her limitations and take up new hobbies: mountain climbing and becoming a paraplegic snowboarder. Ennis has made it her goal to climb the seven tallest peaks on each continent in the world while raising money for the Kirstie Ennis Foundation. Since she began her journey, Ennis has raised over $70,000 for veterans, women, and disabled populations. After she finishes this current goal, she plans on tackling the World Marathon Challenge, where she will attempt to run seven marathons on seven continents in seven days.

From Ennis' story, we can learn the transformative power of being a fear confronter and overcoming our inner critic. When faced with life-altering adversity, she realized that the biggest obstacle standing in her way was her own doubts and self-limiting beliefs. By silencing her inner critic, she unlocked a growth mindset and ventured towards truly innovative concepts.

Ennis' journey is a remarkable example of resilience and determination. Despite the devastating injuries she sustained in a helicopter crash, she refused to give in to despair. Instead, she made a conscious decision to embrace life fully, despite the physical and invisible scars.

Her breakthrough came when she recognized that her challenges didn't define her. She chose not to surrender to her limitations, recognizing that her amputated leg and injuries didn't define her worth. Embracing the difficult journey of recovery, she became an inspiration by taking up mountain climbing and snowboarding, determined to conquer new heights.

Ennis's story resonates deeply because it lays bare the unseen struggles behind her triumphant moments. Her ability to share her challenges, from the daily struggles of putting on her prosthetic leg to the hardships of recovery, underscores the importance of acknowledging one's vulnerability. In doing so, she dismantles the illusion of isolation that often accompanies times of transition and adversity.

It's Easy to Stay the Course and Not Tip the Apple Cart

One of my favorite interviews I've conducted on the *Passion Struck* podcast was with Dara Kurtz.[77] If you looked at Kurtz's life from the outside, you would have thought it was easy. She had an amazing family and a brilliant finance career, and life was going brilliantly until one day it wasn't. She found a lump on her right breast, which turned out to be breast cancer. Isn't that how life often is? One day it is fine, and the next day you are wondering if you will live to see your children get married.

After successfully battling her cancer, Dara could have gone back to her career as a financial advisor, but instead, overcoming her fear of dying led her to question everything about her life and how she was focusing her time. She made the decision to quit her job at a large bank and start a new venture called Crazy Perfect Life. Dara realized that the most important things in life are not represented by a financial statement or balance sheet. Rather they are represented by confronting the fear of doing what you truly are meant to do.

You might ask, what is a crazy perfect life?

Dara explains that "life is messy and full of ups and downs. At the same time, it's precious and something to be cherished. My experiences have taught me what is truly important and I don't take my life for granted."

I was able to ask Dara why it takes people facing an ordeal or struggle to make the choice to confront their fear. In Dara's insightful perspective, she highlights the messy yet precious nature of life, brimming with both challenges and moments to cherish. Her personal experiences have bestowed upon her a profound understanding of what truly matters, instilling in her a deep appreciation for the gift of life itself. She explains:

> There's so many reasons. I think, one is just it's easy to stay the course and not tip over the apple cart. You're living this life and your image, and all of the things that go along with that. And it's not easy to wake up one day and say, "Hey, this isn't actually what I want to be doing." And not everyone's going to like that. Not everyone's going to like the new version of you.
>
> Or maybe making a change will trigger things for other people that they don't want to think about for themselves. So it's safer to stay the course. For me, it really just all came down to redefining success for myself, and deciding what success means to me. And what success means for my life, and what is a

successful life—and after going through cancer, my answers changed completely. I didn't care if my name was at the top of a list anymore. I didn't care how I was perceived.

It just kind of went back to: How do I want to spend my time? Am I spending my time doing things that are worthwhile? That feed my soul? That I'm passionate about? The answer was a hard *no*. And I am so grateful that I was able to pivot and walk away from it. I'm so much happier today than I could have even imagined. And if you had told me ten years ago that I would be doing what I'm doing today, I never would have believed you.

But, that's the thing about life; it doesn't always work out the way we think it's going to work out or the pictures that we have in our mind of the way things "should be." I put that in quotation marks because I strongly dislike the word *should* because I think we can get used to living our lives doing what we should do instead of really what we want to be doing. But often life can be so much better than we could have ever imagined. If we give ourselves the freedom to figure out what success looks like for us and confront our fears.

For Dara, it all came down to redefining success on her own terms, determining what truly mattered in her life. Her battle with cancer transformed her perspective completely. No longer concerned with external validation or societal perceptions, she found herself drawn to the fundamental questions: How do I want to spend my time? Am I engaged in endeavors that nourish my soul and ignite my passion? The answer was a resounding "no," prompting her to pivot and walk away from the expected trajectory.

Today, she revels in the happiness she never could have fathomed. Reflecting on her journey, she acknowledges that life often unfolds differently from the visions we hold and the societal expectations we place upon ourselves. Rejecting the notion of "should" that dictates our choices, Dara encourages us to seek a life driven by our authentic desires. Embracing this freedom to define success for ourselves and confronting our fears, we can unlock a reality that surpasses our wildest imaginations.

Dara's story serves as a powerful reminder that life's true beauty lies in our willingness to explore, challenge, and, ultimately, forge our own paths.

Some Famous Examples of Fear Confronters

Underestimating the potential of underdogs is a common mistake. Novak Djokovic's journey exemplifies this truth. When he first started on the ATP tour in 2004, Roger Federer and Rafa Nadal had a duopoly on tennis. It would have been easy to believe the commentators and TV analysts who said that the deficiencies in Djokovic's game would mean that he could never go on to match them. But instead of accepting the doctrine peddled by those around him, he went back to the drawing board, acknowledged that he needed to work on his weaknesses, and hit the training courts. Today, he has surpassed both Federer and Nadal in grand slam titles, defying all expectations.[78]

Returning to the podcast featuring Hilary Swank, her own journey is a testament to overcoming adversity. At the age of fourteen, she, along with her mother, moved to Los Angeles with nothing more than a van to live in and seventy-five dollars between them. She spent the next nine years scratching around auditions and picking up bits and pieces of work.

However, no matter how many rejections she received, she never lost the belief that she was destined to be an actor. She didn't abandon her beliefs despite almost a decade of failure.[79] She accepted the rejection, embraced it even. She used the repeated setbacks to improve and evolve, culminating in a leading role in a small indie film named *Boys Don't Cry*, for which she was only paid $3,000. A year later, she was giving an acceptance speech at the Academy Awards for winning the Oscar for Best Actress.

Empower the Underdogs

The stories of Kirstie Ennis, Dara Kurtz, Novak Djokovic, and Hilary Swank provide valuable insights into overcoming our inner critic. Ennis's journey exemplifies resilience as she confronted life-altering injuries and emotional struggles, choosing to set personal goals and push past limitations. Kurtz's inspiring story teaches us the profound importance of confronting our fears and redefining success on our own terms. Djokovic's path to becoming a tennis champion highlights the power of self-belief, as he maintained unwavering confidence despite setbacks and doubts. Swank's success in Hollywood was coupled with her humility and authenticity, sharing her inner struggles and vulnerabilities to connect with others. Each story emphasizes the importance of challenging limiting beliefs, embracing vulnerability, and embarking on a journey of self-discovery. By cultivating resilience, self-belief, and authenticity, we can silence our inner critic and unleash our true potential, ready to conquer any obstacle in our path.

Perhaps it's best to leave you with the words of Ethan Kross:

> "[Our] moral compass is a set of beliefs that we have about how to live a good life, at least in the way I would define it. So how do you know the difference between what's right and wrong? And when you're judging, your behavior is giving you a readout on whether you are following that compass or deviating from it, and I think when we detect deviations.
>
> "The challenge is to bring us back on track, and your inner voice can be really helpful in that regard...we use your inner voice to motivate us and

problem-solve. When we detect something's wrong... [we] devise a plan and a solution to get us back on track. So I think having a moral compass is essential, and the inner voice is a way of keeping it properly tuned to where it should be heading."

Scan this QR code for additional resources and insights.

Chapter Exercises: Become a Fear Confronter and Face Your Inner Critic

- Self-Reflection Journal: Set aside time at the end of each chapter to reflect on your own self-critical tendencies. Write down instances when you notice self-criticism arising in your thoughts or actions. Explore the underlying beliefs or fears that contribute to this self-critical mindset.
- Identify Triggers: Identify specific situations, events, or interactions that tend to trigger your self-criticism. Write them down and reflect on why they have such an impact on you. Are there patterns or common themes that emerge? Understanding your triggers can help you become more aware of when self-criticism arises.
- Challenge Negative Self-Talk: Pay close attention to your internal dialogue and identify self-critical thoughts or beliefs. When you catch yourself engaging in negative self-talk,

challenge those thoughts by asking yourself if they are rational, fair, or helpful. Replace self-criticism with more positive and compassionate statements.

- Practice Self-Compassion: Develop a self-compassion practice by intentionally treating yourself with kindness and understanding. When you notice self-criticism, take a moment to offer yourself words of encouragement and support. Practice self-compassion exercises such as writing yourself a compassionate letter or imagining what you would say to a friend in a similar situation.

- Seek External Perspective: Reach out to trusted friends, family members, or a therapist and share your experiences of self-criticism. Listen to their perspectives and feedback. Often, external voices can provide a more balanced and compassionate viewpoint, helping you gain a different outlook on your self-perception.

Remember, overcoming self-criticism takes time and patience. Be gentle with yourself as you work through these exercises, and remember that self-compassion is a powerful tool for fostering self-growth and well-being.

CHAPTER 6

PERSPECTIVE HARNESSER — ZOOM OUT AND TAP INTO ITS POWER

*It suddenly struck me that that tiny pea, pretty and
blue, was the Earth. I put up my thumb and shut
one eye, and my thumb blotted out the planet Earth.
I didn't feel like a giant. I felt very, very small.*
—Neil Armstrong

E go is the enemy of perspective.
    I have always been fascinated by off-world exploration and
the search for extraterrestrial life. Everything from the frequent
Space Shuttle missions in the 1980s and 1990s to the discoveries on the
International Space Station intrigued me. The current era is equally

exciting (or perhaps even more so), especially with the rise of private space companies like SpaceX, Blue Origin, and Virgin Galactic.

Those brave souls who travel into space are signing up for the adventure of a lifetime. Yes, there is the excitement (even terror) of blasting off into space. But after getting into orbit, many astronauts talk about the sheer sense of awe that they experience. That awe centers on the fact that the earth is alive. It is commonly known as the "overview effect."

Edgar Mitchell, who was an astronaut on Apollo 14, once said that this overview effect gave him a profound sense of the universe being interconnected. Along with this, there was a subtle sense of the vanishing of time. Mitchell and other astronauts say that seeing Earth from space creates an important framework that is difficult to get on Earth. That framework is centered on the fact that humanity and our systems are part of a synergistic totality. Man-made boundaries disappear, and these astronauts adopt a new perspective that they carry forward through the rest of their lives.

Ultimately, this is a huge paradigm shift. This cognitive shift in awareness helps these astronauts understand the big picture in their lives. It gives them a better understanding of what is truly important and how they can get the most out of their careers and lives.

This powerful sense of perspective isn't limited to astronauts alone; passion-struck leaders also possess the ability to zoom out and tap into the force of perspective. By wearing another hat and seeing things from different angles, they can overcome challenges and existential crises. Just like viewing the iconic Golden Gate Bridge from above, this fresh perspective reveals its significance as a symbol of human achievement and ingenuity.

It is crucial to understand the value of attention to detail but also recognize the importance of not getting lost in one perspective. Failing to grasp the broader context can lead to missed opportunities and personal discontent. On the other hand, maintaining perspective offers a distinct advantage, helping us to navigate challenges, find positivity even in difficult times, and stay motivated.

Ultimately, perspective adds depth and meaning to our careers and lives. It humbles us, reminding us that we are a small part of a vast universe. This altered lens allows those who are passion struck to be happier, healthier, and more successful in their endeavors. Embracing this power of perspective unlocks endless possibilities for growth and fulfillment.

An Eye-Opening Lesson on Perspective Aboard the USS Kidd

I caught a glimpse of the power of perspective early in my career. It was fall 1995, and I was a lieutenant junior grade in the U.S. Navy. I was temporarily assigned to the USS *Kidd*, which was deployed to support allied forces in the Bosnian War. At that time, President Clinton had reversed America's more reserved approach to the conflict and deployed the USS *Kidd* (among other ships) to support NATO forces in the Adriatic Sea.[80]

It wasn't my first time in the region. I had been on early deployments where U.S. forces had supported humanitarian efforts related to the conflict. Bosnian forces, however, took it too far. Their campaign of ethnic cleansing shocked the world. It was clear that something had to change, especially as the U.S. election came closer. The U.S. government responded in kind, prompting my return to the Adriatic Sea.

Aboard the USS *Kidd*, my eye-opening lesson on perspective occurred on Thanksgiving. It was a typical day except for the fact that it was a holiday. To celebrate the holidays, the ship hosted a five-kilometer Turkey Trot. Halfway through the race, I was struck by an extremely surreal feeling of being out of place. The contrast was stark. Here, my fellow shipmates and I were participating in a seemingly normal activity that plenty of people do on Thanksgiving Day. Yet at the same time, NATO warplanes were screaming past our vessel.[81] They were using it as a rendezvous point to commence their attack runs against Serbian forces.

It was a fascinating change of perspective. It allowed me to view the war in a completely different way and our place in it. Moreover, viewing the war through this new lens made me become a better officer. The game had changed, and I needed to elevate my already high expectations for myself. In effect, this change in perspective was an important catalyst in helping me and my shipmates do the best work possible to support NATO's mission and take the fight to Slobodan Milosevic's regime.

The highest levels of the U.S. government also experienced this change in perspective. The Pentagon believed that the Bosnian Serbs had gone too far after the Srebrenica massacre.[82] U.S. Secretary of Defense William Perry and Chairman of the Joint Chiefs of Staff John Shalikashvili took the lead in pushing for a vigorous air campaign. That said, the real reason for the escalation was the shift of perspective in terms of U.S. foreign policy. According to Anthony Lake, President Clinton's national security advisor, America's credibility was being undermined by what was occurring in Bosnia. America and NATO's failure to end it, along with a presidential election less than one year away, created this shift in perspective that led to increased American intervention.

Perspective can move mountains. It can inspire a group of people in the midst of conflict or even key decision-makers who change the course of international relations. Passion-struck leaders intuitively recognize this fact and call on perspective.

Shattering Echo Chambers by Embracing Diverse Perspectives

On the *Passion Struck* podcast [83], I interviewed Wendy K. Smith, a professor of management and faculty director at the Women's Leadership Initiative at the University of Delaware, and Marianne W. Lewis, the dean of Carl H. Lindner College of Business at the University of Cincinnati, co-authors of the book *Both/And Thinking*. Their insights shed light on the crucial role that embracing the paradox mindset plays in navigating complex issues and fostering meaningful dialogue.

Lewis explains, "We use the analogy, the Hindu parable of the blind men and the elephant. Most issues that are really challenging are complicated, they're messy, they're dynamic. And there's just no way for one person or even one kind of type of perspective to get the whole picture. And so by narrowing ourselves by staying in an echo chamber, listening to others with the same perspective, we're missing all other parts of that elephant. And we're likely to make a really poor decision, because we don't see the complexity."

Acknowledging the peril of making ill-informed decisions due to a limited understanding of complex issues, Lewis delves into the concept of bounded rationality, championed by Nobel laureate James March.[84]

She says, "There was brilliant work by James March, who actually won a Nobel Prize for it around bounded rationality, which just means cognitively, we can't see the whole elephant. It's just not possible. It's too complicated of a system. It's too messy." By recognizing the cognitive constraints that prevent us from comprehending the entire scope of intricate problems, Lewis urges us to adopt a practice she calls triangulation. This involves actively seeking and incorporating diverse perspectives into discussions to gain a more comprehensive and nuanced understanding of complex issues.

Lewis highlights the challenges inherent in embracing diverse perspectives, particularly when our emotions gravitate towards seeking validation for our own views. She remarks, "And it's not easy to do. Because it feels much more comfortable talking to people who say, 'Oh, yeah, exactly. Right.' And you feel this kind of reinforcement for your view. But that's just going to fuel that intensification. If you don't get the other debates in the room, you are going to miss really important elements."

Building upon Lewis's insights, Smith directs our attention to the emotional aspects that influence our perspectives and interactions. She highlights the inclination to align ourselves with individuals who affirm our beliefs, leading to polarizing debates and hindering the search for effective solutions. She uses the example of climate change to illustrate how people's views encompass more nuance than the binary divisions often portrayed. Smith explains, "Climate change is a great example. Because what it points to is the ways in which we have picked a particular perspective lined up with other people who confirm our perspective. And then we get into these polarizing debates."

Contrary to the entrenched positions often portrayed, Smith emphasizes that there is often significant overlap in people's underlying beliefs and concerns. She remarks, "But when you go and talk to people, there's actually a lot more overlap than they actually propose to say when they just identify with a particular perspective." Recognizing this, she encourages us to engage in open conversations that honor different perspectives and considerations.

Instead of framing discussions as a binary choice between belief or denial, Smith urges us to explore strategies that enable dialogue and integrate diverse viewpoints. She states, "It's how we get into conversation with one another so that we can come up with strategies that enable and honor these different perspectives and considerations that we have to do in order to go forward."

Smith's and Lewis's insights underscore the significance of venturing beyond the boundaries of familiar perspectives and embracing the discomfort that comes with exploring diverse viewpoints. They urge us to break free from the confines of like-minded echo chambers and actively seek out alternative opinions. This willingness to engage in open, honest conversations and integrate a range of perspectives becomes the catalyst for fostering greater understanding, generating innovative solutions, and navigating the intricate complexities of our world with more enlightened and inclusive outlooks.

In essence, Smith and Lewis remind us that the power of perspective lies in our ability to embrace diverse voices, challenge preconceived notions, and foster meaningful dialogue. By venturing beyond the confines of narrow-mindedness and incorporating varied viewpoints, we not only enhance our understanding but also unlock the potential for innovative solutions to address the multifaceted challenges we encounter. Through these concerted efforts, we can cultivate a more inclusive and knowledgeable society that harnesses the power of diverse perspectives to shape a brighter and more harmonious future.

Learning About the Power of Perspective from a Legendary Astronaut

One of the best examples of a passion-struck leader who adopted the power of perspective is astronaut and Navy SEAL Captain Chris Cassidy. Chris is a friend and one of my U.S. Naval Academy and Naval Academy Prep School classmates.

After attending the U.S. Naval Academy, Chris decided to become a Navy SEAL. As you likely know, becoming a Navy SEAL is extremely difficult, yet Chris was the honor graduate from the Basic Underwater Demolition SEAL/School[85] (BUD/S) Class 192. After successfully completing one of the most rigorous training programs in the U.S. military, Chris dedicated eleven years of his life to serving as a SEAL. During his remarkable career, he earned several prestigious accolades, including a Bronze Star with the "V" insignia for valor, another Bronze Star, and a Presidential Unit Citation.

As if that wasn't enough, Chris decided to take his post-SEAL life to the next level. He received a Master of Science in ocean engineering from the Massachusetts Institute of Technology and applied for the NASA astronaut program. In 2004, NASA selected him as an astronaut and he became a veteran of three space flights (shuttle mission STS-127, Expedition 35, and Expedition 63 mission). Chris served as NASA's fifteenth chief astronaut, which is the most senior leadership position for active astronauts. He is currently the president and CEO of the National Medal of Honor Museum Foundation.[86]

However, these accolades didn't occur in a straight line. Chris relied on perseverance, hard work, and, yes, the power of perspective to get through the rough times.

Finding the Strength to Survive BUD/S

One great example of how the power of perspective changed Chris's life comes from his experience at BUD/S. BUD/S training is known for being some of the most intense in the U.S. military. The BUD/S dropout rate is extremely high, as approximately 25 percent of graduates make it to graduation.[87] While the entire training is difficult, BUD/S is perhaps most well-known for its dreaded Hell Week,[88] where candidates are challenged with only four hours of sleep and near-nonstop physical activities over five days.

Hell Week challenges every single candidate. It doesn't matter whether you were a star college athlete or whether you can bench-press three hundred pounds. Getting through Hell Week (and the entirety of BUD/S) is about mental strength and keeping perspective. As he told me, getting through Hell Week and BUD/S itself is a true gut check. But along with that gut check comes the realization that trying times end. Everyone thinks about quitting to relieve the pain and get warm. The temptation is always there. But Chris and other successful BUD/S candidates are able to shift their perspectives and understand that BUD/S training is for a defined duration. Compared to a long-protracted health problem that can occur for years, Hell Week is just five days. BUD/S itself lasts twenty-four weeks, not years. It gave him and his graduating classmates comfort as they suffered through near-nonstop pain.

Yes, getting through BUD/S requires physical strength. It also requires teamwork and the commitment to do your job for your teammates. One of the great things about working with other highly motivated people in stressful situations is that they can consciously (or subconsciously) provide you with perspective. Chris and his fellow BUD/S candidates were suffering, but spotting a foreign exchange officer from Thailand gave them extra motivation. As Chris told me, this officer had virtually no fat on him, meaning he had a low tolerance for cold. Everyone was chilly and uncomfortable, but this officer was expending all his might and energy to complete the evolution. His energy in the midst of near-intolerable conditions gave Chris the perspective and energy to keep going. If the Thai officer was getting through the pain without quitting or complaining, Chris and his classmates could do the same. Chris explained his experience to me in this way:

> For me, it was figuring out that your time horizon of the future is like an elastic band. The more available bandwidth you have, that rubber band stretches out further, and you can look for deeper ahead of you. But when you get really into the thick of it in the BUD/S analogy, you're just buried in sand, and you're on your hundredth push-up, and instructors are screaming at you. Your time horizon shrinks to what is just in front of you. At that moment, your perspective shifts to *trying times end*. And so that's where I realized, at the beginning of BUD/S, it's overwhelming to think about the end. It's even overwhelming to think about getting to the end of the first phase. You have to be like a rubber band and stretch this time horizon. In general, I broke it down into chunks of meals: get to lunch, get to dinner.

So, when you are facing some unbearably difficult situation, it helps to think of Chris's experience in Hell Week. It may seem impossible to overcome the pain or stress that you're feeling in the moment. Giving up may seem like the clearest (and, frankly, sanest) option.

Passion-struck leaders resist this temptation. They tap into the power of perspective and keep the bigger picture in mind. While they may be in extreme pain or fear, the pain or fear of failing to accomplish their goal is even greater. They intuitively understand this and use perspective as fuel to bring their dreams to life.

Take Ownership of Your Perspective

Not long ago, there was a time when NASA considered spacewalks to be extremely risky. The Administration feared them. During the mid-1990s, when NASA was preparing to build the space station, some pundits didn't believe that the agency would safely conduct three or four assembly spacewalks on every shuttle mission, several times a year, for a decade. They called the space station's demanding extravehicular activity (EVA) schedule "The Wall," and thought it was insurmountable. This backdrop brings into perspective how impressive NASA's EVA record was (with thousands of hours conducting EVAs) that there had never been a near-death accident until July 16, 2013.

Chris Cassidy and Italian astronaut Luca Parmitano conducted their first spacewalk together on July 9. It was a busy EVA that needed to address some science experiments, relocate equipment, and do prep work—including routing power and data cables—for the arrival of a new Russian lab module.

A week later, on July 16, the two astronauts went out again to finish the tasks from their first EVA and do other maintenance chores. On that fateful EVA, Chris and Parmitano looked death[89] in the eyes. The EVA began smoothly, and the astronauts were a good forty minutes ahead of schedule. Parmitano was moving to his next worksite, an aperture where three of the station's cylindrical modules come together. The timeline called for a quick task. He extended his arm as far as possible into this crevice to evaluate its accessibility. He was conducting the test when he suddenly noticed the feeling of water hit the back of his neck. As the two astronauts assessed the situation, they first thought it might be sweat, which is expected, when conducting these stressful operations. Chris then peered into Parmitano's helmet and could see the water, which looked to him like beads. Parmitano tasted one of the beads, and it didn't taste like sweat. It tasted awful and metallic. At that moment, the criticality of the situation became apparent—Parmitano was drowning and NASA ordered a full abort.

While on the way back into the space station, Parmitano maneuvered to avoid a sharp protrusion and during the movement, his snoopy cap became saturated with water. As the water moved down the cap, it covered his eyes and nostrils. He had to breathe only through his mouth and was unable to see. At that moment, he was facing a life-or-death situation, and before long, he wouldn't be able to breathe. Chris recognized what was happening and acted. Chris described to me what happened next:

> I mean, everything we do, no matter what you're doing, reverts back to training. And if you're experiencing seeing something for the first time, you'll be slower to react. Just think about putting a bicycle together for your kid on Christmas Eve if you get to do three of them. The first bicycle takes you three times as long as the second and third bicycles. And the same thing is true for space training. That's why we train over and over and over for spacewalks in the pool. We train over and over and over for malfunctions in the cockpit with the simulators.
>
> And when that particular EVA happened, I can't remember my actions to get the hatch closed. My hands just did it. And it's so weird. Even right now, I'm trying to think about how I moved Luca out of the way. How did I swing the hatch closed? How did I get the hatch sealed without anything fouled in the seals? It just happened. And it happened because of the perspective of the iteration training we did time and time again. It was just complete memorization. I like to think of it as the thousands of hours over my whole career preparing me to respond quickly and efficiently and do it. And do it right. And that's the perspective that comes with the value of practice.

Perspective isn't something that just appears from thin air. The good news is that we can take control of our perspectives and use them to inspire ourselves and others. Chris's experiences during this EVA are a perfect example of this. Like many of us, Chris spent countless hours mastering his craft. From those experiences, Chris was able to craft a unique perspective filled with principles and maxims. These insights formed the foundation of his perspective and became second nature to him when he was in the heat of saving Parmitano from peril.

From his early Navy SEAL experience, Chris realized that it wasn't his job to be a demolition expert or communication expert. Rather, it was his job to pull everyone together, lead, and give his teammates the support and motivation that they needed. His prior experiences developed a perspective that consistently helped him to understand the mission, deliver the mission's intent, and make quick, thoughtful decisions.

We all have different life experiences. Even if we're on the same mission or completing the same project, our perceptions and thoughts form our perspectives and therefore could be different. But as Chris illustrates, we can take ownership of our perspective. We don't have to approach it passively. By being cognizant of the value of the daily incremental work, we see its value over the long game.

The benefits of this are huge. Ultimately, when the chips are down and we need to respond to some obstacle or problem aggressively, we'll know that we can rely on our perspective and the work we did to reach this point. It'll be an ever-present force that can inspire and motivate us. We just need to actively create it and call on it when we're feeling stressed.

Understanding the Bigger Picture

Between graduating from the U.S. Naval Academy, going through the BUD/S grinder, achieving some of the highest military accolades in Afghanistan, and literally becoming an astronaut, Chris has a resume that is second to none. Many would give anything to have as many accolades as Chris has gathered. That said, Chris is a passion-struck leader because he understands the bigger picture. He understands that we are all part of one "Spaceship Earth" and that we have a responsibility to each other.

Enter the overview effect. In my conversations with Chris,[90] I asked him about the overview effect when he first entered orbit. His first experience in space was more centered on the fact that he was actually in space. Growing up in York, Maine, it seemed surreal to him that his career led him to the International Space Station. But on his second trip to space, Chris noticed this effect. As he told me, space travel changed his perspective on how he makes life choices. Seeing Earth made him feel small—almost like a dot in the grand scheme of things.

This was similar to my discussions with astronaut Captain Wendy Lawrence, USN, whom I will introduce more fully in the next chapter. She takes this overview effect concept even further. Lawrence told me that every astronaut or cosmonaut will say to you that until you look out the spacecraft's window and see your planet with your own eyes, you just can't comprehend how hugely impactful it is. I was fascinated by the fact that, according to Lawrence and Chris, you can independently talk to each astronaut or cosmonaut who has been to space, and invariably they all use the same word to describe what Earth looks like to them. That word is *fragile*.

Lawrence described it as "seeing our planet suspended against an intensely black void of space. It just seems like space wants to swallow up Earth. From this experience, you clearly understand that Earth is our home planet and the only place we know how to live on. And, we have to do a much better job taking care of it. Because we need to help our Earth hold off this void of space that wants to gobble it up. Through this experience, they both learned that we are all connected." Our decisions affect others in our communities and in our world. It is the idea of being world-centric with our beliefs and intentionality.

Passion-struck leaders look beyond themselves—even if they are highly ambitious. They intuitively understand that we are all part of a larger world-centric community. Using our talents to benefit that world-centric view not only makes all of us better off, but it is more satisfying. We become happier and more fulfilled in our day-to-day work. We see how our lives are making a difference to the entire planet.

Grasping the Power of Perspective in Our Own Lives

Now, we come to the $64,000 question: How can I get and leverage this power of perspective in my own life?

It starts with a conscious and deliberate engagement with perspective, both personally and professionally. It may sound abstract at first, but taking this essential step can elevate our journey towards a more fulfilling life. Amidst the hustle of daily routines and to-do lists, we must make the effort to grasp the bigger picture actively.

To begin, reflect on the experiences and lessons learned throughout your life, both positive and negative. Carve out time in your schedule to contemplate your past experiences, goals, and your place in the world. Whether it becomes a part of your meditation practice or bedtime reflections, making perspective a priority will set you apart from others.

When facing challenging moments, draw on that perspective, just as Chris did during his toughest times. Though our challenges may not be as extreme, we can rely on our perspectives to overcome obstacles. Take a moment to step back and remove yourself from immediate stress. Maintaining perspective can make daunting challenges seem more manageable.

Passion-driven leaders understand their role in the world extends beyond material success. They actively seek ways to give back and create a positive impact. Consider your unique skills and how you can contribute to the well-being of others. Prioritize action and embrace opportunities to make a difference, whether in your community or on a larger scale. Cultivating human connections and making a positive impact will give you an unfair advantage as you pursue personal and professional goals.

By adopting these practices and embracing the power of perspective, you'll unlock a new level of fulfillment and success in your life's journey. Don't underestimate the profound impact this shift in mindset can have on your trajectory. Embrace perspective, and let it propel you towards a more purposeful and passion-struck existence.

Maintaining Perspective in Good and Not-So-Good Times

Another leader who talked with me about the power of perspective is Matt Higgins, co-founder and CEO of RSE Ventures, a former guest shark on *Shark Tank*, and author of *Burn the Boats*, whom I mentioned previously. Matt explains in our interview:

> We have a tendency to put ourselves in a box more than anyone else does. So, I've always felt that I was never going to escape my circumstances if I allowed them to define me. The first step in not being defined by your circumstances is to refuse to let anyone else put you in a box and not put yourself in a box. Let me unpack that statement.
>
> At various times in my life, I could have been a high school dropout. But I refused [to take that path]. I was a success story who went to college and law school, I worked for government as the] COO of the Lower Manhattan Development Corporation overseeing the largest development project in the history of the world. So I could have defined myself as a government person, or even as a press person. I could have limited [myself]. But when you zoom out, and I encourage everyone listening to this, zoom out on your experience at any one moment in time, and say fundamentally, What are you doing not specifically in terms of your domain? But fundamentally, what are you doing?

The problem is, rarely do we stop to ponder our perspectives and realign them. Often, brilliant ideas remain unrealized, and individuals find themselves trapped in a cycle of self-imposed limitations. Every obstacle appears insurmountable, and progress feels elusive. However, by taking a moment to reflect and question our own perspectives, we unearth a wealth of self-awareness. By delving into the "whys" behind our actions and opinions, we open doors to adaptability and personal evolution.

The shift toward becoming a "perspective harnesser" holds the promise of profound transformation. It propels us from mere ideation to tangible realization, from self-centered pursuits to a world-centric view centered on serving others. Just as astronauts experience the awe-inspiring "overview effect" when viewing Earth from space, we too can experience a paradigm shift by embracing the power of perspective. This shift empowers us to conquer challenges, navigate uncertainties, and unveil hidden possibilities.

In a world marked by complexity and uncertainty, the ability to zoom out and glean insights from different angles is an invaluable skill. The pursuit of success, fulfillment, and impact is guided by our willingness to explore the broader panorama of possibilities. By unlocking the power of perspective, we embark on a journey of self-discovery, growth, and ultimately, the realization of our full potential.

Scan this QR code for additional insights and resources.

Chapter Exercises: Harness the Power of Perspective

- Reflective Journaling: Reflect on a recent decision or problem, considering the perspectives you used and sources of information you relied upon. Explore how you can expand your perspective in future situations and actively seek alternative viewpoints.

- Engage in Constructive Disagreements: Find someone with a different perspective and have a respectful conversation about a topic you feel strongly about. Practice active listening, ask questions, and look for common ground. Reflect on how this experience influences your perspective.

- Diversify Information Sources: Assess the diversity of your regular information sources (news outlets, social media, books). Identify at least three new sources with alternative viewpoints. Commit to engaging with them regularly to broaden your understanding and challenge preconceived notions.

- Participate in Cross-Disciplinary Discussions: Seek out opportunities to join discussions that bring together individuals from different fields or areas of expertise. Listen to diverse perspectives and contribute your own insights. Notice how these conversations enhance your understanding and inspire new ideas.

- Challenge Confirmation Bias: Deliberately expose yourself to counterarguments and opposing viewpoints on a topic you feel strongly about. Engage with articles, books, or podcasts that challenge your existing beliefs. Evaluate the evidence presented and reflect on how this process shapes your perspective.

These exercises empower us to embrace diverse viewpoints, expand our understanding, and make more informed decisions. Let us embark on this journey of self-discovery and intellectual growth, continuously seeking to broaden our perspectives and foster a more inclusive and interconnected world.

CHAPTER 7

ACTION CREATOR—PERMIT YOURSELF TO DREAM THE DREAM

*The only impossible journey is
the one you never begin.*
—Tony Robbins

Hesitation is the enemy of action.

By this stage in the book, you've witnessed the transformative mindset shifts of passion-struck seekers. They have the ability to scrutinize the prevailing norms and summon the internal courage to pursue unconventional paths. Fear doesn't hold them back; instead, they harness the power of perspective to their advantage. Even when faced with significant failures or setbacks, they boldly reinvent themselves and seize new opportunities without hesitation.

Amidst all these essential attributes, there lies one overarching mindset shift that defines passion-struck individuals. Whether they are rebounding from a colossal public failure or seeking their next triumph, passion-struck people fuel their passion through consistent action, making deliberate micro choices throughout their days. These seemingly small decisions pave the way for their unwavering commitment to their passions and aspirations. This trait is a hallmark of my own leadership and something that has defined my reputation in business, sports, and philanthropic activism. Luckily, I learned early on in my career, that an organization can introduce a new initiative, announce a new marketing campaign, conduct a capital raise, or create the greatest strategic plan—however, without a bias for action, they fail to achieve breakthrough results. This is likely because of the leadership of the organization.

A great example of this was my tour of duty as the executive officer of the National Security Agency detachment at the Joint Interagency Task Force South (JIATF-South), formerly JIATF-East, in Key West, Florida. For those of you who don't know, JIATF-South is a joint command that is focused on America's war on illicit drugs.[91]

The JIATF-South is unique because not only does it contain soldiers from all five military branches, it also has representatives from the DEA, U.S. Customs and Border Protection, CIA, NSA, FBI, and country partners (such as the Netherlands, the UK, and Canada). In fact, the Department of Homeland Security was modeled after it, in part, due to its overwhelming success in creating interagency coordination and cross-functional teams.[92]

With such a large and diverse organizational structure, leadership was absolutely critical to helping JIATF-South achieve its mission. For that reason, a two-star rear admiral is in charge, with an immense responsibility for detecting and monitoring illegal trafficking in the air, on land, and on the water. It operates in waters covering forty-two million square miles of the Western hemisphere, predominantly with its thirty official partner nations.

While coordination is vital, the flag officer is also responsible for ensuring that the entire team is moving in real-time to accomplish its mission. According to General Douglas Fraser, former commander of U.S. Southern Command (USSOUTHCOM), "JIATF-South is the standard for integrating and synchronizing 'whole of government,' 'whole of nation,' and 'whole of many nations' solutions in confronting challenges to our national and shared regional security."

Back when I was detailed to JIATF-South, I was deep-selected as a lieutenant junior grade into a lieutenant commander billet. The officer who improbably chose me, Navy Commander (CDR) William "Bill" Fitzsimmons, had a fascinating and legendary story. He was a so-called Mustang Officer, a military slang term meaning that he started his career as an E-1 (a Navy seaman recruit), became a warrant officer, and rose through the ranks over thirty years to become an 0-5 (a Navy commander). I had heard of CDR Fitzsimmons before I arrived. His reputation preceded him, and I had been warned to avoid working for him. He carried the nickname CDR Fitzhitler, and I was apprehensive about what to expect.

Surprisingly, CDR Fitzsimmons came to be one of the best bosses and teachers that I've ever worked for. The commander was an outstanding leader for many reasons, but one of the most notable was that he was a believer in the need for action. Yes, he would develop well-thought plans to help his team to accomplish its mission, but he was able to take decisive action. He was absolutely the type of warrior you wanted to have in your foxhole in time of battle.

Along with this, he would give his direct reports the latitude to also make independent decisions and expected us to do so. If we were wrong, he would always have our back in public and would give us detailed critiques in private. I remember making an operational call on the watch floor when I gave my opinion to the rear admiral in charge of JIATF-South. Although others in the room told the admiral that I was wrong, CDR Fitzsimons defended me. I later turned out to be correct, but he gave me an ear lashing in private for how I went about delivering the information and stepping on the toes of two

O-6s in the process. It was a valuable lesson, and I would not repeat that mistake.

In the end, however, timely decisions were his forte. He relied on his bias for action to progress his entire career, climbing the ranks farther than anyone would have expected from his initial beginnings. He took advantage of opportunities presented to him in the Navy— even if he made some incorrect decisions on the way. In fact, an overwhelming number of his decisions were correct.

A great example of this occurred in 1996 during a global incident where Cuban fighter jets shot down two small planes operated by a Cuban-American group over the waters north of Havana. Given our proximity, JIATF-South took point on this incident with CDR Fitzsimmons providing vital intelligence all the way up the chain of command to President Clinton. Even when faced with pressure, CDR Fitzsimmons stood fast that U.S. military intelligence revealed that the Cuban fighter pilots knew the planes were civilian Cessnas before firing missiles and downing two of the three aircraft piloted by Cuban exiles.

He also was steadfast in his recommendation that we not counterattack. He was confident that Castro did not authorize the attack, and recommended that the U.S. look at sanctions instead. In the end, he analyzed the facts, made quick decisions, and stood firm with his choice. Ultimately, the U.S. issued a condemnation to the United Nations Security Council and implemented sanctions.

After CDR Fitzsimmons left JIATF-South, ensuing retirement, another officer naturally replaced him. He had a reputation for being a nice guy (and he was). You wouldn't be afraid of being chewed up by this officer, and I would go out running with him almost every day at lunch. That said, he couldn't make a decision without analysis paralysis. He would overanalyze and overthink *every* judgement that came his way. While he was a strategic thinker, he failed to invoke action alongside his ideas. This played out in real-world results, as the team performed at levels far below those under CDR Fitzsimmons.

In the end, there was a clear example of taking action and a clear example of hesitation. The overarching variable separating the two? It was a consistent focus on action, even in the midst of major uncertainty and real-time military operations.

When it comes to fueling your passion, you'll notice that it has a snowball effect. Passion possesses a remarkable quality—it ignites exponentially with each consistent, coordinated action taken towards our goals. Those who are truly passion struck understand this phenomenon. They embody the spirit of unwavering determination, relentlessly moving forward regardless of obstacles encountered.

Why Action Leads to Action

In an engaging interview featured on the *Passion Struck* podcast, I had the honor of conversing with Lydia Fenet, a distinguished former Christie's ambassador, renowned charity auctioneer, and author of *Claim Your Confidence*. Together, we explored the extraordinary phenomenon of why action leads to action, uncovering the transformative power of momentum in our pursuit of becoming passion struck.

During our interview, Fenet conveyed a powerful truth: "Action leading to action is the critical part that so many people are missing in their life and in their business." She challenges the notion that success simply falls into our laps and urges us to actively shape our destinies. Waiting for opportunities to find us is futile; we must take charge and make things happen.

Fenet emphasizes the importance of proactive engagement in our endeavors. She encourages us to examine our actions when we find ourselves in a rut. Are we diligently seeking new clients? Are we investing time in networking and sharing our aspirations with others? Every intentional step we take moves us closer to our goals, expanding our network and attracting potential supporters.

Fenet shares a compelling story of a friend who experienced the profound impact of action leading to action.

"A friend of mine who [had], during COVID, just gone into the cycle about not having money, she was concerned about her family's money and not being able to make any money. But at the core, she's a very talented artist. And she's sitting on so much inventory. And she couldn't see the forest from the trees. And I said to her, 'What are you doing to let people know what you're doing?' She'd gone quiet on social media. And I was like, you just have to let people know that you have plenty of artwork ready to ship and ready to go. And even just having that fifteen-minute conversation with her sparked something in her. You have to be the spark in this entire fire. She just started going crazy. She was doing flash sales. She was doing customized work. I mean, all of a sudden it created this chain reaction, which is what action leads to action means. You start it, you spark it, and then watch it fly."

Fenet's narrative echoes timeless wisdom—action begets action. Her inspiring insights illuminate the remarkable chain reaction that unfolds when we seize control of our lives and pursue our passions with unwavering determination. Each intentional action becomes a catalyst, propelling us into a state of exhilarating momentum, ultimately leading us towards the fulfillment of our dreams.

How to Develop Passion-Fueled Action

Fenet's example showcases the fundamental truth that without action, nothing happens. Action is the epitome of being passion struck. Anyone can be interested in or passionate about a particular subject area, job, or hobby. But without taking action, any passion or interest will remain hypothetical. That may feel safer and more comfortable, but that person will live a life of "what ifs" and regrets.

Passion-struck leaders like CDR Fitzsimmons and Fenet prioritize action, no matter where they are in their careers. They use their passion as fuel to try different things, learn from their success and failure, and continue to take action. And if there is a substantial chance of misfortune? Passion-struck leaders find a way to mitigate as much risk as possible and proceed anyway.

If you are looking to become passion struck in your life, there's no choice but to rise up and take action towards your goals—even if you're fearful or intimidated. Ultimately, action is one of the most valuable strategies to avoid apathy, which you can then use to get closer to your sky-high goals.

Two excellent examples of passion-struck leaders who possess this character trait are Navy Captain and NASA astronaut Wendy Lawrence and billionaire, NBA owner, and philanthropist Mark Cuban. Waiting is anathema to them. They combine passion and action into a killer cocktail that has led to massive career success and trailblazing careers. Learning from their stories, we can begin to understand examples of this important transition and how we can adopt an action-first attitude in our own lives.

Wendy Lawrence: A Passion-Struck Leader and a Trailblazer

Wendy Lawrence is a perfect example of a passion-struck leader who has leveraged bold, consistent achievement throughout her career. She was one of the first women to attend the U.S. Naval Academy, graduating in 1981 with a Bachelor of Science in ocean engineering. Lawrence went on to become a Naval aviator and was one of the first two female helicopter pilots to join a carrier battle group.

Even at this point, Lawrence had achieved career-defining milestones in one of the world's most venerable institutions—the U.S. military. But Lawrence was only getting started. She completed a highly selective master's degree program at MIT and later returned to the U.S. Naval Academy to become my physics instructor. I remember meeting her and realizing there was something different and special about her and the abundance of vitality and conviction she possessed.

It was in 1991, however, while we were both at the Naval Academy, that Lawrence's career went, literally, out of this world. She applied to become a NASA astronaut, eventually receiving the good news that she would become an astronaut candidate in March 1992. After going through the rigors of astronaut training, Lawrence became the first female U.S. Naval Academy graduate to fly into space. She ended up experiencing intergalactic travel on four different missions, including the STS-114 *Discovery*, which was the first Space Shuttle flight after the *Columbia* tragedy.

Her CV is extremely impressive. Like With many other passion-struck leaders, it's natural to think that Lawrence traveled on a straight line from her acceptance to the Naval Academy to doing somersaults in space. However, Lawrence faced her fair share of obstacles, and she used her passion as fuel to take aggressive and decisive action.

Starting the Journey

On July 20, 1969, Lawrence and millions of others watched the Apollo 11 astronauts walk on the moon. She was ten years old, and from that point, she knew that she wanted to be an astronaut. However, Lawrence hadn't seen anyone like her become an astronaut at that time. She had big dreams, but to that point had only seen men become astronauts. However, her passion was fueled by the fact that she knew many of the initial Mercury 7 astronauts.[93] In fact, her father flew with Alan Shepard, and he was involved in the selection process for the Mercury astronauts. He was also a test pilot with John Glenn, the former astronaut and U.S. senator.

She thought she would attend a civilian university to begin the journey of achieving her goal. You see, even though both her father and grandfather were Naval Academy graduates, prior to her senior year of high school, no woman had attended the prestigious institution that has shaped some of the world's top leaders.

However, for many, the thought of achieving a dream that appears to be light years away is enough to deter them from working towards their goal, as they are not prepared to put in the effort to get to their final destination. During our interview Lawrence told me:

> You have got to be willing to try. You have to take those initial steps…. We have created an instant society. We have developed a short attention span in people. You have to figure out how to be resilient. So many people want to have it instantly. Making a dream come true and overcoming significant hurdles—none of that happens overnight.[94]

The landscape seemed daunting, yet Lawrence didn't back down. She didn't overanalyze her predicament or think about all the challenges that were in front of her. Instead, she took action. During her junior year in high school, the U.S. Naval Academy accepted the first female midshipmen. And once she realized it was a viable option, she pounced on the opportunity to kickstart her journey. Even at that point, she began charting out a path that could take her from the Naval Academy to NASA. Her father inspired her to examine the career trajectories of the other astronauts and chart a similar course.

So, upon being accepted, she didn't let up, using forward momentum as fuel to continue the pursuit of her end goal. She made it a priority to set the standard for her fellow midshipmen, and she knew that she had to be head and shoulders ahead of the male midshipmen. Even though she was being watched by many at the U.S. Naval Academy, she didn't get stuck in her own head because her father was the superintendent. She was laser-focused on her goal, which was to graduate from the Academy with an engineering degree and land a coveted pilot slot. She knew that both were prerequisites for attaining her dream of joining the space program.

Fight Through Failure

Becoming a U.S. Naval Academy graduate and trailblazing helicopter pilot would make anyone feel like they've made it. It is tempting to take it easy and rest on your laurels. Wendy Lawrence, however, was different. She kept striving toward her ultimate goal of becoming an astronaut—even when she experienced failures.

Lawrence told me about her pursuit of her master's degree in ocean engineering at MIT. Upon acceptance, she was in awe of many of the graduate students who attended the intimidating academic institution. At first, she didn't think that she could measure up to the other brilliant minds. And reality hit her during her first summer as she was taking a course called "Calculus for Engineers." While she assumed she could handle the course, the content seemed incomprehensible. At that time, she also hadn't been in a classroom for five years. She ended up failing her first test badly. It was the first time that she had ever failed in her academic or professional endeavors.

Like anything in life, when you are knocked down, you have that choice. For Lawrence that meant that she could either continue down the path of failure and self-pity or brush herself off and figure out what she needed to do next to start moving forward again. She chose the latter.

Failure was staring her directly in the face. Even though she was extremely disappointed, Lawrence didn't give up. She knew that getting a master's degree from MIT would substantially increase her odds of becoming an astronaut. She couldn't give up. So, she approached her teacher's assistant and scheduled regular study sessions with him. She was knocked down, but she fully committed to mastering the material. She overcame this obstacle through strong, decisive action and got one step closer to her dream by graduating with a master's degree. Asking for help was a show of strength. She put herself in an uncomfortable position and aggressively acted to get closer to her goal. But it was also a very valuable lesson to her that, sometimes, taking action requires the help of others.

Continue to Dream the Dream

Wendy Lawrence had to overcome failures, frustrations, and dead ends on her way to becoming a NASA astronaut. The astronaut selection process is notoriously competitive, yet Lawrence was able to successfully navigate this gauntlet.

How did she do it? Ultimately, it came down to executing on dreaming the dream. While it's important to dream big, it's not uncommon for people to become overwhelmed by the goals they set. To many, the road ahead is daunting as they forget to focus on the now, what they can immediately work on to get them to their final destination.

Lawrence describes it in this way:

> "If you think about where you want to end up and
> how to get there, you can get paralyzed by how much
> work you perceive it is going to take."

Therefore, to move forward, people must focus on a series of accomplishments that will slowly propel them forward to what they are trying to achieve. Lawrence believes that success is a "progression, a process, a journey."

One example from her career originates with the STS-114 mission. Lawrence and her fellow astronauts were testing safety procedures and repair techniques. While this is always an important task, it was especially relevant because STS-114 was the "Return to Flight" Space Shuttle mission after the *Columbia* disaster. There was significant American public and international scrutiny.

Lawrence flew the space station's robotic arm during two of the mission's spacewalks. As she told me, when astronauts are assigned to a mission, they normally know exactly what they are going to do at the start of their training flow. But this wasn't the case for this mission. Instead, Lawrence and her fellow astronauts had to come up with new ways of doing things in space. They put in the work and developed solutions to the problems they encountered. By taking this approach, they overcame uncertainty and revived U.S. space exploration after a horrific loss.

No matter how large or small your goal is, Lawrence's example illustrates how a large part of achieving your long-term goals is not only goal setting, but practice and putting in the work. Many of us back down when something isn't naturally easy. We make the choice to move on to something else and get stuck in our own heads. We tell ourselves that we'll "never be good at it." We often see the future we long to have; however, we fail to take the needed actions along the way. We face setbacks and too often sell ourselves short of achieving our life goals. Everyone faces adversity during their journey. Failure is something that makes us better. And, you owe it to yourself to try.

In Lawrence's words:

> Many kids think this is what they really want to do [become an astronaut], but then they say this will never happen to them. They immediately sell themselves short. They do a huge disservice to themselves. Dream your dream. You owe it to yourself to try. Have the courage to dream the dream and take the first steps. Then evaluate how well you are doing. If it is not easy at first or you are not doing well, don't quit. Welcome to life. Things you were meant to do were not necessarily made to be easy. If you persist and are willing to work hard and practice, you will generally get better.

Lawrence's journey to space exemplifies that pursuing your aspiration is not easy. It took her twenty-five years to fulfill her dream of flying into space. She focused on those initial steps and asked for help when she needed it. As she tells those asking for career advice, you owe it to yourself to try. One of the worst things is looking back in regret because you never gave yourself the chance to try.

Mark Cuban: Aggressively Pursuing His Goals

Mark Cuban is well-known for his exploits on *Shark Tank* and as the Dallas Mavericks owner, yet it wasn't a smooth path to success. He had to take decisive action to find *and maintain* his success.

Cuban was born with entrepreneurial DNA. He started his first business when he was twelve years old (he went door-to-door selling garbage bags). After graduating from Indiana University, he worked at a bank in Pittsburgh and then moved to Dallas where his true entrepreneurial journey began.

Cuban has been the brains behind several different businesses. MicroSolutions, which was initially a software reseller and systems integrator, sold for $6 million. He then used those proceeds to start Broadcast.com, which was an early Internet radio company. At the height of the dot-com boom, Cuban and his partners sold the company for a whopping $5.7 billion to Yahoo.

Becoming an instant billionaire, Cuban could have taken the easy road and retired on a Caribbean island. Instead, he chose to continue taking action and invest in companies that spoke to him. Not only does he have an established career as a startup investor, but he purchased the Dallas Mavericks and is a regular "shark" on *Shark Tank*.

Cuban's story is one that many entrepreneurs could only dream of. But it didn't come automatically. Mark had to deal with massive amounts of uncertainty and fear. Rather than backing down, however, Cuban was relentless, taking decisive action to accomplish his goals.

Seize Opportunities—Even If They Result in Temporary Pain

One of the defining moments in Cuban's life was when he worked as a salesperson for Your Business Software, which was an early PC software retailer in the Dallas area. As the legend goes,[95] Cuban's duties included not only selling and installing software, but opening and sweeping the retail store in the morning. Cuban wasn't initially opposed to this. He was getting referrals, making cold calls, and generally enjoying his job.

Nine months into his career, a sales prospect contacted Cuban and asked him to come to his office to close a sale. The problem? Mark still had to open the store that same morning. It was decision time. And so often it is the little decisions that have the biggest impact. Mark followed his first instinct: close the sale. He rationalized that you never turn your back on a closed deal. So he called one of his coworkers to come in and open up, and closed the deal. The next day, Cuban was fired. We all have to make that "make or break" call to follow orders or do what you know is right. Mark did what he thought was right and from there went on to create MicroSolutions, which he eventually sold for $6 million.[96]

While it was a seemingly small decision in his early career, Cuban already exemplified the traits of a passion-struck leader. He recognized that bold, aggressive action was necessary to advance his career and pursue this extremely unique opportunity with a new client. Yes, there was the risk of losing his job (which happened). Yet he recognized that he had to aggressively pursue this opportunity—even if there was near-term uncertainty.

To be clear, I'm not saying that you need to immediately quit your job or put it in jeopardy to pursue your dreams. You certainly don't need to undercut your employer for personal gain. That being said, if there's a compelling opportunity out there for you to get closer to your goals, you may want to take it seriously. Once again, action rules the day.

Looking to the Future—and Acting

Throughout his career, Mark Cuban has been known to be an opportunistic entrepreneur and investor, relying on action and speed to make huge returns. He is always analyzing technology trends and changing consumer preferences. He hates meetings and prefers action over groups of people simply talking and planning in a large conference room. Ultimately, while it is easy for billionaire investors like him to sit on the sidelines, Cuban aggressively places bets when he thinks the odds are on his side.

There are plenty of examples of this. Broadcast.com, the startup that made Cuban a billionaire, was founded in response to advancing Internet technology and a growing desire to hear and watch sports content on the Internet. His purchase of the Dallas Mavericks occurred just as the NBA was about to explode with popularity and massive TV deals. Even if you look at his investments on *Shark Tank*, Cuban is always looking around the corner, analyzing how markets are shifting and taking aggressive action when he has an edge.

With so much capital at stake, Cuban has to look forward, mitigate his risk, and take bold action. It's a fine line to walk, and he has his fair share of failures. Even so, Cuban learns from those failures and continues to act—even if the future isn't completely certain.

Resisting the Waiting Game in Your Own Life

As Wendy Lawrence and Mark Cuban both illustrate, passion-struck leaders have ingrained an "action first" mindset into their lives. Whether times are good or bad, they are constantly moving forward. Action is the name of the game, whether you are trying to become the CEO of your company, the senior minister of a church, an astronaut, a military general or to launch a billion-dollar startup.

So how do you both resist indecision and find the strength to take more action towards those goals? I have a few suggestions.

First, don't look for complete certainty or near-complete certainty when making decisions. This is a fool's errand. Passion-struck leaders understand that there will *never* be complete certainty, no matter how long they spend studying a problem, dilemma, or opportunity. They take bold, aggressive action—even if there is a possibility that they may be wrong. While they may be wrong at times, this approach leads to more right decisions and more value in the long run.

This approach, however, naturally leads to the question of, how much certainty *do* you need? Is it 50 percent, 80 percent, or something else? Ultimately, there is no quick and easy formula. It will come with trial and error. But I'd generally recommend that you take action *earlier* than you feel you are comfortable with. Even though it will seem scary, getting into this habit will make it less daunting over time.

From there, make sure that you are taking advantage of real-world data. One of the best parts about taking bold, decisive action is that you get real-world feedback at your fingertips. In the startup world, this is essentially the value of a minimally viable product. Even if you are embarrassed by your first launch, you can capitalize on real and honest feedback about your product or service. This sort of feedback would be impossible to obtain if you were simply thinking about startup ideas or theorizing on potential features for your product.

In effect, by waiting, you are throwing away priceless data that can get you closer to your goal. The short-term comfort of waiting or being more reserved comes at the sacrifice of real-world feedback, which can propel you towards your long-term goals.

Finally, don't be afraid to ask for help. If you are feeling anxious about taking one step towards your long-term goal, taking action can seem less intimidating when others are helping you. Wendy Lawrence saw this when seeking help from her teacher's assistant at MIT, and Mark Cuban saw this when working with a co-founder to start Broadcast.com.

Whether you are subtly procrastinating in starting your own side hustle or are waiting for the right moment to ask for a raise, I encourage you to reach out. Contact friends, mentors, or whoever you think can keep you accountable. Ask them to follow up and confirm that you truly are taking action. Having this sort of accountability buddy can go a long way in forcing you to take action.

The Transformative Power of Micro Choices

On the *Passion Struck* podcast, I had the privilege of interviewing Michelle Segar, a renowned behavior change expert, an award-winning researcher at the University of Michigan, and the author of *The Joy Choice*. Our discussion centered around the significance of intentionality and the transformative nature of conscious action-taking in our lives. During this enlightening conversation, Michelle shared her profound insights on the power of micro choices.

According to Segar, consistent, moment-to-moment choices are the key to lasting change.

> "The secret sauce to sustainable behavior change is our consistent choices throughout our days, weeks, months, and years." It is these micro choices that lay the foundation for transformative and enduring shifts in our lives."

Cultivating a sense of drive and motivation is essential in implementing sustainable behavior change. Segar explains, "To create the foundation for sustainable change and consistent decision-making, the first essential step is cultivating a sense of drive and motivation. This internal fuel becomes the catalyst for transformation. However, it is essential to recognize that having drive alone is not enough. We must also possess the wherewithal to improvise and adapt in the present moment."

While our initial motivation provides the spark, life often presents unexpected challenges and curveballs. No matter how meticulously we plan or how determined we are, circumstances can shift, and our path may veer off course. During these moments of uncertainty, our ability to think on our feet and make spontaneous decisions becomes crucial.

The power to improvise allows us to navigate obstacles and stay on track toward our goals. It enables us to adjust our approach, find alternative solutions, and overcome unforeseen barriers. By embracing this adaptive mindset, we increase our chances of sustaining positive change in the face of adversity.

So, while having drive and motivation is a given, it is equally important to cultivate the capacity for improvisation. This dynamic combination empowers us to create lasting transformations by responding effectively to life's ever-changing circumstances.

Imagine being given a photograph of a person and asked to replicate it using only a pencil and a piece of paper. As someone who doesn't usually draw, your immediate response would likely be a resounding "no." But what if you were tasked with reproducing a simple solid gray square? Suddenly, the answer becomes clear: yes, you can do it.

The truth is, if you can create one gray square, you can create two, then three, and eventually, all the shades of gray squares come together to form the person's image.

This simple illustration serves as a powerful reminder that the barrier between us and our most ambitious dreams and goals has less to do with possessing some elusive talent or skill and more with our problem-solving and decision-making approach.

When we view a task as a daunting whole, its complexity can easily discourage us or diminish our tenacity. However, when we break it down into tiny, manageable bits and focus on the micro choices we can make in each moment, we gain the ability to swiftly complete tasks and build upon each small accomplishment. This concept will be extensively explored in part three of the book, delving into its profound implications. By incorporating these micro choices into our daily routine, they become ingrained, recurring patterns of behavior. Whether you aim to advance professionally or embark on a learning journey, it all begins with that initial step and grows from there. Taking a step forward is something anyone can do. Yet, the true challenge lies in consciously harnessing micro choices' power to elevate your life and career to new heights. Through this intentional practice, you unlock your full potential and pave the way for remarkable success.

Unleashing the Power of Micro Choices: Igniting Passion-Struck Action

Those striving to be passion struck understand that true transformation and the pursuit of our deepest aspirations require more than just introspection and alignment with our passions. It demands strong, decisive action and a commitment to making bold decisions, even in the face of uncertainty. It is in these moments of making deliberate and conscious micro choices that the true power of our passion is unleashed.

Just as Michelle Segar emphasized the significance of micro choices in creating lasting change, passion-struck individuals recognize that the execution of these choices is paramount. They accept that each moment presents an opportunity to make a decisive decision that propels them forward. They acknowledge that uncertainty is part of the journey and are willing to learn from both their successes and failures as they progress towards their goals.

While the initial step towards pursuing our passion may seem daunting, passion-struck leaders understand that it is in these small yet deliberate actions that momentum is built. They embrace the challenge with commitment, courage, and a desire to make bold decisions, even in the face of fear. They recognize that by consistently making these micro choices, they are building a muscle of resilience and determination that grows stronger over time.

Just as a single gray square can pave the way for a complete portrait, each micro choice we make becomes a building block towards the realization of our dreams. By incorporating these intentional choices into our daily routines, they become ingrained patterns of behavior, propelling us closer to our desired outcomes.

So, don't let anything hold you back from unleashing the power of micro choices in pursuit of your passion. It requires commitment and courage, but it is an investment that you cannot afford to overlook. Start strong, take decisive action, and build a wave of momentum that will sweep away any obstacles in your path.

Embrace the mindset of an "action creator" and continuously move forward, regardless of the circumstances. Picture yourself at the end of your life and ask yourself if you would be satisfied with how you lived it. You have the opportunity to live the life of your dreams, and it begins with the conscious choices you make every day.

Now is the time to dream your dream and seize it through the transformative power of micro choices. Unleash your passion, ignite your action, and embark on a journey of fulfillment and purpose.

How are you going to dream your dream?

Scan the QR code for additional resources and insights.

Chapter Exercises: Steps to Start Dreaming Your Dream

- Reflection and Analysis: Think about a situation where you hesitated to take action. What were the consequences of inaction? Reflect on how taking that initial step could have led to a cascade of actions and potentially different outcomes. Write down your insights.
- Embracing the "Action Loop": Explore the concept of the "action loop," which suggests that taking action creates momentum and motivation for further action. Think about an area where you want to create positive change. Start by taking one small action related to that area. Reflect on how that action can lead to a domino effect of further actions. Write down your observations and insights.

- Overcoming Resistance and Building Habits: Choose a new habit you want to develop. Identify one small action you can take consistently to build that habit. Reflect on how this initial action can catalyze further actions and reinforce the habit loop. Write down your chosen action and commit to practicing it daily for the next week.
- Celebrating Small Wins and Adjusting Course: Consider a situation where you realized your initial action was not leading you toward the desired outcome. Reflect on the importance of being flexible and willing to adjust course when necessary. Write down three strategies you can use to evaluate and adapt your actions to ensure they align with your goals.

Remember, the purpose of these exercises is to encourage self-reflection, provide insights, and inspire action. Embrace the power of taking that first step and observe how it can lead to a series of subsequent actions, ultimately propelling you closer to your goals.

PART 2

BEHAVIOR SHIFTS— HOW SELF- REALIZERS NEED TO TAKE ACTION

CHAPTER 8

ANXIETY OPTIMIZER—HOW TO BE ON EDGE, WITHOUT GOING OFF THE EDGE

Don't think about the past, don't think about the future, don't think about anything but that moment and how can you take your best action at that time. There should be no apprehension. There should be no fear.
—David Cameron Lee

I n 1985, Coopers & Lybrand, later becoming Pricewaterhouse-Coopers, was one of the Big Eight accounting firms when a twenty-one-year-old Colgate economics major began working there. Even at that young age, he established a regimen where he would get up early in the morning, go for a six-mile run, and then work.

At lunchtime, when everyone went to lunch, he would go to the gym and bang out a high-intensity interval workout. He had a significant two-and-a-half-hour gap in the evening between the end of work and going to school for his master's degree. So, he wondered what he could accomplish instead of going home and relaxing like most of his peers.

During one of these periods, when he was walking home on 23rd Street near Broadway, he heard shouts coming from the second floor of a building he was walking by. As he stopped to listen and looked up, he discovered the Seidō world karate headquarters. He decided to go upstairs and check it out. He was just blown away by the positive atmosphere of the studio and by the energy given off by Tadashi Nakamura, the founder of this style of karate. He decided to join up on the spot.

It just so happens that Nakamura was also a Zen master, who believed that intentionality and spiritual development were equally as important as physical and mental development. It was the first time the young man experienced this kind of integration of physical training, mental training, intentionality, and stress control using techniques like breathing and meditation.

The young man decided to focus his energy on learning this new path. He consumed everything he could and started reading everything about the technique. He practiced daily. He would go to the Zen Mountain Monastery, a Zen Buddhist monastery and training center on a 230-acre forested property in the Catskill Mountains in Mount Tremper, New York, for four- or five-day retreats. During these sessions, they would do karate for a couple of hours, then meditate for a couple of hours, three or four times a day. As he continued his daily habit, he incrementally got better and fine-tuned this practice into mastery.

And then, after a few years of working on it, he started to get these signals from his internal guidance system, his spirit, that he was heading down the wrong path in his career and life. He started journaling and asking himself questions. From this internal dialogue, he learned that the quality of his life would be determined by the quality of the questions he asked himself. And the vision that came to him from these questions was that he needed to do something different from the business world. The answer he got back was that he needed to become a warrior.

His name is Navy SEAL Commander Mark Divine.

In a discussion I had with Divine, he told me:

I started to juxtapose that with this deep passion I had for physical training, for mental development for this warrior path that I was learning through Nakamura and Zen. And I thought, well, geez, I've got some skills that make sense that I would be a warrior, like in the military sense. But, it's important to understand that you can be a warrior in any setting. It is how you decide to act and show up with the right amount of anxiety and take risks that that are challenging and uncomfortable.[97]

In 1990, now twenty-seven, Divine reported to Basic Underwater Demolition/SEAL[98] (BUD/S) and graduated as Class 170 Honor Man. He earned the nickname "Cyborg" from his teammates for his unique combination of cognitive strength, intentionality, and endurance. He learned how to perform at the edge, without going over the edge.

What might be the most impressive fact is that of the nineteen who graduated, his entire small boat crew of seven were all graduates—a feat that had never happened before in SEAL training. I asked Divine what made the difference between him and his crew graduating and 166 others failing. He explained:

When I showed up to BUD/S, I had the presence of mind to be non-reactionary, to take everything thrown at us, and to be able to take a deep breath. I would activate my deep diaphragmatic breathing,

look at it, and be like, what can we do right now?
That's going to make the most sense to move forward
out of this shitstorm they're creating because they're
trying to cause stress and put us into fight or flight.

So how can I keep my team calm? And how can
we together come up with a solution? And find our
way through this?

He taught his boat crew what he calls "the big four skills":

1. Breath control, which interrupts that knee-jerk fight or flight
    reaction;
2. Positive internal dialogue, which leads to more creative solu-
    tions and better performance;
3. Imagery, which is the ability to visualize the win and under-
    stand what mission success looks like when achieved; and
4. Targeted focus, which is the ability to be present and focus
    your mind on just doing one thing well.

Those four skills allowed Divine and his team to be very present,
be cohesive, solve problems as a team, and get their egos out of the
way. In other words, he was teaching them how to be intentional.

Divine's story offers a fascinating perspective on what it takes to
operate at an optimum state of performance. Being a Navy SEAL is
not for the timid. It is hard to imagine another profession that would
strike more fear into the hearts of people than going into battle, thousands of miles from home, with only a small team around you. And
yet, Mark Divine faced this fear every week of his twenty-year career
as a Navy SEAL.

Why is it that some people, like Divine, can sustain their mental toughness and intentionality while most of us struggle to stay
motivated? The human brain loves a challenge, but only if it exists
when it is not an obstacle too formidable for us to master. If you love
volleyball and play a competitive match against someone much less

skilled, you will quickly become bored. It becomes effortless, and you end up winning by a landslide. In contrast, if you play a professional volleyball player like Karch Kiraly, David Cameron Lee, or Misty May-Treanor, your motivation may quickly drop. That is because you believe your opponent is too challenging to beat, and you stop believing in yourself.

As Karch Kiraly said, "No volleyball play can begin without a serve, and the serve is the only technique that is totally under your control. In other endeavors, you cannot succeed without believing in yourself, and that belief is completely under your control."

Now, imagine playing volleyball with someone slightly better than you. As the match progresses, you win some points, and you lose a few. Victory is within your grasp, but only if you truly put your mind to it and get into the flow zone. When this happens, you narrow your focal point, you believe in yourself, and you become present in the moment as distractions fade away and you become consumed by the vision of winning. At this moment, you have reached the zone of optimal anxiety.

The zone of optimal anxiety is a state in which an individual's performance peaks, when their anxiety level and intentionality are within or near their optimal zone. When an individual falls outside the optimal level, performance deteriorates. It is a concept that was first introduced in 1908 by psychologists Robert Yerkes and John Dillingham Dodson, when they studied the phenomenon in mice. In Figure 5, I have updated it to reflect a correlation between anxiety and intentionality.

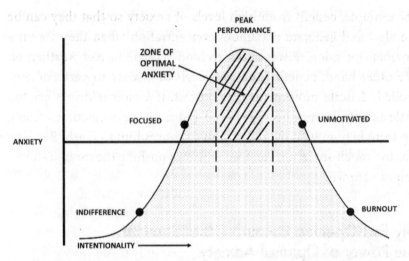

FIGURE 5: Optimum anxiety occurs when anxiety and intentionality are brought into proper alignment of operating on edge, without going off the edge and experiencing burnout. It is the midpoint between anxiety and intentionality.

Mark Divine's Navy SEAL career is an excellent example of the zone of optimal anxiety in practice. Each year, he incrementally expanded his daily routine of the big four ideas of aligning breath control, positive internal dialogue, imagery, and targeted focus. Along the way, he continued to build skills that allowed him to master being fully present and getting his ego out of the way. He demonstrated grit through emotional turmoil and physical setbacks throughout his career but always managed to keep his eyes on the prize of mission success. He learned to put himself in a repeat state of optimal anxiety where he continuously focused on minor continuous behavioral improvements. Divine discovered that once he learned a behavior, it was essential to keep it as simple as possible and advance it incrementally. By doing so, he could learn how to hit the zone of optimal anxiety and use it to drive the momentum needed to achieve long-term peak performance.

Every person's individual zone of optimal anxiety varies based on the different activities he or she is performing. Soldiers like Divine, for example, benefit from high levels of anxiety so that they can be on alert and generate maximum concentration when they are on a combat operation. Pilots about to land a plane in bad weather, on the other hand, benefit from low levels of anxiety to perform controlled, delicate movements. In contrast, if a racecar driver has too little anxiety, he may become bored and miss the competitor coming up from behind who overtakes him or causes him to crash. But if he has too much anxiety, it can lead to fear of pushing the car to its limits required to win.

My Eye-Opening Encounter that Showed the Power of Optimal Anxiety

Even after launching headlong into pursuing your passion, it can be easy to fall into the trap of following a "safe" routine. One that may yield progress, but at a rate that will see you left behind by others. Self-doubt, comfort, and, most of all, fear, lead us to say "no" to opportunities when we should say "yes." But peak performance comes with learning to live in that state of optimal anxiety—and embrace it, rather than run away from it.

I once almost lost one of my most significant business breakthroughs when I was an associate at Booz Allen due to the temptation to say no to a life-changing opportunity. I had recently transferred to the San Diego office and was building out Booz Allen's technology practice. A few months later, I happened to attend a conference and saw a gentleman wearing a Corvette jacket during a break. I was always fond of Corvettes and couldn't resist the temptation to talk to him about his jacket. We immediately hit it off and shared our passion for the mighty beast. We got to conversing about his 1963 Chevrolet Corvette Stingray before eventually exchanging pleasantries on why we were both at the conference.

After giving him my rehearsed spiel about my company, he asked whether Booz Allen offered distance learning and whether it was a core competency. Before providing him the answer, I asked him what organization he was with, and his response completely caught me off guard. He said, "Hi, I am Wayne Hameloth, the civilian head instructor for the Navy's Top Gun program," whose official name is the Strike Fighter Tactics Instructor (SFTI) program.[99]

Hameloth revealed that fighter pilots needed a better training program to prepare for potential combat missions while on deployment. He was proposing to his boss that distance learning could be a solution that would allow SFTI to train deployed fighter pilots better. I became suddenly aware of the enormity of the situation and the prominence of his authority. I quickly realized that achieving his goal could be a colossal win for Booz Allen—if we had the off chance of winning it. At that time, our firm did not have a relationship with SFTI, so I knew it could be a meaningful opportunity for the company long-term.

I had to reply to him with either "yes," Booz Allen does have a distance learning experience, or "no," we do not.

It just so happens that the week before that conference, I was back in Reston, Virginia, at our headquarters. I decided to stay a few days extra to go through some sales briefings for engagements we had recently delivered. As fate would have it, one of those engagements was the Army National Guard distance learning (DL) program that Booz Allen just implemented. Not only was it a distance learning program, but it was also the largest ever to be built in the world.

I had no idea at that point what we would face or how to overcome the technical challenges of delivering distance learning to a deployed carrier group. I took a deep breath, and with positive intent, visualized us winning the contract, focused on the task at hand, and went with my gut. I said, "Yes. Booz Allen just delivered the largest distance learning program for the entire Army National Guard. It is absolutely a core offering."

As far as opportunity goes, that was one of the most pivotal yesses of my entire career. But my work didn't end there. I courted Hameloth with intense focus and passion for the opportunity and established a friendship with him. Booz Allen won an initial $5 million contract to build the Strike Fighter Online Distance Learning program eighteen months later. Two years later, the deal transitioned into a $15 million program and expanded beyond the fighter community into other aircraft types in the Navy and Marine Corps.

Thinking back, I sometimes wonder what caused me to say yes because I could have just as easily taken the safer route and said no. At the time, I had no idea how I would pull it off. I just knew I could. And, within five years, that fateful encounter turned into an ongoing $80 million to $100 million contract for Booz Allen that has continued to grow to other branches of the military.

I'm sure many people would have given a much more cautious response, telling Hameloth the usual "I'll have to find out," or "Let me check and get back to you." Had I done that, I believe that the universe would have delivered a completely different outcome. You see, at that moment, I had just the right amount of confidence, motivation, and anxiety to proceed into the unknown.

Why Is It So Hard to Find the Zone of "Optimal Anxiety"?

As singer, songwriter, and actor Justin Timberlake said, "You're not meant to do what's easy; you're meant to challenge yourself."

"Yes" may be one of the most common words in the English language. Yet, many of us struggle even to utter it in response to what matters most in our lives. I do not believe it is for fear of the word itself. Instead, it's the consequences that saying that word may bring. Rather than run from potential failures or difficult decisions, passion-struck individuals know that real growth and opportunities arise from moments filled with anxiety and the intentionality of focusing on the task at hand.

Now, let us consider the story of award-winning producer, author, and creator Shonda Rhimes. She devoted an entire year to saying "yes," not just to trivial things but also to the things that frightened her.[100] It is a decision she credits with changing her life. Rhimes explains in her best-selling book *Year of Yes* that her journey began at Thanksgiving when her sister uttered six words to her: "You never say yes to anything."

Before that moment, Rhimes described herself as an introvert and someone who stayed in the realm of comfort. However, those six words led to a personal challenge. She told herself that

> [f]or one year, I would say yes to all the things that scared me. Anything that made me nervous, took me out of my comfort zone—I forced myself to say yes to it. And a crazy thing happened: the very act of doing the thing that scared me undid the fear, made it not scary. My fear of public speaking, my social anxiety, poof, gone. It's amazing, the power of one word.[101]

Because of humankind's evolution, our basic human instinct is to push away from high-anxiety-inducing situations. We need and want to take on new challenges, but the fear of failure and self-doubt prevent us from jumping in with both feet. Once the trepidation to say yes subsides, we fall into a sense of status quo, and that, unfortunately, is where we stay. Profound breakthroughs rarely come from a state of comfort.

I am not going to sugarcoat it. It can be scary to have the courage to say yes to an opportunity about which you are unclear or you have never done before. By saying yes and finding a way to push into the anxiety-optimizer behavior, you stare failure in its face and adapt and evolve, just like Mark Divine and Chris Cassidy did during their BUD/S training.

We become prone to head in the other direction of fear because it's our neurological default. From the dawn of time, we've been hardwired to be risk-averse, to protect what we have, and to avoid putting ourselves into discomfort. In essence, we are afraid to cross the chasm of uncertainty that often comes with saying yes to change and being motivated to tackle it. But it's precisely that chasm of uncertainty that we should be seeking out, for it's where the most significant opportunity for self-improvement lies.

Unleashing Flow: The Key to Optimal Engagement

In the quest for optimal performance, one mental state stands out as the pinnacle of engagement, enjoyment, and peak performance: flow. Coined by psychologist Mihaly Csikszentmihalyi[102] in the 1960s, flow refers to a state of deep, sustained focus, where time seems to disappear and individuals effortlessly excel at their tasks.

In an insightful *Passion Struck* podcast interview with Steven Kotler, renowned author of *The Rise of Superman* and *The Art of Impossible* and an expert in flow psychology, we delved into the essential elements required to access the flow state. Kotler emphasized the significance of both cognitive and physical dimensions in achieving peak performance. According to Kotler, "In the Peak Performance Equation, there are four categories of essential cognitive skills: motivation, learning, creativity, and flow. Underpinning these cognitive skills are five essential physical skills: strength, stamina, agility, balance, and flexibility."

Flow is a mental state characterized by unwavering focus and optimal engagement. As Kotler describes it, "Flow is the state of optimal performance, where everything goes through the roof, including learning." When in a state of flow, individuals experience a sense of effortless immersion, heightened performance, and a profound sense of enjoyment. Flow is characterized by a seamless merging of action and awareness, where time seems to dilate, and individuals become fully absorbed in the present moment.

Kotler shared valuable insights on the triggers that ignite the flow state, stating, "If you're trying to onboard a new skill, you want to maximize your time in flow. One of the big insights is that flow states have triggers. If you want more flow in your life, the [twenty-two known] triggers are your toolkit." In his book, *The Art of Impossible*, Kotler categorizes these flow triggers into four groups: internal, external, creative, and social. While these triggers may vary, they all share a common thread—the complete concentration on the present moment. Kotler highlights the challenge-skill balance as a crucial trigger, where the challenge slightly exceeds our skill level, directing our attention to the task at hand.

The practical application of flow psychology lies in intentionally pursuing actions that bring us closer to our goals. Flow enhances the learning process, maximizing our time and immersion in acquiring new skills. Here, the Pareto Principle,[103] also known as the 80/20 rule, comes into play. By identifying the critical tasks or elements that contribute to achieving a flow state, we can prioritize them and create an environment that enhances the likelihood of entering and sustaining flow.

When we integrate the principles of the Pareto Principle and the flow state, a powerful synergy emerges. By effectively allocating our resources, focusing on the vital few, we increase our likelihood of consistently entering the flow state. This alignment leads to heightened productivity, creativity, and fulfillment as we tap into our full potential.

Unleashing flow becomes a transformative journey—one where we harness the power of deep focus, align our actions with our goals, and harmonize the principles of flow and the Pareto Principle. By embarking on this path, we unlock our potential for optimal engagement, extraordinary performance, and a profound sense of fulfillment in all aspects of life. As Kotler wisely states, "Flow is about the complete concentration on the task at hand, and that's what all the triggers do—they drive our attention to the present moment."

How Do You Find Your Individual Anxiety Optimizing Zone?

Let's examine this question through the lens of Eleanor Roosevelt, who said: "Do one thing every day that scares you."[104]

As discussed throughout this chapter, this anxiety-optimizing state is responsible for driving our performance. If you want to become passion struck, you're going to have to get used to saying yes and the discomfort that comes with it. It is essential to reach the state of flow you achieve by becoming an anxiety optimizer. A way you can do this is by working on goals that are just beyond the level of your current comfort zone—then building upon those actions daily and achieving an incremental gain.

Whatever it is that scares you, choose to confront it. Step into your sharp edges. This could be fear of activities like ballroom dancing, public speaking, playing a sport against someone better than you, having a hard talk with your partner, or making an appointment to seek counseling. Deliberately put yourself into uncomfortable situations because you will gain confidence, strength, and courage through every experience.

An example of this comes from my high school running career. What separates a good athlete from an elite athlete? I believe it comes down to how they approach the routine of daily practice and incremental improvement. Is it done with intentionality and with the right amount of motivation to overcome the stress?

When I first started running, I experienced terrible pre-race nerves, and I performed sub-optimally. However, I began to approach practice every day as a race. I saw the practice sessions as an opportunity to challenge myself and compete with my teammates. I would go to the track for a workout and imagine that the eight-hundred-meter repeats we were doing were the same as an actual meet. I would then take a step back and analyze my performance, process what I had learned, and then refocus on my task of improving my performance.

After several weeks, things started to change. I began to think about things differently, and it impacted my daily intentions. I began to want to improve, and I did steadily over time. When I visualized the race or practice, I was mindful, focused on the moment, and envisioned myself improving, I unlocked the best performance from myself. I became an anxiety optimizer.

Once I learned what the zone of optimal anxiety looked and felt like, it became something I could revert to throughout my career. I learned how to put myself in a place to push my performance to the edge while making enough progress to stay driven.

Like Mark Divine and me with my running, through daily practice and incremental steps, you learn how to create the proper level of anxiety and intentionality by building up habits over time. You gain momentum based on your actions to achieve what you fear most because you can now do the things you once thought unimaginable.

Research supports this assertion. Studies have demonstrated that we perform at our best when faced with anxiety and fear of failure. One of the most famous studies was conducted by psychologists Robert M. Yerkes and John D. Dodson back in 1908.[105] The two discovered that sub-optimal performance was achieved during a state of comfort. In contrast, peak performance levels arise when we are in a relative state of anxiety, with heightened stress levels.

The key here is to reach an optimal point of heightened anxiety without taking on so much that you become completely overwhelmed. Too little, and we don't achieve peak performance. Too much, and our performance begins to diminish. It's about saying yes to the opportunities that make you nervous, while deep down, you have the confidence in your abilities to pull them off.

Just think of the leading sports stars that need to be nervous before a game to perform at their best, despite already being professional athletes with years of training behind them. A professional soccer player will feel anxious shooting a penalty shot but will still have the underlying confidence to make the shot. But put them in a situation to kick the winning field goal for an NFL team, and they likely become overwhelmed entirely and fail despite their range of transferable skills.

Deploying an anxiety-optimizer mindset helps you continuously to push the envelope, discover opportunities, and grasp innovations available only for the brave. Once that initial fear subsides, you will quickly see that the pain wasn't that bad and that what you're left with is potentially life changing.

However, achieving the zone of optimal anxiety requires a delicate balance: meaning you shouldn't say yes all the time to everything. By contrast, it's also about learning when to say no to distractions that will throw you in so far over your head that you have little chance of succeeding. During my career, I've seen many peers, superiors, and subordinates alike plateau and turn their careers upside down because they became paralyzed under the enormity of the challenges they had agreed to take on. They became burned out.

It's a scenario that happens all too often, and I am sure many of you have witnessed it. You have a peer or maybe a partner who says yes to several new initiatives or assignments until the obligations become stacked into a pile so high that they fail to deliver on any of their goals. I am sure you have seen what happens next. They usually start to blame those around them instead of learning from their mistakes, saying no, and pushing back. I've seen more than one person lose his vocation to this pattern.

It all comes down to picking and choosing the right opportunities for your goals and aspirations. When we say no, we should instead say yes to other pursuits on our path to achieving excellence. When we produce average results because we have taken on too much and are burning out, it isn't getting us closer to our dreams. It's the reverse. By contrast, completing a personal goal may catapult your growth journey to the next level.

In other words, don't just say no to a situation because it may be scary and an enormous challenge. Say no to something because you are saying yes to another opportunity, one that gets you closer to your future self.

Jesse Iwuji — Pulling it All Together by Learning to Be on the Edge

As we discussed at the beginning of this chapter, one of the biggest obstacles anyone faces is learning to visualize success and focusing on the steps to reach it. It's learning how to have a positive self-narrative and bust through the status quo set by our circumstances.

Consider the story of NASCAR Xfinity driver Jesse Iwuji,[106] who achieved his unlikely dream of transitioning from Naval officer to professional race car driver. I interviewed Iwuji on how he learned how to be an anxiety optimizer. Iwuji explains:

> So many people have these big goals, these big dreams that they're too scared to go after, and they go to the grave with them. I went to my first two ships for four years. While on deployment, I kept on having this vision of me racing in the cup series and walking out onto driver intro. When I was on a second deployment, I made that decision that NASCAR was where I was going to go.[107]

Some years ago, when he was deployed to the Arabian Gulf, he began to learn to sit with his thoughts and what he wanted to accomplish. Like Mark Divine, he learned how to visualize the future he wanted, perfected the intense focus to get there, and the positive intentionality to achieve it.

There were many times he wanted to quit. He wrecked out of six of his first seven races. After each one, he could have easily said to himself, "Why am I doing this? I should quit." But instead, he told himself, "Now it's going to get better." Iwuji began to learn how to improve incrementally and to control his stress level.

Iwuji credits much of his success to his time at the Naval Academy and his experience as a four-year starter on the varsity football team:

One of the biggest lessons I learned, especially at the Naval Academy, from my coaches, was a very simple thing: *nobody cares*. And the reason why they would say that is we would face opponents like Notre Dame and Ohio State, who outsize us, have better speed than us, they're stronger, and have better training facilities. But at the end of the day, no one feels sorry for us. We still have to line up just like they do every single down and fight for that win. And what did we do when we put our mind to it? We beat Notre Dame twice, a team that should have stomped us every single year, but they didn't. And that's because we never felt sorry for ourselves, and we learned how to focus on the task at hand and envision winning. Even though the other team might have these five-star recruits, future NFL stars, whatever it is, it didn't matter. Nobody made excuses for us.

He took that "nobody cares" philosophy and applied it to everything else he did in life, whether it was his career as a Naval officer or starting the journey into NASCAR and working his way up the ranks. He didn't have many resources when he began NASCAR, but guess what, nobody cared. And he learned to push forward.

He explained it in this way: "You've got to begin walking and keep walking and then start running and then learn how to sprint. You keep grinding even when you trip and fall and get up, and you go. And, anytime someone tells you, you can't, look the other way, and you keep going."

Similar to what Iwuji experienced, emotions and feelings can be either helpful or a hindrance. While being a little relaxed can be beneficial, being relaxed to the point you are bored is probably not. Essentially, there is a psychological component to achieving an optimal anxiety zone that can affect performance regardless of physical ability or skill.

Iwuji explains it in this way:

> It's a balance because you have to be on edge with the race car. It's essential to find that edge where the race car is not entirely spinning out. But it's on the edge, where at any moment it could, but you are in such control that you're in complete command of keeping it on that edge that you don't let it spin out. But then you're not driving it too slowly. And that's the challenging part about being a high-caliber driver. It is finding the zone of optimal anxiety, which is literally *on edge, without going off the edge.* You're in control of being out of control. It is the challenging zone of excellence that the best drivers regularly achieve.

Jesse Iwuji's journey teaches us how to be on edge in our lives. By visualizing success, maintaining a positive mindset, and persevering through setbacks, we can push boundaries and achieve greatness. It's about finding the delicate balance between control and pushing our limits, embracing the zone of optimal anxiety where excellence thrives. So let's embrace the challenge, stay on edge, and unlock our full potential.

How to Be on Edge in Your Life

You may feel that you do not have the education, the experience, the ability, or the potential to succeed. You may not be fully engaged in your own life. However, Mark Divine and Jesse Iwuji illustrate that our most significant limiting factor is how we approach the vision of the future we want to achieve.

As you go on any journey in life, when you're trying to accomplish something more significant than where you're at, there are many sacrifices along the way. If you are going to elevate your life and try to achieve something you never achieved, you will have to do things you've never done. This will require you to show up in the right way to sustain momentum. For Divine, this was learning karate, researching everything he could about breathing techniques, discovering imagery, and creating a positive intention to build an unbeatable mind. For Iwuji, conducting the mosquito audit (we talked about that in Chapter 4) and getting rid of the baggage holding him back were initial steps he had to take. And from there, he researched how to gain sponsorships, practiced for hours daily on the simulator, talked to different business owners from racing teams to learn how to build a team, and did anything he could to practice his driving. It is an excellent example of how each gained mastery through incremental actions of self-betterment.

It takes sacrifice to get anywhere in life. You need to create your future vision, clearly seeing yourself become what you're supposed to become. And then, from there, it is the daily activities to maintain momentum to make it happen. Sometimes, during your journey, it's going to be dark—very, very dark. Sometimes, even when you are nearing your end goal and can see the light at the end of the tunnel, you won't feel like you can reach it. It's still dark where you are.

When you're taking risks and leaps of faith, life rewards the actions you take, even if it doesn't work out at that moment. So that's why it is important to say yes to many different things. But, at the same time, you have to analyze which of these opportunities will be quality opportunities so that you stop merely making movement and start making progress.

Will you allow yourself to be knocked down by your self-doubt and fears? Or will you take advantage of the unique opportunities you have been granted?

Standing on the precipice of a new opportunity can be scary, but if you don't start saying "yes," and learning how to reach the zone of optimal anxiety, you'll live your life in the status quo. You'll never solve new problems; you'll likely struggle to find your "why," and you'll spend most of your career flatlining.

Similar to Divine and Iwuji, you also need to settle on a decision. You will either keep deceiving yourself—many do their entire lives—or you can be honest with your inner voice. You have a choice. Our behaviors are influenced by our beliefs. They are potent beliefs, but they are just something in your mind. Become an anxiety optimizer and start taking deliberate steps to change how you react to the opportunities thrown your way.

Only your opinion of yourself matters. Only you can see the vision, where you're supposed to go, what you're supposed to become, and who you're supposed to be. God gave us each an individual vision of where we're supposed to be in life. And guess what, He didn't give it to anybody else. He didn't give you my vision. He didn't give me your vision. So, I can't even see your vision for myself, but I can see my vision for myself. And because I can see it means that I can achieve it.

Anyone reading this book can accomplish big goals and dreams. You were the only one given your vision. Nobody else has any right, or any say so, or any validity to ever tell you differently or doubt your vision for your life. When your dream comes, and you become a mission angler, that means it is achievable by you. You just need to learn how to achieve the zone of optimum anxiety to keep up your forward momentum.

As Dale Carnegie said, "Most of the important things in the world have been accomplished by people who had kept on trying when there seemed to be no hope at all."

Scan the QR code for additional insights and resources.

Chapter Exercises: Becoming an Anxiety Optimizer

Exercise 1: Breath Control—Explore a breathwork technique called "Box Breathing" to interrupt the knee-jerk fight or flight reaction associated with anxiety. Follow these steps:

- Find a comfortable seated position or lie down in a quiet space.
- Close your eyes and take a moment to connect with your breath.
- Begin by inhaling slowly through your nose to a count of four, filling your lungs completely with air.
- Hold your breath for a count of four, maintaining a sense of calm and stillness.
- Exhale slowly through your mouth to a count of four, releasing all the air from your lungs.
- Hold your breath again for a count of four, embracing the empty space.
- Repeat this box breathing pattern for several rounds, focusing on the rhythmic flow of your breath.
- As you continue, imagine the breath traveling in a square shape: inhale along one side, hold at the top, exhale along the opposite side, and hold at the bottom.
- Allow yourself to fully immerse in the present moment, letting go of any tension or anxiety with each exhale.
- Gradually increase the count of your breath if comfortable, but always maintain a smooth and steady rhythm.

Exercise 2: Positive Internal Dialogue—Engaging in positive internal dialogue can lead to more creative solutions and better performance. Complete the following exercise:

- Choose a challenge or problem you are currently facing.
- Write down three negative thoughts or self-criticisms related to this challenge.

- Reframe each negative thought into a positive and empowering statement.
- Practice repeating these positive statements to yourself whenever you encounter the challenge.
- Reflect on how this shift in internal dialogue affects your mindset and approach to the challenge.

Exercise 3: Imagery—Develop your ability to visualize success and understand what mission success looks like when achieved. Follow these steps:

- Close your eyes and bring to mind a specific goal or outcome you desire.
- Create a vivid mental image of yourself accomplishing this goal, paying attention to the details of your surroundings, emotions, and actions.
- Engage all your senses to make the visualization as realistic as possible.
- Spend a few minutes immersed in this mental image, embracing the feeling of accomplishment.
- Reflect on how this visualization affects your motivation and confidence in pursuing the goal.

Exercise 4: Targeted Focus—Enhance your ability to be present and focus your mind on one thing at a time. Practice the following exercise:

- Choose a simple task or activity that you can fully engage in, such as washing dishes or taking a walk.
- Before starting the task, set an intention to focus your attention solely on the present moment and the task at hand.
- Pay close attention to each action and sensation as you perform the task, without letting your mind wander.

- Whenever you notice your thoughts drifting, gently bring your focus back to the task.
- After completing the task, reflect on your experience of targeted focus and how it influenced your engagement and performance.

These exercises will help you cultivate the necessary skills to become an anxiety optimizer by entering the flow state. Remember to practice them regularly and observe the positive impact they have on your ability to overcome challenges and achieve optimal performance.

CHAPTER 9

ORIGINALITY EMBRACER—
REALIZE THAT ORIGINALITY
NECESSITATES ADAPTABILITY

It is better to fail in originality than
to succeed in imitation.
—Herman Melville

In today's ever-changing world, you need to be open to change if you want to thrive. Embracing originality and adaptability isn't just a choice; it's crucial for success. You might worry that you must be more naturally creative or that change is intimidating. I've been there too. But I've realized that growth is impossible without change, much like expecting a plant to grow without water—it's just not feasible.

The vital connection between originality and adaptability lies at the core of leading a passion-struck life. These qualities work hand in hand to ignite our inner passions. Simply following the well-trodden paths of those before us won't cut it.

So, what does originality mean in this context? While we generally understand the concept, its specifics can vary. At its heart, it's about pursuing novel ideas and breaking free from existing molds, redefining entire industries and the smaller, meaningful transformations we make in our personal journeys. Passion-struck individuals possess the ability to blend diverse concepts seamlessly, leading to unique and innovative ideas.

But ideas don't appear out of thin air. They evolve from existing seeds. Passion-struck individuals blend concepts from different areas, capturing notions that might otherwise elude them. Achieving originality requires developing behaviors and habits that encourage not only the trait itself but also adaptability. It's the interplay between these qualities that propels us forward.

The interplay between originality and adaptability becomes the driving force behind passion-struck lives. This journey demands the courage to push boundaries and explore unexplored realms. By adopting behaviors that embrace change, nurturing insatiable curiosity, and honing adaptive skills to confront the obstacles that come with innovation, we unlock originality's true potential. This connection between originality and adaptability becomes the driving force behind our passionate lives, propelling us to new heights of creativity and fulfillment.

Unleashing Originality and Adaptability: Decoding the Rise and Fall of Groupon

Captivating headlines often celebrate entrepreneurs who are touted as "changing the world" in the realms of business and technology.

While some of these visionaries are genuinely revolutionizing their industries and leaving a lasting impact, it is disheartening to witness a surge of entrepreneurs working on seemingly "game-changing" start-ups that are nothing more than replicas or derivatives of already successful ventures.

Enter the rise and fall of Groupon[108]—an undeniable case in point. By now, most of you are familiar with Groupon, the collective-action platform that delivered massive discounts to email subscribers for local merchants, enticingly known as "daily deals." This innovative concept took the United States by storm, with Groupon achieving a billion-dollar valuation within a mere sixteen months in business.[109] The astonishing success of Groupon spawned a flood of competitors offering similar daily deal services, lacking any meaningful differentiation. Among these contenders were LivingSocial, Gilt City, BuyWithMe, Tippr, and We Give to Get.

However, Groupon's downfall came with its failure to adapt to evolving consumer preferences. The company's business model, heavily reliant on deep discounts and steep commission rates, proved unsustainable for many local businesses. Consequently, merchant participation declined, and the quality of deals suffered. As the novelty of daily deals wore off, consumers sought more personalized shopping experiences, gradually diminishing Groupon's appeal.

This cautionary tale sheds light on the scarcity of originality in the startup landscape. It highlights the distinction between passion-struck leaders and those who merely mimic established ideas for short-term gains. Novice entrepreneurs often aim to replicate successful business models, hoping to build, scale, and sell them. In stark contrast, passion-struck leaders embrace the power of originality, subscribing to Peter Thiel's philosophy of moving from "zero to one"[110] rather than settling for incremental improvements on existing concepts.

Granted, original ideas are rarely born in isolation; they often spring forth from the foundation of prior ideas. It is an arduous task to conceive a wholly unique and groundbreaking concept. However, we must acknowledge a crucial caveat: certain ideas, such as the

Groupon clones, lack the essential spark of originality to the point where one questions the existence of imagination itself. While execution undoubtedly plays a vital role in the success of any startup, the idea itself holds significance. A passion-struck founder who wholeheartedly embraces their originality possesses the potential to amass immense wealth and genuinely reshape the world.

In the realm of entrepreneurship, the symbiotic relationship between originality and adaptability is undeniable. To truly thrive, innovators must not only generate novel ideas but also possess the agility to adapt those ideas to meet the ever-changing demands and preferences of consumers. By embracing intentional behavior choices that celebrate originality while staying attuned to the winds of change, we unlock the true potential of groundbreaking entrepreneurship, paving the way for transformative ventures that endure the test of time.

In this chapter, we embark on a profound exploration of the interplay between originality and adaptability, drawing inspiration from the remarkable journey of Jeff Bezos and the unparalleled success of Amazon. As we delve into Bezos's extraordinary career, we uncover invaluable lessons that shed light on the power of original thinking and its transformative impact. These lessons extend beyond business and startups. They remind us of the importance of embracing our authentic selves and being open to originality and adaptability in our personal lives. The journey towards a passion-struck life involves breaking free from the constraints of conformity, pursuing meaningful endeavors, and continuously evolving in response to life's challenges and opportunities.

At the heart of Bezos's triumph lies the fusion of originality and adaptability. By conceiving a novel idea of an online marketplace that would redefine retail, he embarked on a journey that demanded unwavering adaptability in the face of an ever-evolving business landscape. Bezos recognized the need to constantly adapt to technological advancements, changing consumer behaviors, and emerging market trends, positioning Amazon at the forefront of innovation.

Forging Originality: The Bezos Blueprint for Success

Amidst the realm of entrepreneurial legends, Jeff Bezos's founding of Amazon.com[111] has already etched its place in the annals of Internet history. However, there is a compelling case to be made that Bezos's idea for Amazon was not a singular stroke of genius but rather a fusion of several unique designs. It all began during Bezos's tenure (1990-94) at D. E. Shaw,[112] a renowned hedge fund in New York City, where he stumbled upon a staggering statistic that would change the course of his career. The Internet was experiencing an unprecedented growth rate of 2,300 percent per year—a revelation that ignited Bezos's entrepreneurial spirit and propelled him to capitalize on this remarkable trend.

While Bezos is most known for selecting books as Amazon's first e-commerce product, he is less known for having the initial idea of an "everything store."[113] As he told his former boss David Shaw, Bezos's goal was to create "an Internet company that served as the intermediary between customers and manufacturers and sold nearly every type of product, all over the world."[114] Moreover, he wanted to do it by delivering the best possible customer experience. However, Bezos understood that Amazon couldn't emerge as the dominant Internet retailer overnight. It required a strategic approach of targeting a specific niche, establishing dominance within that niche, and then expanding further.

This is where the convergence of books and originality played a pivotal role. While the idea of a new bookstore wasn't groundbreaking, Amazon was far from a mere clone of existing giants like Borders Books or Barnes & Noble. Bezos harnessed the disruptive power of the Internet, creating an entirely online bookstore that boasted an expansive inventory, 24/7 accessibility, and, in the beginning, exemption from sales taxes. Undoubtedly, this approach meant sacrificing certain features like easy browsing or allaying customers' concerns about online transactions. Yet, Bezos remained resolute in his pursuit of a unique customer proposition: offering an unparalleled selection, doorstep delivery, and competitive prices. As you can see, the essence of originality lies not in reinventing the wheel but in skillfully combining disparate ideas. Bezos used his knowledge of technology and the Internet to combine a limitless inventory, excellent customer experience, fast shipping, and low prices for book lovers around the world.

Thus, take solace in the quest for originality. While undoubtedly demanding, it is a challenge embraced by those who dare to think differently. Remember this: the true key to unlocking your wellspring of originality lies in the fusion of ideas. Embrace this perspective as you navigate your current pursuits, lay the groundwork for future ventures, and embark on the boundless voyage of creation.

Embracing the Power of Originality and Adaptability: Thriving in the Age of Change

To be truly original is to unlock the depths of your inner creativity and venture fearlessly into the boundless realm of imagination. It demands audacity—the audacity to challenge conventions, dismantle existing ideas, and pave new paths. Originality beckons us to explore uncharted territories, surpassing the confines of familiarity and venturing into the unknown, where true innovation and discovery await.

Yet, the journey toward originality is intricately entwined with adaptability. It requires a willingness to take risks and embrace the uncertainty accompanying unexplored terrain. Stepping outside our comfort zones, we encounter the discomfort that often accompanies growth. Originality demands the fortitude to perceive failure as a stepping stone to success, recognizing that it is through experimentation and learning from mistakes that groundbreaking ideas are born.

In her enlightening 2019 TED Talk,[115] US venture investor Natalie Fratto shed a luminous spotlight on the escalating significance of adaptability in our swiftly changing world. As she eloquently proclaimed, "the world is speeding up, thrusting each of us into a tumultuous sea of change unparalleled in human history. Technological progress has been a driving force behind this rapid tempo, compelling individuals to swiftly acquire new skills and adapt to the ever-evolving landscape."

In a compelling interview on the *Passion Struck* podcast featuring Claude Silver, the Chief Heart Officer of Vayner Media, the significance of this imperative became distinctly clear. Silver illuminated the transformative nature of the present paradigm shift and emphasized the indispensable role of emotional elements in the era of adaptability.

Silver expressed,

> "We all encounter a multitude of adaptations throughout our lives. Currently, we stand on the precipice of a profound paradigm shift. We transitioned from an era defined by physical work, navigated the vast realms of the information age, and are now embarking upon an era that resonates with the heart's intuition, emotional optimism, and adaptability."

Expanding upon this notion, Silver introduced the concept of the multiple "brains" within us—our cranial, cardiac, and gut intelligence. These interconnected sources of wisdom shape our decision-making processes, ultimately determining our capacity to adapt or falter in the face of change. Delving into the depths of these internal faculties unravels the enigma of our responses to challenges, illuminating the intricate tapestry of our adaptive nature.

In the complex world we live in, it is imperative to acknowledge that embracing change surpasses the mere acquisition of knowledge or skill. It demands the cultivation of emotional intelligence, resilience, and a profound connection with our shared humanity. The ability to adapt emerges from an authentic core, nurtured by empathy, self-awareness, and a deep understanding of our values, passions, and distinctive perspectives.

Being original also entails embracing diversity and celebrating the differences that make each individual unique. It recognizes that true innovation and progress often arise from the intersection of diverse ideas, perspectives, and experiences. By embracing and valuing the contributions of others, we create a rich tapestry of originality that fuels collective growth and development.

Acknowledging change instead of resisting it brings numerous benefits that contribute to personal growth. One such benefit is increased creativity. Novelty and diversity, both products of change, stimulate our brains to think differently, leading to innovative ideas and solutions. Embracing adaptability makes us more flexible, a highly sought-after quality in today's dynamic landscape. It equips us to handle unexpected situations efficiently and avoid getting overwhelmed by sudden shifts.

In a world where conformity is the norm, originality stands out like an impressive note no one else can match. It's about authentic self-expression rather than being different for the sake of it. Encourage yourself to express your unique ideas and break away from the status quo. Innovation doesn't happen by following others' footsteps.

Nurturing original thinking starts within our own minds, particularly through positive self-talk. This internal dialogue can be either our biggest cheerleader or worst critic. But when used positively, these words become catalysts for creativity and confidence. Studies show that consistent use of affirmations improves problem-solving skills under pressure—crucial traits required when dealing with complex issues.

For instance:

"I am capable."
"My thoughts matter."
"I embrace failure as an opportunity."

These simple sentences can unlock new pathways for thought and action when feeling stuck or uninspired. The journey of embracing change teaches us that failures are not roadblocks but stepping stones on the path to success. As organizational psychologist Adam Grant suggests: embrace them.

The essence of embracing originality lies in its capacity to accelerate growth and deepen understanding. It champions the concept of iterative learning, where each stumble becomes a stepping stone toward mastery. As Grant aptly puts it, "The mark of higher education isn't the knowledge you accumulate in your head; it's the skills you gain about how to learn."

This philosophy finds resonance in various fields, from scientific research to artistic pursuits. Innovations and breakthroughs often emerge from the crucible of failures and setbacks. Pioneers of science, such as Thomas Edison, approached each failed experiment as a discovery of a way not to do something, bringing them closer to the ultimate solution. Similarly, artists refine their craft through countless iterations, each brushstroke or note contributing to their mastery.

In essence, the embrace of failures fosters a mindset that embraces change and adaptability as allies on the journey to success. By viewing setbacks not as detours but as integral components of the path, we cultivate resilience, sharpen our problem-solving abilities, and fuel our innate capacity for innovation. Just as a pearl is formed through the gradual layering of nacre around an irritant, the embrace of failures enriches our experiences and ultimately yields the pearls of wisdom and accomplishment that adorn the tapestry of our lives.

Originality Embracer: A Lifelong Journey of Self-Discovery, Creativity, and Growth

A lifelong journey of embracing originality intertwines seamlessly with adaptability—a transformative path that shapes various aspects of our lives. It isn't just about being different for the sake of standing out; rather, it's a profound exploration of our authentic selves, unearthing the true essence of who we are and what we have to offer.

At its core, embracing originality means acknowledging and embracing our uniqueness. Each of us is born with a distinct set of qualities, talents, and perspectives that make us unlike anyone else. By recognizing and honoring these individual traits, we begin to understand that our originality is a gift waiting to be discovered, developed, and shared with the world.

The journey of self-discovery lies at the heart of embracing originality. It involves introspection, self-reflection, and a willingness to delve into the depths of our being. Through this exploration, we uncover our passions, values, and aspirations, gaining clarity about our purpose and the path we wish to tread. It is a lifelong process that evolves as we grow and change, requiring us to continually reevaluate and rediscover ourselves.

Creativity is an integral part of embracing originality. It is the vehicle through which we express our unique perspectives, ideas, and emotions. Whether through art, music, writing, entrepreneurship, or any other form of creative expression, we channel our authenticity and present it to the world in ways that resonate with others. This act of creation not only brings us joy and fulfillment but also connects us to a larger community that appreciates and values our contributions.

Embracing originality also entails continuous growth and development. It requires us to cultivate a mindset of curiosity and open-mindedness, always seeking new experiences, knowledge, and skills. As we expand our horizons, we gain fresh insights, challenge preconceived notions, and evolve as individuals. It is through this ongoing growth that we push the boundaries of our originality, constantly refining and expanding our creative potential.

When we fully embrace our originality and nurture it, we unlock the transformative power of innovation. Original thinkers and creators have shaped the course of human history by challenging the status quo, inventing new technologies, and revolutionizing various fields. By honoring our unique gifts and contributing them to the world, we become catalysts for change, inspiring others to tap into their own originality and create a ripple effect that spreads throughout society.

Following Jeff Bezos's Lead

Bezos is one of the most game-changing and innovative entrepreneurs in history. Starting with the idea of an "everything store" in the 1990s, Jeff created a trillion-dollar company that makes our lives more convenient. He is the epitome of a passion-struck leader who was able to leverage originality into a massive success.

Even though we may not achieve the same scale or success as Bezos, we can follow in his footsteps here. Originality is something that we can access—so long as we put in the work and stay committed through thick and thin. The road is tough for everyone, and coming up with original ideas isn't instantaneous.

However, it *is* possible.

It is something that can take our businesses to the next level.

And yes, it is a crucial trait of being passion struck.

Those who are passion struck let their enthusiasm for their underlying work power their originality. From the moment these leaders wake up to the moment they go to sleep, they are thinking about their businesses and how to differentiate themselves. Through this obsession over the underlying problems that they are trying to solve, they adapt and create unique ideas that others cannot see. In other words, they become an "originality embracer."

If you cannot solve a novel problem, all you can do is copy.

Scan the QR code for additional resources and insights.

Chapter Exercises: Become an Originality Embracer

Exercise: IdeaFlow Exploration

- Step 1: Set aside dedicated time and create a conducive environment for brainstorming. Find a quiet space free from distractions where you can focus and let your creativity flow.
- Step 2: Familiarize yourself with the concept of IdeaFlow as presented by Jeremy Utley and Perry Klebahn. IdeaFlow is a dynamic process that involves generating a large quantity of ideas, encouraging rapid ideation, and embracing both quantity and quality.
- Step 3: Choose a specific problem, challenge, or project you would like to explore. It can be related to any aspect of your life, such as work, personal growth, or a creative endeavor.
- Step 4: Set a timer for ten minutes and aim to generate as many ideas as possible within that time frame. Remember, the goal is quantity over quality, so don't censor or judge your ideas during this phase. Let your imagination run wild and write down every idea that comes to mind, no matter how unconventional or seemingly unfeasible.
- Step 5: After the initial ideation phase, take a short break to clear your mind and reset your focus.
- Step 6: Review the list of ideas you generated and identify a few that stand out to you. Look for ideas that have the potential to be developed further or resonate with your goals and values.
- Step 7: Choose one idea from the selected list and explore it in more detail. Consider its feasibility, potential impact, and how it aligns with your desired outcomes. Use the IdeaFlow process to refine and expand upon this idea, exploring different angles, variations, and potential implementation strategies.
- Step 8: Reflect on the experience of engaging in IdeaFlow. What did you learn about your creative process? How did the quantity-focused approach impact your ideation? Did

you discover any unexpected or innovative ideas during this exercise?

- Step 9: Select one or more ideas that you find particularly promising or exciting. Create an action plan outlining the next steps you can take to further develop and implement these ideas in your life or work.

Remember, IdeaFlow is a dynamic and iterative process. Feel free to revisit and repeat this exercise whenever you need a fresh burst of creativity or when faced with new challenges and opportunities. Embrace the power of IdeaFlow to nurture adaptability and originality in your approach to problem-solving and innovation.

CHAPTER 10

BOUNDARY MAGNIFIER— UNDERSTAND THAT SOMETIMES BEING RIGHT MEANS BEING ALONE

*The lonely road to greatness is better than
the crowded road to mediocrity.*
—Matshona Dhliwayo

One of the potential side effects of being passion struck is being alone. That's not meant in the literal sense of the word, although there will be plenty of times that you may find yourself literally alone, working on your idea with only yourself for company.

But more often than not, you'll be alone in your belief in an idea or a concept rather than physically alone. When you challenge the norm by introducing a new approach or product, resistance and fear of the unknown are bound to arise. However, the solitude encountered in this context often stems from standing alone in your conviction of an idea or concept, rather than mere physical seclusion. When you disrupt the status quo by presenting a fresh approach or product, resistance and apprehension towards the unfamiliar are likely to emerge. Individuals instinctively fear what they cannot comprehend and gravitate towards maintaining the familiar and predictable patterns in which they feel secure. There's no escaping it; pushing boundaries can be a tough and lonely road. We are social creatures, and it's in our nature to want to be with others.[116] But sticking with the herd breeds mediocrity. If you can't take a stand for something you passionately believe in, despite the possible social reprisals, then you don't have what it takes to become passion struck.

Let's make no bones about it; many people will doubt you, actively resist you, and even cast you out. But amidst these challenges, you'll need to muster the courage to embark on unconventional paths and dare to take action. You must step beyond the familiar confines of what feels secure and acknowledge that even those closest to you may not accompany you on your voyage towards success. But don't let the naysayers deter you; forge your own path and reap the rewards for doing so later down the line. The benefit, of course, is that your courage will pay off in spades. But that doesn't mean that you won't have to navigate several mental challenges, particularly at the beginning when you're a long way from witnessing the results of your initial hard work.

Embracing solitude also necessitates being comfortable with being alone and accepting your true self. As I wrote in the introduction, we often wear masks to hide our shadows—the darkest parts of ourselves—in the presence of others. However, solitude forces us to confront our deepest, most authentic selves. This can be an arduous process, particularly for those who lack self-awareness.

There's a saying that "you are your own worst enemy," and this rings true when someone lacks self-awareness. Being alone reveals the truth about who you truly are, beyond any façade. It reminds you that there is no one to share your thoughts with except yourself.

Furthermore, solitude plays a crucial role in boosting creativity and productivity. When you are alone, you have the freedom to prioritize yourself and take charge of your time. While humans naturally crave social interaction, being alone encourages proactive engagement with your own life. It provides you with the opportunity to meditate, reflect on your aspirations, and chart your desired path.

Consider the last time you found yourself in solitude—what did you accomplish during that time? Now, contrast it with a scenario where you were in the presence of a group of five or more people— what did you achieve then? Odds are, you were more productive when alone, as solitude enables you to concentrate on yourself and your goals without external distractions. Forge your own path and you will ultimately reap the rewards in the future. Embracing behaviors that magnify boundaries demands acknowledging that you may not always be precisely on target, but it also requires having the courage to take action, iterate, and persist in pursuit of your goals.

Boundary Magnification: Unveiling the Path to Happiness Through Self-Knowledge

In an engaging episode of the *Passion Struck* podcast, Gretchen Rubin, the renowned author and observer of happiness and human nature, offers valuable insights into the crucial role of self-discovery in the pursuit of success. Rubin underscores that happiness cannot be encapsulated within a one-size-fits-all formula; rather, individuals must navigate their own path, embracing their distinct temperament, values, interests, and innate qualities.

As Rubin articulates, the challenge of knowing oneself is both profound and essential: "To know ourselves is the great challenge of our lives." She imparts wisdom gained through personal experience:

"There is no magic, one-size-fits-all solution. We each have to decide for ourselves…what is going to make me happier, what's going to work for me?"

However, knowing ourselves can be difficult amidst societal pressures, the longing to be something we're not, and assumptions about who we are. Often, we fail to notice the discrepancy between our assumed identity and our true selves.

To embark on a journey of self-discovery, Rubin suggests posing introspective questions like: "What do you lie about?" Lying often reveals a disconnect between our values and actions. "Whom do you envy?" Envy, though uncomfortable, can serve as a guidepost, signaling unacknowledged desires.

Another avenue to self-knowledge lies in revisiting the joys of our childhood. Rubin suggests the simple yet profound question: "What did you do for fun when you were ten years old?" Amidst the busyness of adulthood, we often lose sight of what truly brings us joy. Reconnecting with the activities that once delighted us, whether wandering through a park with a faithful companion or creating with our own hands, can rekindle our passions and offer guidance.

Rubin concludes with an unwavering declaration: "Knowing ourselves is absolutely essential if we want to create a happier life for ourselves." Embracing the challenge of self-awareness opens the door to a life that resonates with authenticity and fulfillment.

Breaking Boundaries: Unleashing the Power of Core Values and Convictions

In a world dominated by mediocrity, where asserting our genuine convictions often becomes a daunting task, the importance of self-knowledge and pushing boundaries emerges with heightened significance. This profound journey of exploration, as revealed in the enlightening insights of Gretchen Rubin, empowers individuals to transcend limitations and unlock extraordinary rewards.

At its essence, pushing boundaries requires us to tap into our core values and conquer the fear of being wrong. This characteristic stands as a defining trait among the transformative leaders I have extensively researched. Steve Jobs, the co-founder of Apple, serves as a prime example of mastering being a boundary expander.

Jobs's impact and enduring legacy are rooted in his unwavering commitment to his core values, even in the face of standing alone. This resolute determination played a pivotal role in his monumental success, revolutionizing the realms of work, media consumption, and interpersonal communication. Jobs's unwavering belief in his convictions empowered him to challenge the status quo and create groundbreaking innovations. By integrating his core values into his decision-making process, he shaped a vision that resonated with millions and propelled him to unprecedented achievements.

While Jobs's brilliance was unquestionably exceptional, we can extract valuable insights from his habits and behaviors that enabled him to conquer the fear of being wrong. By aligning our actions with our core values, we can approach boundary-pushing endeavors with unwavering confidence, knowing that we are staying true to our authentic selves. This commitment to living in alignment with our values bolsters our resilience, allowing us to persevere through the inevitable challenges and setbacks along the way.

A Personal Lesson from a Business Titan

Before describing how Steve Jobs mastered the art of being a boundary magnifier, I want to share how intimidating this process can be—even if we aren't creating products that will be placed in the annals of tech history.

I previously worked as a CIO at Dell.[117] When I was at Dell, we were in the middle of a strategic inflection point in our transition from a hardware provider to a solutions provider. As part of that transition, my colleagues and I were acquiring numerous services and software businesses. We were simultaneously in the middle of the most extensive global implementation of Oracle Quote to Cash (Q2C) by any company. This initiative would replace thousands of our systems globally. It was the most significant internal project in the company, so it was definitely a big deal.

Now, I inherited this project from a predecessor who was promoted to become the president of one of Dell's business units. Upon taking over the project, I discovered that the solution to navigating this transition wouldn't meet the requirements of our new software business (specifically, it wouldn't allow subscription billing and many other nuances for the new business).

The stakes reached staggering heights as we embarked on this monumental transition, pouring over $100 million per year into Dell's largest program at the time. It was imperative that my team and I executed it flawlessly. Recognizing flaws in the existing plan, I assembled a select group of experts to assess our alternatives. This task force comprised eight exceptional individuals from Dell, top talent from Salesforce and Zuora, as well as representatives from Boomi, a newly acquired vendor. Together, we forged a compelling solution that not only met our requirements but also came at a fraction of the cost and could be implemented with remarkable speed. On the surface, the choice seemed obvious. We needed to go with this new solution. It was a better and more viable solution for Dell employees and Dell shareholders. That said, the decision was much more difficult because the prior solution was widely supported by the senior executives on the IT executive steering committee and its internal sponsors. The only senior executives who seemed to fully understand the dilemma were the president of Online, Ron Rose, and the SVP of Corporate Strategy, Dave Johnson. But neither was a member of the steering committee.

Therefore, I had a stark choice before me.

Do I follow the crowd or remain true to my fundamental principles and advocate for the choice that serves the best interests of Dell's shareholders?

Typically, I would run into Michael Dell in the private cafeteria that catered to him, the CFO, the chief human resources officer, and the general counsel. Drinking coffee with Michael one morning, I told him about my dilemma and asked him for some advice. What he said has stuck with me ever since. He told me, "When I started Dell, there were many doubters who told me I was barking up the wrong tree by catering directly to consumers."

He then revealed, "Sometimes being right means being alone."

This was not the first time that I had heard this phrase. One of my favorite passion-struck leaders, mentors, and former boss Jay Skibinski spoke the same phrase years before as we were undertaking a controversial global initiative.

Reflecting on Michael's advice, I thought about countless examples in my career where I faced this fork in the road. I could either take the popular path, or take the lonelier and harder path. The latter approach often has much more significant consequences and a significantly higher return. The mental challenges are real. Many will doubt you. Amidst these challenges, you'll need to muster the courage to do something different and dare to act.

So, what happened here? In the end, I put Dell and its shareholders first. I decided to pursue a new solution because it was the right decision for the company. Unfortunately, I lost my CIO role because several senior leaders on Dell's technology committee felt like they had pie in their face and made it their mission in life to see me removed from Dell. But something curious happened about one year after I left. My replacement sent me a message from a recent meeting with Dell's CFO Brian Gladden.

The crux of his message? "[John] Miles was right all along, and we should have trusted his judgment."

Essentially, pushing boundaries requires embracing the inherent solitude and being prepared for the potential consequences that often come with embarking on such a journey. It requires charting a path that deviates from the crowd, sometimes enduring temporary isolation along the way. Yet, by summoning the audacity to tread this uncharted territory, fueled by our unwavering commitment to our core values, we position ourselves for transformative success. The fear of being wrong must be overcome, replaced by an unwavering belief in our convictions and the resolute willingness to act upon them. It is through this steadfast commitment to pushing boundaries, grounded in our core values, that we transcend mediocrity and forge a remarkable legacy of innovation and achievement.

The Prime Example of "Being Right by Being Alone"

As you can tell from my experience, being right may have consequences. It can include everything from being shunned within your company to being removed from your current position. Because of this, it's all too easy to back down and stick within the herd.

Below, I'll mention some strategies for how you can get more comfortable being right by being alone. There are ways to get over the fear of being wrong. To better understand this power, I want to first highlight arguably the most renowned and game-changing entrepreneur in Silicon Valley history. Yes, it is Steve Jobs.

It's ironic. Jobs is almost a God-like figure in Silicon Valley for so many reasons. He was the consummate designer, having the courage to create and distribute some of the most game-changing products in technological history. He also wasn't afraid to challenge established practices and business models. You could make a good argument that he disrupted industries like personal computing, music, television, and more.

When he was doing his work, Jobs did not have an overwhelmingly positive reputation. In fact, he spent plenty of instances in his life on a metaphorical island. Employees complained about his leadership style. Others thought he was aloof. There are many stories of him eating lunch alone and how employees would drift away upon seeing him.

But along with that was the fact that Jobs would stick to his guns when he felt extremely strongly about a product that he was creating.

He wouldn't budge, because he *knew* at his core that his vision was going to resonate with the customer. There are countless examples of Jobs acting this way. I want to talk about two of them. The first is Jobs leaving the company that he co-founded. The second is the introduction of iTunes and the way that the combination of the iPod and iTunes would reshape the music industry.

The Removal of a Legend

Steve Jobs left his own company in the 1980s. Both Jobs and Steve Wozniak founded Apple in 1976,[118] and in 1985, the company faced a crossroads. Apple had recently released Lisa, the first computer that contained a graphical user interface. The company later released the well-known Macintosh computer, and while both of these products pleased Apple customers, Apple didn't see that enthusiasm translate into a higher market share.

Then-CEO John Sculley and the Apple board of directors weren't satisfied. A power struggle emerged between Sculley and Jobs. Sculley favored[119] a vision that embraced open-architecture computers that would be sold to schools, small business, and home markets. Jobs, meanwhile, wanted Apple to focus on the closed-architecture Macintosh, as it could be a compelling business alternative to the leading IBM personal computer (PC).[120]

Ultimately, Jobs stuck with his vision. Whether he was fired or left voluntarily is still in dispute.[121] And granted, there was prior history between Jobs, Sculley, and Apple's board of directors that may have contributed to Jobs's departure. Nonetheless, Jobs wouldn't compromise on his vision. He intuitively knew that his vision for Apple products and the company itself was going to pay off—even if the financial returns weren't promising at first.

Jobs continued to work on his idea at NeXT and then returned to Apple more than a decade later. He introduced the iMac, and the rest is history.[122]

Jobs was right in the long run. But by sticking to his vision in Apple's early days, he ended up losing his job. His leadership run at NeXT was no picnic either.[123] Many people would have capitulated and joined the herd. Jobs wasn't typical, however. He significantly tempered his fear of being wrong and aggressively pursued his vision. In the end, it paid off.

Changing the Music Industry

Beyond his departure from Apple, another example of being right by being alone was Jobs's creation of iTunes and the iPod. The iPod wasn't the first digital music player. For instance, the Walkman and Discman were popular music players that let users listen to their favorite tracks on the go. That said, Jobs felt like this space had a significant amount of untapped potential. Not only would the iPod provide significantly more storage (up to 1,000 songs),[124] but users would be able to purchase and download individual songs.[125]

This á la carte way of consuming music was game-changing. No one had done it before, yet Jobs felt that it would provide a better consumer experience. The music industry, on the other hand, was horrified. It was used to selling music in the traditional album format and argued that á la carte purchases for ninety-nine cents would decimate the industry.

Jobs wasn't immune to this criticism. He needed the record labels to license the music that would be sold on iTunes. Jobs stuck to his guns.[126] Yes, he could have been wrong. He could have been too bullish on consumer demand for á la carte music purchases. Nonetheless, he got over his fear of being wrong and proceeded with his plan.

Eventually, the music industry appreciated Jobs's vision.[127] iTunes (now Apple Music) became a critical tool for musicians and labels to monetize their work. Customers were enthusiastic about á la carte purchases, using the low price point of ninety-nine cents to find new artists that they otherwise wouldn't have noticed. While the world of music has changed again since then (due to the rise in streaming), Jobs's initial vision of how customers would pay for music way paid off.

Embracing Solitude: Nurturing Convictions, Core Values, and Behavioral Science

In a world where mediocrity often prevails, it is no surprise that many individuals shy away from asserting their genuine beliefs. However, embarking on a transformative journey toward self-assurance and resilience involves transcending the boundaries of our familiar terrain. This pursuit aligns with the principles of behavioral science, where core values play a crucial role in shaping human behavior, motivation, and decision-making.

Core values serve as guiding principles that influence various aspects of our lives. They empower us in several ways:

- Goal Setting and Prioritization: Our core values serve as compasses, helping us discern what truly matters and enabling us to set meaningful goals. We establish a solid foundation for personal growth by aligning our actions with these values.
- Moral and Ethical Decision-Making: Embedded within our core values is a moral compass that guides us in navigating complex ethical dilemmas. Honoring our values ensures that our choices align with our principles and integrity.
- Emotional Well-Being: Living harmoniously with our core values enhances emotional well-being, happiness, and satisfaction. It brings a profound sense of purpose and meaning to our lives, positively impacting our overall contentment.
- Relationships: Our core values shape our interactions with others, influencing our choices in friendships, partnerships, and social circles. We foster deeper connections and create a supportive network by seeking relationships with individuals who share our values.

- Organizational Culture: Within organizations, core values define the culture, guiding policies, practices, and decision-making processes. When an organization's core values align with employees' personal values, it fosters a positive work environment, promoting employee satisfaction, commitment, and performance.

Understanding and identifying our core values requires breaking free from the confines of our habitual patterns. It necessitates consciously cultivating new behaviors and establishing empowering habits that align with our convictions.

Drawing inspiration from the remarkable journey of Steve Jobs, we can glean a valuable lesson in embracing unfamiliarity even when it means venturing into solitude. Jobs exemplified the ability to overcome the fear of being wrong, as evidenced by his audacious decision to part ways with the company he had founded. Although such a choice may have appeared daunting and insurmountable to many, Jobs persevered.

Now, the question arises: How can we foster behaviors akin to Jobs and embrace the reality that being right often requires stepping beyond our comfort zones? There is no quick fix; it demands deliberate behavior change and consistent practice. Although this may seem challenging, forming empowering habits can support our journey.

To embark on this path, it is crucial to acknowledge a fundamental truth: it is impossible to please everyone. Whether we are entrepreneurs, nurses, attorneys, or managers, we must recognize that not everyone will share our perspective or be satisfied with our choices.

Criticism can be challenging to endure. Ideally, we would meet everyone's expectations, but it is essential to compartmentalize the voices of critics and naysayers. This involves accepting the presence of dissenting opinions, including those that challenge our work or personal decisions. While constructive criticism may hold valuable insights, acknowledging and embracing this reality helps overcome the fear of being wrong.

Become the Passion-Struck Boundary Magnifier Others Want to Follow

In a compelling episode of the *Passion Struck* podcast, I had the privilege of interviewing Sandy Stosz, a retired United States Coast Guard Vice Admiral and the author of *Breaking Ice and Breaking Glass: Leading in Uncharted Waters*. Our conversation delved into the essence of becoming a leader of character, someone others genuinely want to follow.

During our discussion, I emphasized to VADM Stosz the significance of daily choices and intentional commitment in achieving long-term aspirations. Whether it's transforming an eating habit or aspiring to the rank of admiral, it is the small choices we make consistently that pave the path to success. I asked her about the importance of core values and convictions in how we lead our lives.

VADM Stosz eloquently explained, "Personal core values are the foundation of your character, the cornerstones of who you are and how you will behave in various circumstances. Without core values and the grounding they provide, you will be tossed around by the prevailing winds. We have all witnessed leaders who lack this grounding, constantly shifting their stance to align with popular culture. I love the saying, 'If you don't stand for something, you'll fall for anything,' because core values provide that grounding. When you know what you stand for, you won't compromise your principles or fall prey to unethical practices."

She continued, sharing her own personal core values, instilled in her during childhood. "Honesty and humility form one pair of my core values, while hard work and perseverance make up the other. These values are the cornerstones of my character, and I acquired them from my parents, coaches, and teachers when I was young."

VADM Stosz described these core values as an anchor to windward in a tumultuous sea. They provided her with stability, allowing her to navigate through challenges and make sound decisions. Having core values as her foundation, combined with a clear North Star to steer towards, enabled her to remain steady and resilient in the face of adversity. Core values were so integral to VADM Stosz's leadership philosophy that she made them a priority in every interaction.

As we reflect on Steve Jobs and VADM Stosz's insights, it becomes clear that becoming a leader of character others want to follow requires more than just ambition or long-term aspirations. It demands a daily commitment to make choices aligned with our values, a persistent pursuit of our passions, and an unwavering intentionality in our actions. By cultivating and living by our core values, we lay the foundation for principled leadership, earning the trust and respect of those we seek to lead.

Walking the Solitary Path

The solitary path is solitary for a reason. It can be scary to break away from the pack and take a stand on a particular project or initiative. That said, getting over this fear of being wrong can go a long way in helping you to accomplish your career goals and is a core attribute of passion-struck leaders. It is a skill that can pay off in spades—so long as your thesis or perspective is correct.

Because of this, I encourage you to study passion-struck leaders like Steve Jobs. While none of us can be exactly like Jobs, he didn't hesitate to be right by being alone. He undoubtedly felt fear, but he took action and left an indelible mark on Silicon Valley.

My question for you is this: Are you willing to accept the same challenge?

Scan the QR code for additional insights and resources.

End of Chapter Exercises: Become a Boundary Magnifier by Learning to Apply Core Values to All Aspects of Life

- Reflect on Your Core Values: Take some time to reflect on your personal core values. What principles and beliefs are most important to you? Identify at least three core values that resonate with you deeply.
- Identify Areas of Life: Consider the different areas that make up your life, such as personal, family, professional, social, health, and finances. Take a moment to think about how your core values can play a role in each of these areas.
- Aligning Core Values: Connect each of your core values to its relevance in each area of your life. For example, if one of your core values is integrity, think about how you can demonstrate integrity in your personal relationships, at work, in your financial decisions, and in your overall lifestyle.
- Action Plan: Now that you have identified the connection between your core values and various areas of your life, it's time to create an action plan. Determine specific actions or behaviors that will allow you to honor your core values in each area. Set realistic goals, establish timelines, and consider accountability measures to keep yourself on track.
- Commitment and Reflection: Implement your action plan and make a commitment to living in alignment with your core values. Regularly reflect on your progress and evaluate how well you are incorporating your values into different aspects of your life. Adjust your action plan as needed and continue to make conscious choices that reflect your values.

By intentionally integrating your core values into every aspect of your life, you cultivate authenticity, purpose, and a greater sense of fulfillment. Embrace these exercises as a transformative journey towards living a values-aligned life, and let your core values guide you towards a life that is meaningful and true to who you are.

CHAPTER 11

OUTWARD INSPIRER—SPEAK (OR ACT) WITH YOUR FEET

I no longer listen to what people say, I just watch what they do. Behavior never lies.
—Winston Churchill

In the last chapter, we started this discussion of how passion-struck leaders need to look at both sides of the coin. Essentially, they must not only focus on the work that affects their mindset and "internal game." They must *also* focus on their thought processes and actions that affect their "external game," and their ability to push their boundaries.

Yes, mindset is important. It is why I spent so much time talking about things like being a mission angler, brand reinventor, fear confronter, mosquito auditor, perspective harnesser, and action creator. Even so, mindset doesn't mean much without inspiring others to act. Those who become passion struck can develop the habits, and learn the behaviors and skills, that can inspire others to follow them on their journey.

While most of the journey towards becoming passion struck revolves around recalibrating your internal workings, you also need to master your external signals. Rarely, if ever, does a passion-struck leader achieve enormous success without the help of others. It is essential to cultivate relationships that inspire others to act, follow, and join you on your mission.

That means that you'll have to develop habits and skills that inspire others to act, follow, and join you on your journey to achieving your mission. You need to cultivate a legion of fans that will follow you to the ends of the earth and figuratively die for you and your cause. You need to foster an environment of implicit trust and loyalty.

But how can you achieve those outcomes? By acting with your feet.

Jay Skibinski is the former CIO of many companies, including Lend Lease Corporation,[128] an Australia-based multibillion-dollar international financial service, property, and infrastructure group. Along with being an extremely successful businessman, Jay was my former boss at Lend Lease.

Jay taught me so much, but one of the most important lessons can be boiled down to one idea: people speak or act with their feet.

Essentially, he meant that you need to watch people's actions rather than relying solely on their words. Anyone can talk a big game. It is easy to share extensive platitudes about your company goals or a new project that can change your organization's course. Your employees may seem enthusiastic about these projects and ready to take on the world. However, true commitment and dedication are revealed when faced with difficult choices and the need for aggressive action.

As someone who is striving to become passion struck, you must pay attention to how people back up their words with action. It's easy to be swayed by charismatic speeches or grand promises, but true dedication is demonstrated through consistent action and follow-through. Building trust and loyalty within your team requires a focus on deeds, not just words.

By observing people's actions, you can identify those who truly align with your vision and mission. These individuals are the ones who consistently act in support of your goals and are willing to go the extra mile. Nurturing such relationships and surrounding yourself with these committed individuals is vital to achieving your mission and creating a lasting impact.

Take a moment to recognize the power of your actions in inspiring those around you. Leading by example, through your unwavering dedication and commitment, has a profound impact on others. As you demonstrate your values and principles in action, you ignite motivation in others to follow suit.

To better understand what speaking and acting with your feet means, I want to share one anecdote from my life and another from the life of Susan Wojcicki, the former CEO of YouTube. With these insights in mind, you can get in the habit of leading with your feet and inspiring others to do the same.

A Personal Experience from Lowe's Home Improvement

During my time at Lowe's Home Improvement, the company was driven by a passionate mission to become the leading global home improvement retailer. With over 1,400 stores and a fierce competition with Home Depot, Lowe's had experienced significant growth. The company culture was vibrant and enthusiastic, making it feel like being part of a close-knit family despite its massive Fortune 50 status.

Top executives, including CEO Robert Tillman, CFO Robert Niblock, and COO Larry Stone, were visible and approachable, regularly interacting with employees, and providing updates on various aspects of the company. This open and connected environment fostered a sense of pride and loyalty among employees, who felt deeply connected to the organization's core principles, mission, and customers.

However, things started to change when Lowe's relocated its headquarters to Mooresville, North Carolina, just sixty miles away. This move led to a dispersion of employees and executives across multiple locations. Previously accessible leaders now resided in an exclusive executive suite with limited interactions with non-executive colleagues. The shift in physical proximity began to impact the company's culture negatively.

As a result, employees started disengaging, and the sense of pride in the company eroded. Project teams became less cohesive, a sense of urgency dwindled, and the company's strategy grew more confusing. Lowe's lost its way and struggled to keep pace with its competitor, Home Depot. The disconnect from the company's past and core values became more pronounced.

The lesson from the experience with Lowe's is clear: leaders must actively engage with their employees and maintain a strong connection to the organization's values and culture. Leading with their feet means being present, accessible, and fostering a sense of belonging. It requires leaders to prioritize face-to-face interactions, create opportunities for collaboration, and continuously reinforce the company's core principles. By doing so, leaders inspire loyalty, maintain a cohesive workforce, and drive sustained success even in times of growth and change.

Speaking with Your Feet: A Primer

The Lowe's story serves as a clear example of the detrimental effects that arise from failing to align actions with words, both financially and culturally. But how does the concept of speaking with your feet apply to our personal lives and relationships?

Speaking with your feet means conveying your thoughts, emotions, and intentions through your actions rather than mere words. It's the notion that actions have a more profound impact than verbal declarations—an embodiment of the adage "actions speak louder than words." Instead of relying solely on what you say, speaking with your feet emphasizes demonstrating your commitments and beliefs through tangible behaviors.

I learned this idea of speaking with your feet from Jay Skibinski. However, it isn't a new concept. In fact, it can be found in the Bible. Looking at Proverbs 6:12-15 ESV, you can see the following passage:

> A worthless person, a wicked man,
> walks with a perverse mouth,
> winking his eyes, speaking with his feet,
> and pointing with his fingers.
> With deceit in his heart he devises evil;
> he continually sows discord.
> Therefore calamity will come upon him suddenly.[129]

Passion-struck individuals embody the principle of speaking with their feet in all aspects of life. In essence, it boils down to action. Those who resist or fail to support an endeavor tend to manifest hesitation in their actions. On the other hand, those who genuinely champion a cause or vision eagerly embrace opportunities and wholeheartedly tackle challenges. You can discern these subtleties by observing the choices they make and the paths they take.

By authentically speaking with your feet, you inspire those around you to do the same. This concept becomes a compass guiding you to create meaningful connections, nurture growth, and establish trust in your interactions with others. Ultimately, the principle of speaking with your feet becomes a cornerstone of fostering authentic relationships, cultivating personal growth, and nurturing an environment where actions and intentions align harmoniously.

Susan Wojcicki: A Stellar Leader Who Speaks with Her Feet

Throughout this book, we have encountered numerous passion-struck leaders who possess this remarkable quality. However, I would like to shine a spotlight on a specific leader in the tech industry: Susan Wojcicki, the former CEO of YouTube. Her unwavering dedication to embodying this principle in her daily work made her one of the most remarkable and passion-struck leaders I have had the privilege of encountering. Wojcicki[130] has a long and storied career with Google. In fact, when Google was first incorporated, Larry Page and Sergey Brin worked out of Wojcicki's garage.[131] She became Google's first marketing manager, contributing to iconic products and features like Google Doodles, Google Images, Google Books, and Google AdSense.[132] As if that wasn't enough, Wojcicki oversaw the acquisitions of DoubleClick and YouTube.

Wojcicki became the CEO of YouTube in 2014. YouTube was already popular at the time of the acquisition, but under her leadership, it has become the second-most visited website on the Internet (after Google).[133] While the precise value of YouTube is unknown, one analyst believes it can be worth up to $300 billion.[134]

Wojcicki has plenty of traits that helped her to turn YouTube into the massive success that it is. Putting those aside, however, let's talk about her ability to speak with her feet.

One of the clearest examples is something that Wojcicki personally experienced throughout her career in the tech industry. It's not controversial to say that males dominate tech. There are few women in leadership positions (although the tide is slowly turning). As Wojcicki told CNBC,[135] she would often find herself in situations where she needed to go the extra mile to get some much-deserved respect and attention. She says that she experienced many microaggressions. She was talked over and had her ideas ignored in meetings. In response, she had to call others out on the spot while simultaneously stating her opinion in a direct and confident way.[136]

So as Wojcicki rose through the ranks at Google and became the CEO of YouTube, she advised her colleagues to take a direct approach. Not only that, but she has made it a priority to hire more female staffers at YouTube. By bringing more gender diversity to YouTube, Wojcicki signals that bridging this gender gap and eliminating gender discrimination in the workforce is critical. She told CNBC that this type of leadership "has to come from the top."[137] The leader not only has to mean it, but must live it out in her day-to-day work. Doing this inspires other team members to do the same.

Wojcicki's commitment to leading with her feet extended beyond her role as CEO of YouTube; it also manifested in her dedication to the growth and financial success of Google, a company she had been a part of[138] since its early stages. Having witnessed the sacrifices and unwavering effort required to build a thriving tech company, Wojcicki possessed a deep understanding of the journey to success. She once emphasized this point during a discussion on gender disparity in the workplace, stating, "At the end of the day, both men and women who become CEOs have showed tenacity and hard work to succeed in their careers. It takes not just skills but also extreme dedication and commitment. And regardless of gender, CEOs are measured by the same criteria—the growth and success of the business."[139] Her words reflect her belief in the essential qualities of dedication and commitment that drive CEOs, regardless of gender, towards achieving remarkable outcomes.

Wojcicki consistently embodied this behavior throughout her time as the CEO of YouTube. Her unwavering determination and tireless efforts were evident as she led the company through substantial growth. Even though she has transitioned from her role at Google, her legacy continues to foster the ongoing expansion and success of YouTube.

Leading by example, Wojcicki fostered a culture that prioritized sustained growth and inspired her colleagues to follow in her footsteps. Her significant contributions have left an indelible mark on the tech industry, and her ability to lead with her feet continues to inspire the creation of products that resonate with billions of people worldwide.

Get Out There and Speak with Your Feet

Susan Wojcicki is a legend for a reason. Adopting these crucial attributes of a passion-struck leader, she became an instrumental force in one of the most disruptive companies of all time.

Leading with your feet is a prerequisite to becoming a passion-struck leader. But how can we transition from theory to practice? Like the other passion-struck attributes in this book, you can learn how to speak with your feet.

The following are examples of four passion-struck leaders who learned how to speak with their feet. I encourage you to adopt these behaviors as you travel the path to becoming a passion-struck leader yourself.

Leading with Empathy: Transforming Lives Through Genuine Connection

Passionate leaders who lead with their feet understand the transformative power of empathy. They possess a deep intuition that treating people with kindness, compassion, and respect is paramount to earning their trust and loyalty. This type of leadership goes beyond mere words; it is rooted in heartfelt actions. When you genuinely care for your colleagues and create an environment that prioritizes their well-being, your leadership becomes authentic and influential.

Embracing empathy as a guiding principle has the potential to transform not only the way we lead but also how we navigate life's journey. When we choose to lead with empathy in all aspects of our lives, we open ourselves up to profound connections and create a more compassionate and understanding world.

Passionate individuals who embody empathy understand the immense impact of treating others with kindness, compassion, and respect. They recognize that actions speak louder than words, and genuine care can bridge gaps, dissolve barriers, and uplift those around them.

Throughout history, remarkable individuals have exemplified the power of empathy in shaping lives. Mahatma Gandhi, renowned for his leadership in the pursuit of Indian independence, stood as a living testament to the transformative nature of empathy. By treating his followers as equals and truly understanding their experiences, he forged deep connections and fostered a collective sense of purpose.

To lead a life grounded in empathy, we must strive to understand the perspectives, emotions, and needs of others. By genuinely putting ourselves in their shoes, we cultivate a deep sense of compassion and forge connections based on mutual respect and understanding.

Embracing empathy extends beyond our interactions with colleagues and acquaintances; it influences the way we approach every aspect of life. When we embrace empathy, we become better listeners, seeking to understand rather than simply waiting to respond. We become more attuned to the needs of those around us, offering support and comfort in times of struggle. Empathy guides our actions, inspiring us to lend a helping hand and make a positive difference wherever we go.

In all our relationships, personal and professional, empathy allows us to build trust, foster open communication, and create an environment where everyone feels valued and heard. It enables us to navigate conflicts with grace, seeking resolutions that honor the feelings and needs of all parties involved.

Beyond our immediate circles, empathy helps us address broader societal issues, fostering inclusivity and promoting understanding across diverse communities. By seeing the world through the eyes of others, we can challenge biases, bridge divides, and work towards a more harmonious and compassionate society.

Embracing empathy as a way of life requires continuous commitment and practice. It involves staying open-hearted and actively seeking to understand the experiences and emotions of others. By doing so, we not only transform our own lives but also inspire those around us to embrace empathy as well.

Harnessing the Power of Hard Work

Next, leading with your feet involves hard work. Words mean little when we are talking about hard work. Luckily, you don't have to talk a big game about hard work. Instead, doing the work and getting real, measurable results will speak volumes. Your colleagues will intuitively understand that hard work is not only expected in your organization, but that it will be rewarded.

This is especially good news for introverts and those of us who don't feel as "charismatic" as some of our peers. Your actions do the talking, and those actions can speak volumes. One of my favorite examples of this trait is Derek Jeter. Jeter is one of baseball's most legendary players, having led the New York Yankees to five World Series. He was elected to the Baseball Hall of Fame in his first ballot with 99.7 percent of the votes[140] (the second-highest percentage in baseball history).

One of the most interesting things about Jeter was his leadership style. His teammates latched onto the fact that Jeter led by example. According to his former teammate Tino Martinez:

> [Jeter] led by example. His whole career has been that way. Plays hard, plays to win. Expects the most from his teammates. When you're in battle with a guy like that, it's important not to let him down. From superstars to the 25th man on the roster, we all felt a responsibility to play hard and play to win because of Jeter. That's rare.[141]

As the captain, Jeter knew that his teammates were watching him. This was even truer as his career progressed and his legend grew. Even though he could have rested on his laurels, Jeter arrived at Yankee

Stadium ready to work. He knew he didn't need to talk about his work ethic to inspire his younger teammates. Rather, his actions would do the talking. As the Yankees continued to be World Series contenders throughout Jeter's career, they certainly did.

Jeter's approach to leadership offers valuable insights for building strong relationships. Just as he led by example in baseball, his unwavering commitment to excellence applies to fostering deep and meaningful connections. By investing time, energy, and effort into your relationships, you communicate that you genuinely care about the people in your life. Your dedication becomes the foundation of healthy and fulfilling connections.

As you navigate the various dimensions of your life, remember the importance of leading by example and embracing hard work beyond the confines of your job. Let your actions demonstrate your commitment, loyalty, and genuine care for those around you. In doing so, you create a positive ripple effect, inspiring others to follow suit and cultivating lasting bonds that endure the test of time. Leading with your feet not only transforms your own life but also empowers you to make a profound impact on the lives of others.

Selling Thoughts and Creating Impact

Leading with your feet means selling your thoughts directly. Yes, setting a great example through hard work is essential for passion-struck leaders. Actions in nearly every circumstance trump words. That said, words are not irrelevant. Words are an inevitable part of leadership—including passion-struck leadership.

When using words to lead their colleagues, passion-struck leaders don't hesitate to sell their thoughts directly. Wojcicki embraced this axiom, directly calling out her colleagues when they weren't taking her seriously. Even though it may make you uncomfortable, directness with your words is essential for leading with your feet. Being direct with your words *and* taking direct, decisive action is a killer combination.

Bono, the U2 frontman and renowned activist, is one of the world's greatest leaders[142] for a number of reasons. He sells his thoughts by leading by example, meaning that he doesn't just talk about the issues he cares about, but he actively works towards creating positive change in the world.

For example, Bono has been a vocal advocate for debt relief in developing countries, and he co-founded the organization ONE,[143] which works to end extreme poverty and preventable diseases. Bono has also used his platform to raise awareness about the importance of combating HIV/AIDS, and he has worked closely with organizations such as (RED) to support the fight against the disease.

A major reason why Bono is so effective is because he sells his thoughts directly. He is able to communicate complicated topics and issues in a simple way.

One well-known story about Bono is that he was once standing on stage between songs. He prompted the audience to start clapping their hands at a specific pace. After some time of repeated clapping, Bono said: "Every time I clap my hands, a child in Africa dies." While one audience member eventually yelled out,[144] "Then stop f***ing clapping!" the point is that Bono is skilled in selling his thoughts directly.

Beyond his words on stage, Bono's directness has moved the needle in global philanthropy. Everything from directing concertgoers[145] to sign up on their cell phones "to make poverty history" to lobbying members of Congress and U.S. presidents to fight poverty and disease across the world.[146] Ultimately, action is extremely important, but words matter. Directness can go a long way in spurring people to follow in your footsteps and act.

By actively engaging in these causes and using his platform to raise awareness, Bono inspires others to take action and make a difference in their own way. He doesn't just sell his thoughts through words, but through his actions and the impact he has made in the world.

Leading with your feet entails more than just actions—it involves effectively selling your thoughts. Directness, coupled with impactful actions, can drive individuals to follow your lead and create meaningful change. By embracing direct communication, you can leave an enduring impression, inspiring others to join you in making a difference and leaving a lasting impact on the world.

Embrace Optimism—Even on the Darkest Days

Finally, those who are passion struck, who lead with their feet, embrace optimism. Moreover, they do so in peaceful times and on the darkest days. It's axiomatic that people want to follow optimistic leaders. Yes, language is an important part of optimism. Passion-struck leaders use optimistic and positive language to inspire their colleagues to act. Optimism is also represented through action. Optimistic action involves passion-struck leaders taking bold, aggressive action in the midst of huge obstacles. They are willing to experiment and try different things—even if failure is a real possibility. Underneath all their action is a cool, collected confidence in their team's ability to get the job done.

An exceptional example of embracing optimism in the face of adversity can be found in the leadership of Franklin Delano Roosevelt (FDR). Countless books and articles have been written about FDR's leadership prowess, yet one of his most remarkable qualities as a passion-struck leader was his unwavering optimism, determination, and enthusiasm. In his acceptance speech, Roosevelt declared, "I pledge you, I pledge myself to a new deal for the American people... This is more than a political campaign. It is a call to arms." The American people saw FDR as a leader who would not surrender in the face of seemingly insurmountable odds. Instead, he was prepared to fight. Inspired by his resolve, the American people rallied behind him, and the course of history was forever altered. Historian James MacGregor Burns said it best:

The president stayed in charge of his administration...by drawing fully on his formal and informal powers as Chief Executive; by raising goals, creating momentum, inspiring a personal loyalty, getting the best out of people...by deliberately fostering among his aides a sense of competition and a clash of wills that led to disarray, heartbreak, and anger but also set off pulses of executive energy and sparks of creativity...by handing out one job to several men and several jobs to one man, thus strengthening his own position as a court of appeals, as a depository of information, and as a tool of co-ordination; by ignoring or bypassing collective decision-making agencies, such as the Cabinet...and always by persuading, flattering, juggling, improvising, reshuffling, harmonizing, conciliating, manipulating.[147]

In applying the lessons from FDR's leadership, it becomes evident that embracing optimism is not limited to the realm of professional leadership. It holds relevance in our personal lives as well. By approaching life with optimism, we inspire others and create an environment conducive to growth and progress. Optimism becomes a guiding force in our interactions, infusing our relationships and friendships with hope, positivity, and resilience.

Leading with your feet in a passion-struck life involves embracing optimism. Through positive language, bold actions, and unwavering confidence, those who are passion struck inspire and uplift others. Franklin Delano Roosevelt's ability to exude optimism on the darkest days serves as a testament to the transformative power of optimism. By adopting an optimistic mindset and embodying it in our actions, we can navigate life's challenges with resilience and inspire those around us to do the same.

Let Your Feet Do the Talking

Mark Twain's timeless quote, "Action speaks louder than words but not nearly as often," holds even more relevance in today's word-dominated, social media-driven world. A profound truth emerges from Twain's wisdom: actions speak with greater honesty and authenticity than words alone. This principle manifests in diverse aspects of life, where body language often reveals more about one's true emotions and honesty than verbal expressions.

Applying this principle to self-understanding is illuminating. If you seek to uncover your genuine preferences, beliefs, and values, observe your actions. Your behavior unveils the core of your identity, surpassing the limitations of verbal communication. In this introspection, you may uncover surprising revelations about yourself, enriching your understanding of your true self.

Speaking with your feet takes on a personal dimension, embodying this principle of action-oriented conduct. As an "outward inspirer" in your personal life, your actions align seamlessly with your words, engendering trust and respect. Genuine leadership extends beyond mere words; it demands a commitment to promises and a consistent display of your convictions. Leading by example, supporting loved ones during challenging times, and staying true to your values garner admiration and esteem.

When you speak with your feet, you create an atmosphere of trust, support, and inspiration. Your actions reflect your intentions and values, setting a profound example for those around you. By actively demonstrating your care, empathy, and dedication, you create meaningful connections and nurture lasting relationships.

The good news? Leading with your feet is within your control. Nothing is stopping you from taking that first step. So, get in the habit of leading with your feet. You'll quickly discover that your team is more motivated, inspired, and optimistic.

The best time to get started is today.

Scan the QR code for additional insights and resources.

Chapter Exercises: Develop the Ability to Speak with Your Feet

- Lead by Example: Identify an area of your life where you want to inspire change or improvement. It could be in your personal relationships, health and wellness, or community involvement. Set a positive example by taking decisive action and demonstrating the behaviors you wish to see in others. By consistently embodying the qualities you value, you will inspire and motivate those around you to follow suit.

- Engage in Active Listening: Practice active listening skills to truly understand and empathize with others. This involves giving your undivided attention, maintaining eye contact, and demonstrating genuine interest in their perspectives. By listening attentively and responding thoughtfully, you can foster stronger connections and build trust, ultimately leading with your ability to understand and support others.

- Take Ownership of Mistakes: Accept responsibility for your actions and acknowledge when you make a mistake. Instead of deflecting blame or making excuses, embrace accountability and apologize sincerely. By demonstrating humility and a commitment to learning and growth, you set an example for others to take ownership of their own actions and mistakes.

- Support and Uplift Others: Look for opportunities to support and uplift those around you. Celebrate their successes, offer encouragement during challenging times, and provide assistance when needed. By actively promoting a positive and supportive environment, you demonstrate your commitment to the well-being and growth of others, inspiring them to do the same for their own communities.
- Practice Self-Reflection and Self-Awareness: Regularly engage in self-reflection to assess your words and actions. Ask yourself if they align with your values and intentions. Cultivate self-awareness to understand how your behavior impacts others and make adjustments as necessary. By continuously striving for self-improvement and aligning your actions with your values, you can lead by example and inspire others to do the same.

Remember, speaking with your feet and leading with your actions is a lifelong journey. These exercises will help you develop the necessary skills and mindset to make a positive impact in your own life and the lives of those around you.

CHAPTER 12

GARDENER LEADER—PRACTICE EYES-ON, HANDS-OFF LEADERSHIP

What leaders have to remember is that somewhere under the somnolent surface is the creature that builds civilizations, the dreamer of dreams, the risk taker. And remembering that, the leader must reach down to the springs that never dry up, the ever-fresh springs of the human spirit.
—John W. Gardner

Once you've assembled your talented, motivated, and loyal team, your focus as a passion-struck leader should be on how to get the most out of your team members. Those who are passion struck aren't individuals who micromanage and control every single aspect of their companies or organizations. They understand the perils of such an approach to management.[148]

In today's interconnected world, micromanagement hinders your ability to become the influential leader you need to be. In the past, leadership often required hands-on involvement and direct oversight. However, in the era of rapid change and connectivity, effective leadership involves shaping the entire environment, guiding the collective rather than every individual piece of the puzzle. This transition requires a shift from heroically controlling to fostering a culture of collaboration and progress.

In order to lead others while remaining focused on the bigger picture, you need to practice an eyes-on, hands-off style of leadership that is similar to that of the humble gardener. Adopting the role of a "gardener leader" entails nurturing the growth of your team, providing them with the necessary tools, guidance, and support to flourish. Just as a gardener tends to their plants, you plant the seeds of inspiration, offer mentorship as nourishment, and eliminate obstacles that hinder progress.

In our discussion of passion-struck leaders, it is easy to focus on these leaders' "internal" qualities. By this, I mean things like these leaders' mindsets and internal drives. It encompasses a focus inward rather than a focus outward.

Mastering this internal game is critical. Without it, your chances of becoming a passion-struck leader are nearly gone. The internal game, however, is only one side of the coin.

The highest-performing passion-struck leaders are not micromanagers who control every aspect of their organizations. They understand the importance of mastering the internal game while also valuing the external aspect of leadership.

I witnessed this approach through the lens of Larry Stone,[149] the former president and COO at Lowe's. Stone is a retail legend whose brilliant career at Lowe's lasted more than forty years. Stone's tenure started as a mailroom clerk, and along the way he progressed through almost every job in the organization. I worked with Stone for six years during some of the most transformational times in the retailer's history.

To say Stone was highly ambitious was an understatement. With every waking breath, this passion-struck leader dedicated his career to building the best company possible and winning the war against his nemesis, Home Depot. It was normal to see Stone arrive at the office at 5 a.m. and not leave till well after 7 p.m. And the Lowe's employees loved him. He was one of the most down-to-earth leaders in the company. The rank and file at the store found him easily approachable—not because he was the president, but because he had performed their jobs and knew them inside and out, and they trusted that he had their backs.

Stone's humility allowed him to gather feedback from the trenches and listen to the customer's voice at the store level. And, even though he was at the headquarters, he didn't micromanage the stores. Instead, he used this feedback loop to analyze data (which he did all the time) and make operational adjustments to merchandise, supply chain, and customer experience. It was not uncommon for Stone to call individual store managers to coach them based on the data he was seeing. That said, he let them run their stores and trusted them to do their jobs.

Listening to this example, it sounds simple to implement, but many leaders find it difficult to adopt this approach. All too often, it is tempting to get into the weeds and complete important projects or initiatives "the way that they should be completed." Even though you may feel some relief in the short-term, the long-term effects are harmful to your organization. Your work product is poorer, employee morale declines, and you are more stressed.

This chapter further discusses why passion-struck leaders practice eyes-on, hands-off leadership through some lessons and insights from two passion-struck leaders, General Stanley McChrystal and serial entrepreneur and former under secretary of state for economic growth, energy, and the environment Keith Krach. Along with being outstanding leaders, I know each of them personally.

Some Basics about Eyes-On, Hands-Off Leadership

Eyes-on, hands-off leadership is relatively self-explanatory. You can break it down into two parts. The eyes-on portion can be summed up in one word: vigilance. Passion-struck leaders have an excellent sense of what is happening in their organization. From reading reports to walking the floor of their offices, eyes-on leaders embrace granularity. Ignorance is the enemy here. They want to know what their employees are doing, who they are working with, their deadlines for certain projects, their KPIs, and how those projects are furthering the organization's mission.

The second half of this mantra is hands off. While passion-struck leaders must have an intimate understanding of their employees' work, they are primarily observers. They trust that their managers and employees will do their best work, whether it is a small routine task or a mission-critical task for the organization. Micromanaging is the enemy here. Instead, the passion-struck leader embraces intelligent delegation, only inserting himself or herself into lower-level work if it is truly necessary. Instead of doing the job that colleagues should do, the passion-struck leader spends more time strategizing and focusing on the larger picture.

This hybrid of eyes on and hands off leads to a highly effective management style by empowering employees while simultaneously letting the passion-struck leader focus on the most mission-critical tasks for the company.

Critical Attributes of Eyes-On, Hands-Off Leadership

As you can see, eyes-on, hands-off leadership prioritizes widespread observation, while simultaneously trusting that employees will get the job done.

McChrystal and Krach are the epitome of passion-struck leaders. They have displayed strong but firm leadership throughout their careers, whether it occurred on the battlefield (in McChrystal's case) or the boardroom (in Krach's case). To them, eyes-on, hands-off leadership wasn't just a slogan. It was a real-life way of overcoming the inevitable challenges that occurred in their professional lives. They adopted this leadership philosophy because the results spoke for themselves.

One of my favorite quotes on what makes a tremendous eyes-on, hands-off leader comes from the late General Colin Powell, who said:

> A person who understands that they're leading fol-
> lowers. A person who understands that they are there
> to put a group of human beings into work that has
> value, that has a purpose, and that the leader will give
> them the inspiration needed to achieve that purpose,
> and the leader will make sure they have everything
> they need to get the job done. That is what leadership
> is all about—inspiring followers.

I want to highlight several attributes that are critical to this philosophy:

- Delegating to the right level,
- Effectively hiring for your weaknesses,
- Becoming "humbitious,"
- Putting the team first—at all costs, and
- Inspiring colleagues through a noble mission.

Delegate to the Right Level

Eyes-on, hands-off leadership requires delegation. Though there is some nuance here, passion-struck leaders delegate yet ensure that they have all the necessary information to make strategic decisions.

Someone who leads through delegation is General McChrystal. McChrystal has built an extremely impressive career[150] after graduating from the U.S. Military Academy at West Point and quickly rising through the ranks to eventually command the Joint Special Operations Command (JSOC),[151] where he spent his time commanding special operations in both Afghanistan and Iraq. As if that wasn't enough, McChrystal was later promoted to general and served as commander of U.S. and ISAF forces in Afghanistan. In total, he served thirty-four years in the U.S. military.[152]

It goes without saying that McChrystal faced leadership challenges that most, if not all, of us will likely never have to face. Not only did he command a force as large as U.S. and ISAF forces in Afghanistan, but did so under life-and-death circumstances where one mistake could get people killed.

This type of high-pressure work environment is inevitably stressful. Along with this, the temptation to micromanage is all too real. Because the stakes are so high, it's tempting to take extreme control over operations to save lives and get the job done. McChrystal inevitably felt those pressures and still chose to act differently.[153]

I interviewed McChrystal a few years ago to learn about his leadership philosophies on an active battlefield and how they relate to the civilian world. The bottom line? He told me that it was critical to delegate to the right level. Meaning, it is impossible for a leader in the White House Situation Room to have the same perspective as the warfighter in the caves of Afghanistan. Those in the room need to place their trust in the fact that these soldiers are properly trained and will make appropriate decisions based on what the battlefield presents to them.

For instance, serving as commander of the JSOC, McChrystal recalled having dozens of screens depicting military operations in the field. The U.S. military has some of the most sophisticated technology in the world, and McChrystal and his direct reports were relying on it for a birds-eye look at what was happening on the ground. However, McChrystal did not use his all-knowing position to interfere with much of the decision-making. In fact, McChrystal told me that he was not always in the best decision-making position despite all this intelligence.

This is an important point. Even though McChrystal could have jumped into the weeds and micromanaged, he proceeded cautiously.

He recognized that although he had a tremendous amount of information at his fingertips, he had to trust that his leadership on the ground would do their jobs to the best of their professional abilities. His belief that those warriors in the thick of an operation were better informed than he allowed him to take a hands-off approach. Although he was eyes on, he delegated, at the same time keeping a close eye on what was unfolding in front of him. If necessary, he could intervene, while remaining more passive and relying on his soldiers in the thick of the fight.

Striking this balance is critical. While you may not be dealing with life-and-death situations, the same applies to our worlds outside of the military. Passion-struck leaders trust their leaders on the ground, the ones on the front lines.

Effectively Hire for Your Weaknesses

Eyes-on, hands-off leadership also requires individuals to effectively hire for their weaknesses. They know both their inherent strengths and weaknesses and dare to find stellar talent to compensate for their weaknesses.

Keith Krach has had a stellar business career. At twenty-six years old, Krach was named the youngest-ever vice president at General Motors.[154] After his time at GM, he pursued a more entrepreneurial career, co-founding Ariba[155] and serving as its chairman and CEO from 1996 to 2003. Later on, he served on boards for companies like XOJet, Ooma, and Angie's List, which he helped to take public in 2011. He also served as chairman and CEO of DocuSign, where he drove dramatic global growth, turned it into a verb, and also engineered a successful IPO in 2018. Krach then took on his most recent leadership challenge serving as the under secretary of state for economic growth, energy, and the environment[156] and was most recently nominated in 2022 for the Nobel Prize.

I first met Krach more than twenty years ago when he was the CEO of Ariba. He is an extremely talented and motivated individual, one who defines what it means to be a passion-struck leader. There are many reasons why Krach is so successful, but one of the most important is that he always pushes himself and everyone in his organization to "hire the best people, especially if they're better than us." He applies this rule to himself as well. Krach believes that building high-performance teams is his number one priority as a leader, and he is relentless when it comes to finding, recruiting, and hiring team members that exceed his own capabilities.

This requires him to have both a dispassionate assessment of his own capabilities *and* the ability to objectively analyze his team members' skills and motivations.[157] This is challenging, but Krach is single-minded in his pursuit of motivated individuals who can constantly raise the bar for performance across the entire organization. Ultimately, Krach is a student of people,[158] and a self-professed people collector. It is a huge advantage, and one that has ensured his success.

For example, in the early days of Ariba, Krach and his colleagues hit a dry patch in sales.[159] While he and his colleagues were focused on diagnosing the problem, he developed an idea to hold an offsite meeting to motivate his team.[160] At that meeting, Krach encouraged a third-party facilitator to ask his team about the organization's strengths and weaknesses[161] and Krach's own strengths and weaknesses. He was determined to model a willingness to admit faults, and demonstrate an openness to feedback. Surprisingly, his team came up with a list of seven strengths and a whopping twenty-one weaknesses for Krach.[162]

This exercise forced Krach into an extremely vulnerable position. Not many people would be happy to hear from their peers that they have three times as many weaknesses as strengths, but it was just what he wanted to drive a culture of openness, honesty, and vulnerability across the entire company. During the offsite, Krach acknowledged his weaknesses and openly committed to work on them. Krach set the example that made Ariba a safe environment for everyone to admit their "fears, flaws and failures." This opens the door to self-improvement and helps drive organizational improvement as everyone, from the CEO on down, is unafraid to hire people who are better than themselves.

That's why a big part of eyes-on, hands-off leadership is being honest with yourself. Identify where you are weak and seek out talented people who can make up for your weaknesses. You'll thank yourself later.

Become "Humbitious"

You may not be familiar with the term *humbitious*, yet it is essential to becoming an eyes-on, hands-off leader. The term *humbitious* originated at IBM several years ago, where the company described its best leaders as being one part humble and one part ambitious.

Passion-struck leaders possess intellectual humility along with a burning ambition to achieve their goals. Ambition is a given for all high strivers. However, passion-struck leaders use this intellectual humility to reflect on setbacks, listen, and adjust to critical input. While superstar entrepreneurs like Elon Musk and Steve Jobs might not initially be described as humble,[163] they *do* practice intellectual humility. In other words, they accept critical feedback and make adjustments that have profound impacts.

General McChrystal, whose ambition helped him to reach some of the highest levels of the U.S. military, is also humbitious. He practices intellectual humility[164]—both when he is alone practicing mindfulness and when working with colleagues. This tendency toward "humbitiousness" most likely saved lives. As McChrystal said:

> Successes I credited to a decision I'd made felt less impressive once I recognized the myriad factors and players who often had far more to do with the result than I had. We weren't on the ground. We didn't know how cold it was. We didn't hear the crack of the bullets. You can't pretend that you know more than you do. So what we did was we got much more humble.

I witnessed this humbitious leadership trait firsthand. During our interview, McChrystal consistently pointed out that although he was the leader of the McChrystal Group, which bears his name, he was not the most important element of the business. I watched as he sought out the input of his employees across all levels and listened intently to the other business leaders who were visiting for a leadership training session. What was most impressive to me was that McChrystal, given his prominence, could easily leap to judgments or conclusions, but does not. Instead, he chooses to listen with intent, absorb the feedback, and adjust his outlook.

Don't get me wrong. The general is ambitious and strives to build a winning company just as he was taught to win on the battlefield. Still, he remains one of the most humble senior military leaders that I have ever met. He continuously made the point that I needed to interview various others on his team in addition to talking with him. Because, he said, without them, there would be no McChrystal Group. These interviews ranged from those who were in the top circle like Chris Fussell, its president, to many other subordinates, including a junior business analyst, who was normally out on client engagements. During our entire time, McChrystal repeatedly spoke of the McChrystal Group in terms of a "Team of Teams," the name of his book.

Therefore, it's important to understand that to embrace the eyes-on, hands-off style of leadership, those who are passion struck must also be humbitious. While you can shoot for the stars, it's vital to stay intellectually humble. It is important to be willing to change tactics as necessary. These traits make you a better leader who is much more likely to accomplish your goals.

The Team Comes First—At All Costs

Next, the eyes-on, hands-off leadership style requires you to take responsibility for your team *at all costs*. Passion-struck leaders know that they can't be a leader (let alone a legendary one) without guiding and developing their team. They understand that reputation, relationships, and results are interconnected. These leaders also know when to take the blame for a mistake.

McChrystal understands that relationships determine your success or failure as a leader. As the man in charge of all U.S. and ISAF forces in Afghanistan, he didn't hesitate to take responsibility for his team's actions. While he couldn't control every single action of his troops on the battlefield, he recognized that the buck stopped with him. This awareness led to increased trust among his team, which inevitably led to more positive results on the battlefield.

Krach has also consistently demonstrated this approach at every organization he's run. At Ariba, Krach worked tirelessly to build and model a culture where humility, vulnerability, and openness were prized above all. Putting the team first was an operating principle at the company. These were more than just words. Krach's founding VP of sales at Ariba did a terrific job—closing all the original deals with FedEx, VISA, and Bristol-Meyers. But one day he approached Krach and said, "I've done a good job up to this point. But, you know, I'm more of a startup kind of a guy. To take this to the next level, I think we should get someone who has done this before at a much higher level." Krach was astonished, but it was exactly what the company needed. The same kind of humility and selflessness led the founding head of engineering to announce to everyone one day that, "This is a bigger opportunity than I ever thought possible. I think I should step aside and focus on strategic partnerships."

This culture of putting the team first, modeled by Krach himself, is what enabled both Ariba and DocuSign to succeed and grow at an unprecedented rate—becoming the fastest growing software company in history.

Passion-struck leaders recognize how important it is to put the team first. The key? Building a culture where it's okay literally to step aside when someone else can do the job better. Because that way everybody wins.

Inspire Through a Noble Mission

Finally, passion-struck leaders adopting eyes-on, hands-off leadership inspire their teams through a noble mission. This mission is something that their colleagues can rally around. In those inevitably stressful moments, the mission gives the entire team a boost, which may be just the thing that determines success or failure.

In my career, I have worked alongside great passion-struck leaders like Krach, who recently reminded me of the importance of inspiring colleagues through a noble mission. It all comes down to combining this noble mission with a passion-struck force behind it. As he told me, "Success happens in direct proportion to the passion behind your commitment to making a difference."

Your company or personal mission doesn't need to be literally saving the world. It can be something as simple as providing the best possible customer service to clients or creating the most beautiful piece of hardware. Whatever it is, keep it close and use it to inspire your colleagues.

How You Can Adopt These Elements

The eyes-on, hands-off leadership style is essential for being a passion-struck leader. The good news is that this leadership style leads to better results, happier employees, and less stress for you. Whichever way you look at it, embracing a eyes-on, hands-off philosophy is a good idea.

You may be asking yourself, "How do I actually do this in practice?"

Granted, McChrystal and Krach seem to naturally embrace this leadership style's qualities. But this was not always the case. Like them, you can adopt it yourself by keeping a couple of things in mind.

First, many of the attributes listed above require honesty. There are two facets to honesty. You need to be honest with yourself *and* honest when interacting with your team members. Being honest with yourself requires self-examination. It is critical to determine your strengths and weaknesses and to be humbitious. Honesty with your team is also imperative when you are delegating critical and not-so-critical tasks.

Being honest with ourselves can be difficult. All humans have biases, and it is all too easy to succumb to those biases. Nonetheless, passion-struck leaders aren't afraid to take long, hard looks at themselves in the mirror. They are dispassionate observers, recognizing the areas where they are less adept and looking for others to make up for those shortcomings. It's an ongoing process, but embracing honesty goes a long way in becoming proficient in the eyes-on, hands-off leadership style.

Along with honesty, you want to embrace active practice of these attributes. Most of us aren't born humbitious, nor do we naturally feel the need to take responsibility for all our team's work. Leadership is a learned skill. The quickest way to learn is through practice.

As with learning any skill, you are bound to fail sometimes. There will be moments when you weren't clear when delegating an important task to a colleague. There will be other moments where you subtly throw one of your direct reports under the bus. These are all learning experiences, but it's essential for you to embrace them as such actively.

When you face a setback when pursuing eyes-on, hands-off leadership, don't hesitate to write it down. Create a leadership journal where you can identify your mistakes and develop safeguards so that those mistakes won't happen again. Don't think this needs to happen in a day. The most important thing is to start making small changes and realize that you're investing in the long term. So, while you may not see results right away, have faith that they will pay off in the future.

Embracing Eyes-On, Hands-Off Leadership

Over my career, I have observed that eyes-on, hands-off leadership isn't always the easiest leadership style to obtain because at first it seems like you are letting go of power. And that is oftentimes where the problem lies. We confuse power with authority. This often results in leaders who micromanage until they are overwhelmed and immobilized. I've found countless times that there's that one boss or friend who is incapable of being wrong or the coworker who takes on too much and then deflects blame when it all comes crashing down. We all have these types of individuals in our life. They feel that admitting to a few cracks in the image they want to portray is akin to failure, so they fail to let go of control.

That is why the eyes-on, hands-off leadership style requires a boatload of honesty, drive, and trust in your team members. But, even more so, one of the first steps in achieving this style is to have the courage to allow yourself to be vulnerable. That is often not easy to do. No matter who you are, we all have an image of ourselves within our own minds. The truth is that our perception of ourselves is of a person who is a little smarter, more confident, and just a little bit better all-round than we really are.

That was certainly the case for me in my early career. I was too proud of my projected self-image to be vulnerable. Part of that was attributable to my initial personal feelings that vulnerability wasn't something that was part of my DNA as a man. Another stemmed from my naval training and subsequent service, which wasn't conducive to vulnerability. I felt that admitting I was wrong wasn't an option, and that being the "true" version of myself would have negative consequences.

When I came to start my life in the corporate world, I retained that attitude. But as I matured as both an employee, leader, and human being, I began to realize that vulnerability is beneficial in many ways. Rather than being wrapped up in insecurities, being vulnerable is actually a dominant trait that enables more effective leadership and closer relationships. I was reminded of this fact after spending some time with Sara Blakely, the founder of Spanx. Similar to the examples of Krach and McChrystal, she told me that vulnerability is one of her core values, and is a significant driving force of her success in business.

Today, I treat being vulnerable as one of my most significant assets as a business leader and in my personal life. It requires unveiling your genuine authentic self, acting, and feeling as you naturally do, as opposed to putting up a façade to either fit a projected self-image, a person we long to be with, or to fit in with an audience.

Vulnerable leaders who practice eyes-on, hands-off leadership inspire teams, create closer and more meaningful bonds, and facilitate improved business performance as a result. It can create untold wealth for you, your colleagues, and your organization. Enthusiastically embrace it as you advance on your journey to becoming a passion-struck leader.

This method of operating is not limited to business. You can implement it during personal passion-struck transformations too. For instance, if you're on a weight loss journey, it makes no sense to obsesses over every single meal and calorie you put into your body. You're likely going to put so much energy into creating detailed meal plans and scanning every food item with a calorie-counting app that you run out of time to exercise or get the correct amount of sleep.

By simply tallying rough calorie amounts for each meal, and keeping your mind focused on the bigger picture of burning more calories than you can consume, you can keep your trajectory on the correct path. You can also find the time to work on the most important aspects of your fitness regime that secure the biggest leaps forward.

This bigger-picture thinking allows visionary passion-struck leaders to achieve their goals faster since they manage to avoid the pitfalls of being sucked into the minutiae of day-to-day details.

Scan the QR code for more insights and resources.

Chapter Exercises: Practicing Gardener Leadership

- Reflection and Self-Awareness:
    1. Take some time to reflect on your leadership style and identify areas where you tend to be more hands on or hands off. How does this approach impact your team and their development?
    2. Consider situations where you can practice the eyes-on, hands-off approach. How can you create an environment that encourages autonomy and growth while still providing support and guidance when needed?
- Delegation and Empowerment:
    3. Identify tasks or projects that you can delegate to your team members. Choose tasks that align with their skills and interests, and provide clear instructions and expectations.
    4. Practice empowering your team by allowing them to make decisions and take ownership of their work. Resist the urge to micromanage and trust their abilities to deliver results.
- Developing Trust and Communication:
    5. Reflect on your communication style and how it affects trust within your team. Are there any areas where you can improve transparency and open dialogue?
    6. Implement regular check-ins or team meetings to provide updates, gather feedback, and address any concerns. Encourage open and honest communication, and actively listen to your team members' perspectives.
- Providing Guidance and Support:
    7. Find opportunities to offer guidance and support to your team without taking over their tasks. This could involve providing resources, sharing knowledge, or offering mentorship.
    8. Practice active coaching by asking questions that help your team members think critically and find their own solutions. Avoid jumping in with immediate answers or solutions unless necessary.

- Continuous Learning and Improvement:
  9. Read books, listen to podcasts, watch videos, or attend workshops on leadership and hands-off management styles. Look for insights and strategies that resonate with your leadership goals.
  10. Seek feedback from your team members on how you can improve your hands-off leadership approach. Actively incorporate their input to enhance your leadership effectiveness.

Remember, becoming a gardener leader takes practice and commitment. Through these exercises, you can begin to develop the necessary skills to empower your team, foster autonomy, and create a culture of growth and success.

CHAPTER 13

CONSCIOUS ENGAGER — KEEP THE MAIN THING THE MAIN THING

Business and human endeavors are systems....
We tend to focus on snapshots of isolated
parts of the system. And wonder why our
deepest problems never get solved.
—Peter Senge

I n the last chapter, I discussed the concept of a gardener leader. A leader's primary role is to ensure that the main thing remains the main (or most important) thing—the essential core of your work. This requires aligning one's purposeful choices with the true focal point. In theory, the concept sounds so easy. Yet, it is not nearly as simple as it sounds.

During my interview with Dandapani, a Hindu priest, entrepreneur, author of *The Power of Unwavering Focus*, and former monk of ten years, we delved into the profound connection between purpose and focus.

Dandapani emphasized the interplay between these two elements, stating, "Focus needs to go hand in hand with purpose. It is about leading a purpose-focused life and being intentional in our actions. How can we lead an intentional life if we are uncertain about what we truly want? It all starts with the mind and our ability to sustain focus. Without the ability to focus and engage in self-reflection, how can we discover our life's purpose? Focus becomes the foundation that allows us to uncover our purpose and, more importantly, stay committed and devoted to leading an intentional life."

As I listened to Dandapani's wise words, I couldn't help but be reminded of Stephen R. Covey, the acclaimed author of *The Seven Habits of Highly Effective People*.[165] Covey's book has resonated with millions of individuals across the globe and has become a timeless guide to personal and professional growth. One of Covey's most powerful concepts, which echoes the essence of Dandapani's message, is the notion that "the main thing is to keep the main thing the main thing."

This profound principle lies at the core of Covey's teachings and permeates his entire work. It serves as a powerful reminder that in our complex and fast-paced lives, we often get caught up in distractions and lose sight of our true priorities. Yet, by consciously focusing on what truly matters and aligning our actions with our core values and purpose, we can achieve remarkable clarity and effectiveness.

Dandapani's insights beautifully complement Covey's teachings, underscoring the importance of purposeful focus in our quest for personal and professional fulfillment. They remind us that by cultivating behaviors and habits that prioritize what truly matters and eliminating distractions, we can navigate life with intention and achieve extraordinary results. Embracing these behavioral changes empowers us to align our actions with our purpose, to overcome challenges, and to create a life that is both meaningful and impactful. I believe purposeful focus is even more relevant to our lives today than when Covey wrote the book more than twenty-five years ago. That is because our world is becoming so incredibly demanding of our time and how we focus it. Digital addiction, new ways of working, social media, AI, the growth in freelance work, and near-constant distractions progressively increase the daily challenges we face. Our schedules are so tight that figuring out how to fit it all in is becoming much more complex, and thus we seek comfort and routine.

Taking a step back and prioritizing what is really important takes enormous work and conscious effort. While it's true that our thoughts make our reality, it's not true that we do this alone. In fact, we are part of an infinite loop (giving, receiving, possessing, and discharging) of transactions with everything around us. Therefore, the way we engage with the world around us makes a fundamental difference between our success or failure at keeping the main thing the main thing:[166]

- We often allow our unconscious mind to be the master over our daily interactions (being on autopilot);
- We transact in a delayed-return society,[167] yet we've been conditioned by evolution to focus on engaging with what appears urgent and provides immediate results;
- We are stuck in our routines and habits, which causes us to be extemporaneous in our interactions; and
- We lack systems that reinforce our daily actions in pursuit of long-term goals and allow us to track progress.

This actuality causes us to go through life spontaneously engaged with our daily actions and intentions versus practicing conscious engagement or focus. In fact, I think this is one of the most significant factors in why so many people are disengaged at work, in their relationships, and with their physical and mental health, spirituality, and moral development.

The challenge we often face is that the growing reality of what is consuming our lives is far different from what we are genuinely passionate about and our priorities. This reality sets us up for all kinds of conflicts, struggles, and failures, both personally and professionally.

What Does It Mean to Be Unconsciously Engaged?

In Chapter 2, I introduced Jim McKelvey, the founder of Square, and the concept of becoming a "mission angler." Jim told me that one of the biggest mistakes he sees organizations and people make is losing focus on the underlying problem (the main thing) that was the genesis of their idea. And, he often finds that entrepreneurs he encounters are in constant motion with the world around them but not taking intentional, deliberate actions.

Said differently, they spend most of their day on autopilot, stuck in a spontaneous routine of doing what appears to create immediate impact instead of intentionally focusing on actions that take them closer to their end goal. Over time, they veer off course and venture into other conundrums that take focus away from their original issue. Without even realizing it, they are moving farther and farther away from their goals and ambitions.

But this isn't just about entrepreneurs. Unconscious engagement is all around us. It consumes our relationships with others, our daily work routine, our family interactions, and our pursuit of our dreams.

Let me describe this phenomenon in a different context.

Growing up, I always loved playing pinball machines, and I think it is a great way to explain the concept of spontaneous engagement. A pinball on its own has no intentionality whatsoever. It constantly reacts to its environment and goes in a particular direction until it bounces off the next object it touches. Ultimately it takes many twists and turns on its way to the drain. It's a never-ending pattern.

The same is true for unconscious engagement in our daily lives. You see, pinball is like life itself. Pinball machines are a study in distraction, pitching up bright bells and whistles to distract the player from the game. What happens is that the players become so distracted by what is around them that they don't take the deliberate actions to keep the ball in play, and that is when the ball sinks down the gutter. Like pinball, when we allow the game to play us, we are instinctively interacting with the game. We do it without intentionality. In other words, our routine and habits are on automatic replay without our conscious involvement.

During a captivating episode of the *Passion Struck* podcast, I interviewed Gloria Mark,[168] the chancellor's professor of informatics at the University of California, Irvine, and author of *Attention Span: A Groundbreaking Way to Restore Balance, Happiness, and Productivity*. Irvine explains life's pinball-like distractions:

> We tend to think that the primary cause for distractions for us to shift our attention is from algorithmic ads and notifications. And it turns out that people are just as likely to interrupt themselves forty-nine percent of the time. So these self-interruptions originate from within ourselves. We are conditioned in a lot of ways. We have urges that we want to look something up. And we're sitting in front of the world's largest candy store, where we can access information within milliseconds. You have a memory to do something. About a hundred years of psychological research is traced back to Bluma Zeigarnik,[169] the first researcher who looked at interruptions, who found that when you have an interrupted task, it tends to stay in your mind. We don't forget interrupted tasks.

Mark's groundbreaking findings expose distractions and interruptions as originating not only from external triggers like algorithmic ads and notifications but also from our own self-imposed interruptions. The lingering urge to accomplish interrupted tasks becomes a constant companion, fueling our internal distractions. Moreover, cognitive fatigue further heightens our vulnerability to both external and internal disturbances. The very design of the Internet, influenced by visionary concepts such as the Memex, sets in motion a whirlwind of associative thinking that effortlessly draws us into intricate digital rabbit holes.

When we lead a pinball life, we are not focused on solving world problems, nor are we really practicing vital leadership. We are living a life that is necessary but not strategic. Valuable but not value-added. It's apathy at its pinnacle, and it puts us in survival mode without us even realizing it is happening. It is being stuck in an infinite loop of spontaneous transactions with the world around us.

Our increasing reliance on technology and living a pinball life can cause us to disengage from creating a fulfilling life in several ways. One of the most significant ways is through distraction. Technology, particularly smartphones and social media, can be a source of constant distraction, taking our attention away from the present moment and disrupting our ability to focus on the things that truly matter to us. Furthermore, social media platforms often promote a culture of comparison and competition, leading us to feel inadequate and dissatisfied with our lives. This pressure to conform to societal norms and expectations can cause us to disengage from our true passions and interests, leading to a lack of fulfillment and purpose. Additionally, technology can create a false sense of connection and intimacy, leading us to prioritize virtual interactions over meaningful face-to-face relationships.

All these factors can contribute to a disengaged and unfulfilling life. Why would you want to live your life this way without intention and with constant distraction?

But so many of us do. We are disengaged from our lives and continually react to what the universe throws at us out of routine instead of intentionally engaging with it on purpose. This is spontaneous engagement. It happens simply because it happens. And, over time, this automatic loop becomes increasingly detrimental to your overall aspirations.

Why? The way you act or respond in various situations directly impacts your life, career, and family; thus, thoughtful participation is required to be successful in life.

Criticality of Aligning Importance with Urgency

Ask Apple CEO Tim Cook what he believes the tradition of the esteemed innovation company will be, and the appropriate response he gives may shock you. While he considers the iPhone an essential part of Apple's legacy, Cook also believes that it has undesired consequences for the way people engage with the world around them.[170] Let me illustrate this point through an example.

When I am out for a meal, I like to observe people's interactions. I find it ironic how few interact with each other versus how many are on their phones. We naturally tend to focus our attention on what appears to be urgent at that moment, just like in pinball. We are consumed with the spontaneous: someone trying to reach us, checking email, looking at chats, or staying abreast of social media. This scenario plays out at home with our families, with our friends, or in our interactions at work.

We have a growing societal problem where too many choose to live by our smart devices and the appointments on our calendars. This cross-generational issue invades all social, economic, and ethnic norms.

Tim Cook reflected on his own tech habits during a CNN interview[171] that illustrates his personal wake-up call after a newly unveiled app showed him his usage data. It is called Screen Time and provides detailed reports of how much time you spend on your iPhone and iPad. Through self-analysis, Cook came to an important conclusion: "I've been using it, and I have to tell you: I thought I was fairly disciplined about this. And I was wrong. The device is not addictive in and of itself. It's what you do on it."

And that is the problem. Technology fosters convenience and distraction. And that is why Tim Cook never wanted users of the technology to be spending so much time on the devices that it became their primary focus. The Apple iPhone's original intention was to be a tool to assist us in living our lives, not spontaneously consuming our lives. Yet, for so many, it has.

This was highlighted further in my interview with Isa Watson, the CEO of Squad and author of *Life Beyond Likes*. Watson explained:

> I think that the differentiation between engaging and addictive is really about escapism. When you are addicted to something, you engage with it to escape. For example, my friends who are the most depressed at any given point are the ones on social media the most, and I can always tell because they're "liking" more stuff.
>
> If I want to escape or kill time, that's where addiction comes in. If you are waking up in the morning, and the first thing you do is check your social media or the last thing you do before your head hits the pillow at night is check your social media, that's an addiction. The average millennial has nine social media accounts. And people are spending between three and a half and four hours on social media each day. So when you add eight hours of sleep and eight hours of work, people are spending a third of their waking hours on social media. Where does that leave time for genuine connection, spending time with your family, cooking, cleaning all the things that you have to do every day?[172]

Our lives become what is programmed into our schedule and the constant distractions from the digital world around us. We are so caught up with what appears urgent on our devices and in our calendars that we forget what is most important outside of them. It's analogous to trying to reset the deck chairs while the *Titanic* is sinking.

Stephen Covey outlined the following guidance for how we deal with the urgent versus the important:

> If something is important and it is urgent, then you need to do it.
> If it is important, but it is not urgent, then plan it.
> If it is urgent, but it is not important, then delegate it.
> If it is neither urgent nor important, then eliminate it.

Covey's words are a fundamental but straightforward lesson if you desire to become passion struck and learn how to break free from spontaneous engagement. Sometimes we need to take a step back and look at our lives from a different perspective.

An easy way to do this is to conduct a self-reflection of your habits. Examine your calendar over a three-month to four-month period instead of just looking at today or tomorrow. Don't focus on what to do next, but ask yourself, "How am I prioritizing my time and activities?" "Is what I am so busy with the main thing I should be occupied with?" "How am I interacting with the world around me?" "Is what I am doing in those interactions essential or urgent?"

Make the necessary changes in your life to focus on what is essential, not what appears urgent.

What Is Conscious Engagement?

Conscious engagement refers to the deliberate and regulated activities we consciously undertake in our daily routines. It is a learned behavior shaped by our habits and actions. Unlike casual or instinctive actions, conscious engagers perform tasks with objectivity and purpose. It involves being intentional and mindful in our actions, making thoughtful choices rather than simply going through the motions.

Let's go back to the analogy of pinball. When we are unconsciously engaged, we are letting the pinball machine play us. When we consciously engage, we play the game on our own terms and with deliberate focus and intentionality. In this state of mind, we learn the behaviors and patterns that the game creates and adjust our interaction to compensate for them accordingly.

Most people play pinball like an amateur, only trying to keep the ball in play and from falling off the board. The result is that the game appears random instead of one carefully crafted by its designers to beat the player. Pinball is actually a set of minigames, which cohere into a set of clues of how to beat it. Being cognizant of these clues and overcoming the pitfalls of the game is a lot more satisfying than just keeping the ball from going down the gutter.

The same is true about being a conscious engager. Like the game of pinball, our real life is full of immersive sensory attraction to our complex, all-digital world that I illustrated with the Tim Cook example. And it is easy to get distracted. Conscious engagement is all about controlling your actions and playing the daily game of life as you intend instead of allowing it to play you.

It takes practice and patience to be present and go about your day with intentionality. It is all about information processing and aligning your priorities with the information thrown at you, like playing pinball. But doing so consciously and not spontaneously.

Principles of Conscious Engagement

I want to unpack the three principles of conscious engagement. Let's discuss them in detail.

1. Through our evolution as a species, we are hardwired to act out of our own safety. From the moment we are born, a set of responses are continuously feeding into our subconsciousness to protect our

beliefs, societal standards, and self-identity. This knee-jerk reaction is often caused by us being threatened or by uncertainty about our surroundings. When that occurs, we're thrust into an environment that may appear to our senses to be hostile and punitive. This can create a cognitive, physical, and spiritual impact on us, during which we must remain conscious of our choices and their consequences.

Consider this: If you seem trapped in a risky setting, your mind begins to take actions according to the command of your subconscious instinct. If you touch a hot skillet, for example, you immediately pull your hand back without wasting a second and without involving any conscious control. This is called the subconscious reflex path. The same happens with your everyday interactions, habits, and actions. Being consciously engaged is an exercise in personal growth and in controlling these reflexes. It is having the self-awareness to understand where we are, who we are interacting with, and our intentions for our actions.

2. Anticipatory regulations give rise to continuity of conscious engagement.[173] Those who are conscious engagers don't conform to other people's ideas of happiness or contentment. Through harnessing this anticipatory perspective, they allow themselves to live in the moment and appreciate the beauty of each interaction.

Nikola Ilankovic, M.D.,[174] a professor at the University of Belgrade, explains it this way: "Without anticipation of future and memory for past, we have no continuity of our consciousness and our self. So we are living in the past, in the present, and in anticipation of the future. So have we the continuity of consciousness!"

Consider this: You are watching someone walk down the street when he unexpectedly trips and becomes disoriented and falls. As we observe the fall, it is often the case that we, too, feel suddenly disoriented as a result. The anticipation of what is happening is so central to our cognitive processes that when our subconscious expectations are not realized,[175] it can momentarily throw our own cognition into chaos. It also illustrates our own mind's vital role in comprehending everyday situations and why we react spontaneously to them.

3. Throughout our lives, we become accustomed to other people doing things for us that we are not skilled at or trained to do for ourselves. An illustration of this could be hiring a professional to install new windows in your house or having a software developer code your company's new customer relationship management system. Despite the number of times we experience these encounters, we generally grow unconscious of our emotional dependence on them. This is where changing that reality becomes extremely important to how we interact with others around us. Author and therapist Sue Thoele illustrated this third concept when she wrote,

> Emotional dependence is the opposite of emotional strength. It means needing to have others to survive, wanting others to "do it for us," and depending on others to give us our self-image, make our decisions, and take care of us financially. When we are emotionally dependent, we look to others for our happiness, our concept of "self," and our emotional well-being. Such vulnerability necessitates a search for and dependence on outer support for a sense of our own worth.[176]

Consider this: Dr. Martin Luther King Jr. challenged his followers to become conscious of their interdependence. In other words, he told them not to allow themselves to be emotionally dependent on other people. They shouldn't stay satisfied with their current situation because it doesn't have to remain this way. They can change it by consciously engaging the world around them in an infinite loop to break the cycle of dependence through emotional strength.

Abraham Lincoln: From Humble Beginnings to Becoming U.S. President

President Abraham Lincoln is a prime historical example of a leader who suffered from spontaneous engagement and later became a conscious engager. Widely regarded as the best U.S. president,[177] his rise from humble beginnings to achieving the highest office in the land is a truly remarkable story. But his start could be considered anything but impressive. The young Lincoln ironically described himself as "a piece of floating driftwood," and he was just that for many years.

Like a pinball, he bounced around in an infinite loop of unconscious interactions with the world around him that led him to become a shopkeeper, postmaster, general store owner, and state legislator, before eventually becoming a lawyer at the age of thirty-three.[178] His law partner, William Henry Herndon, affirmed that Lincoln believed in spontaneous engagement. What this meant for Lincoln, as Herndon discovered, was that Lincoln thought that "there was no freedom of the will," that "men had no free choice":

> Things were to be, and they came, irresistibly came, doomed to come; men were made as they are made by superior conditions over which they had no control; the fates settled things as by the doom of the powers, and laws, universal, absolute, and eternal, ruled the universe of matter and mind.... [Man] is simply a simple tool, a mere cog in the wheel, a part, a small part, of this vast iron machine that strikes and cuts, grinds, and mashes, all things, including man, that resist it.[179]

A few years later, this belief continued to permeate him when Lincoln served a single term in the U.S. House of Representatives with an unremarkable attempt at national politics, which ended in 1849. Most would have thought his political career was over, and it almost was.

However, seven years later, in 1856, Lincoln finally found his main thing. His views on slavery moved from acceptance to moral outrage. Lincoln joined the Republican Party on an anti-slavery platform because he believed that America's forefathers intended to create all men with certain inalienable rights. He won his U.S. Senate seat by making slavery his central issue and declaring that "a house divided cannot stand."

At this point, he realized that his actions could be controlled with his intentions, and it wasn't all random. He realized that there are stages that we go through on our life's journey, and that we must recognize that our starting point doesn't have to be where we finish.

As author and consultant Simon Sinek wrote, "What good is it having a belly if there's no fire in it? Wake up, drink your passion, light a match and get to work."

Lincoln spoke about abolishing slavery, debated it, and breathed its importance to all who would listen, every chance he got. His main thing was driving his infinite loop of engagement. He had become a conscious engager. He understood that mastering his emotions, listening, and communications skills was vital to his daily transactions with the world around him.

He empowered his leadership by consciously engaging with the American society of that time and bringing rivals into his closest circle. He used that engagement to consider the opinions of others, to self-correct mistakes, and take actions that improved his public image. Once he understood his mission (the main thing), he realized that you can never ignore the physics of progress in attaining it.

On November 6, 1860, a few short years later, Lincoln won the presidential election without the support of a single southern state. Lincoln once said, "I will prepare, and someday my chance will come." It certainly did.

But, even before Lincoln's inauguration in March 1861, seven southern states had seceded from the Union. On January 1, 1863, Lincoln delivered the Emancipation Proclamation, and later the Gettysburg Address. Both reshaped the cause of the Civil War, from saving the Union to abolishing slavery, which was his vision for the future.

From all around him, Lincoln faced condemnation and opposition. He was often at odds with his party, his generals, his Cabinet, and a majority of the American people. He continually fired his generals leading the war until he found the man who could. Lincoln understood that he must win over those he interacted with by having a never-say-die attitude built on resilience. Through his keen vision and relentless drive, the Union, as we all know, won the war, and with it, slavery was abolished.

Lincoln's path to becoming a conscious engager was not linear. It went from the game of life playing him to becoming a true passion-struck leader with a clear, compelling vision. The transition involved him mustering the power to do something more, reinventing himself, realizing that being right meant standing alone, fueling his passion, and sticking with it in the most trying of times. Although we will likely never encounter the scenario Lincoln did, his life illustrates the importance of a clear and unwavering vision and the difference that conscious engagement can make. Lincoln mastered the importance of dreaming the dream.

Keeping the main thing the priority is like a porous bucket—it leaks, which is why we need to create an infinite loop of conscious engagement to put it into daily practice. Take a step back, create a compelling vision for the future, and then set a path for it; practice daily conscious engagement and stop reacting to external distractions that deter from it. Just as Lincoln, you can also learn to take deliberate actions every day to get comfortable with discomfort.

When you say "no" to a hundred other missions, you say "yes" to the most crucial mission. You keep the main thing the main thing.

Consciously Communicate Your Main Thing to Everyone

When examining potential examples of conscious engagement to write about, I realized there is no better example of deploying it than

Winston Churchill. Since I was a young boy, he has always fascinated me because he is one of my father's heroes and a painting of him was in our home. When Churchill became prime minister of Great Britain in 1940, fascism looked likely to triumph in Europe during a tremendous international crisis. Churchill used the power of engagement to boost morale, rally resistance, defy Hitler, and build alliances with Russia and the United States.

Churchill, in many ways, is an improbable person to become the most revered leader in English history because he had many personal flaws and made some huge mistakes in his long political career.[180] These include putting the country back on the gold standard, which many experts feel caused the Great Depression; supporting Edward VIII during his abdication; opposing India as a nation; and making several critical mistakes during World Wars I and II.

But it was his extraordinary direction in World War II when his country desperately needed it that brought his leadership to the forefront. Churchill was bold, courageous, and tireless in his resolve to unite his country and take on the might of Nazi Germany. He inspired a nervous and uncertain Great Britain through his sheer energy and engaging speeches to defy stark odds, keep going, and win the war. He used engagement in its ultimate form to keep the main thing the main thing and pull Britain back from the brink of disaster.

By doing so, no other British prime minister can even remotely match the scope of Churchill's results. When he died in 1965, the historian Sir Arthur Bryant said: "The age of giants is over." Bryant was right—and yet that, in a way, is a measure of Churchill's success.[181]

Just as England needed conscious engagement during the trials of World War II, today more than ever, organizations rely on the energy, commitment, and engagement of their workforce to survive and thrive in our modern world. As I discussed in Chapter 1, according to Gallup's "State of the Global Workplace: 2022 Report," workplace productivity is low globally. In fact, it states that, "Worldwide, the percentage of adults who work full time for an employer and are engaged at work—they are highly involved in and enthusiastic about their work and workplace—is just 15%."[182]

Through its extensive research, Gallup realized the same thing that Churchill did decades before: organizations that orient their performance around basic human needs for engagement get the most out of their employees. Gallup found that only "1 in 3 working-age adults (23-65) worldwide believe they have a 'good job.'"

How can this possibly be the case? The obvious answer is that the main thing is not the main thing in their environments. And there is a path forward that we can learn from Churchill's life. Jack Welch, the former CEO of GE, realized this same point:

> There are only three measurements that tell you nearly everything you need to know about your organization's overall performance: employee engagement, customer satisfaction, and cash flow. It goes without saying that no company, small or large, can win over the long run without energized employees who believe in the mission and understand how to achieve it.

Passion-struck leaders use words as weapons. Churchill did so by warning his people about the hard road ahead. He famously said, "I have nothing to offer but blood, toil, tears, and sweat."[183] He then committed himself and the nation to all-out war until victory was achieved. Behind this simplicity of words lay an elaborate strategy of engagement, which he followed with incredible consistency throughout the war. Hitler and his Third Reich were the enemies; nothing should distract the entire British people from the task of effecting its defeat. We can apply this approach to our present pursuits by emphasizing what truly matters through our speeches, briefings, pep talks, and mentoring. These diverse avenues provide opportunities to consistently prioritize and reinforce the essential elements, ensuring their continuous application.

The nation took Churchill to its heart because he and they were on their mission together. Faced with the potential demise of France, Churchill repeatedly went to the French government in person in an attempt to keep France in the war.[184] When this failed, he didn't give up. Instead, he used it to his advantage. He appeared on the front lines, whether it was at headquarters, inspecting coastal defenses or antiaircraft batteries, visiting scenes of bomb damage throughout the country, smoking his cigar to show calmness, giving his famous "V" finger sign, or broadcasting frank reports to the nation. Similar to Churchill, passion-struck leaders bring their missions together with their employees or followers. By being on a mission together, we engage those around us to focus on the main thing.

Lastly, Churchill knew that he could not do it on his own. He knew that he had to engage others in his mission and to form strategic alliances. When Hitler suddenly launched his attack on the Soviet Union, Churchill's response was swift and straightforward. He used it to engage the Russians and insisted that "the Russian danger…is our danger." More important, he pledged aid to the Russian people when, at the same time, the English people also needed much support. Later, he did the same thing with President Roosevelt. Churchill had the foresight to construct a "grand alliance" incorporating Russia and the United States. It became a turning point to his success and kept his mission of ultimate victory at the forefront.

So often, we think we can do things by ourselves. We often overlook the importance of building strategic alliances in our own lives. Especially those with people who will tell us the truth regardless of the consequences.

Keeping the Main Thing the Main Thing

As I have outlined throughout this chapter, Winston Churchill and President Abraham Lincoln consciously kept the main thing the main thing. I wanted to expand on its significance by looking at other examples from the book. Jim McKelvey was consciously engaged in solving mobile payments through the DNA of problem-solving[185] that unified Square's various product groups. Jeff Bezos created an "everything store" by his intentionality in delivering the best possible customer experience. Steve Jobs founded Apple on the belief that the power of human creativity can solve even the most significant challenges.[186] And Elon Musk, whom we will discuss in Chapter 16, believes he needs to consciously save humanity from itself.

You might think that these "main things" are grand and ambitious, and indeed they are. However, it's essential to note that all these leaders started as mission anglers, pursuing their passions and convictions. Your own "main thing" doesn't have to be any less significant; it's about what deeply matters to you and what impact you wish to make. Success comes to those who are willing to explore new territories and embrace change, as it is through these ventures that we shape the future and leave a lasting mark on humanity.

In the midst of the overwhelming demands of life and career, becoming a conscious engager calls for self-reflection and a focus on your true goals. By keeping the main thing as your guiding principle, you can stay on course and make meaningful progress towards what truly matters to you.

The main thing is *truly* keeping your main thing the main thing.

Scan the QR code for additional insights and resource.

Chapter Exercises: Become a Conscious Engager

- Self-Reflection: Take some time to reflect on your current priorities and commitments in life. Identify the main thing or the most important aspect that you want to focus on. Write down why it is important to you and how it aligns with your values and long-term goals.

- Prioritization Exercise: Make a list of all the tasks, projects, and responsibilities you currently have. Evaluate each item and determine its importance in relation to the main thing you identified in the previous exercise. Prioritize the items based on their relevance and impact on your overall goal.

- Distraction Awareness: Pay close attention to the distractions that pull you away from the main thing in your daily life. Notice the triggers and patterns that lead to these distractions. Keep a journal or use a mobile app to track your distractions for a week. At the end of the week, analyze the data and identify the most common distractions. Brainstorm strategies to minimize or eliminate these distractions moving forward.

- Intentional Focus Practice: Choose one specific activity or task that is directly related to the main thing you want to focus on. Practice giving your full attention and concentration to this activity for a set period of time each day. Eliminate any distractions during this focused time and be fully present in the moment. Observe the impact of intentional focus on your performance and progress.

- Accountability Partner: Find a trusted friend, colleague, or family member who can serve as an accountability partner. Share your main thing and discuss your strategies for maintaining intentional focus. Regularly check in with each other, provide support, and hold each other accountable for staying on track.

Remember, intentional focus and keeping the main thing the main thing require consistent effort and practice. By incorporating these exercises into your life, you can begin to cultivate a mindset and behavior that prioritize what truly matters and lead to greater fulfillment and success.

PART 3

THE MOST IMPORTANT PIECE OF THE PUZZLE — THE PSYCHOLOGY OF PROGRESS

CHAPTER 14

THE FIVE TRANSITION POINTS
ON THE JOURNEY TO BECOMING
PASSION STRUCK

The will to win, the desire to succeed, the urge to
reach your full potential...these are the keys that
will unlock the door to personal excellence.
—Confucius

I n the preceding chapters, we delved into the mindset and behavior shifts necessary to become passion struck. Now, in the next five chapters, I will guide you in implementing these shifts and bridging the gap from where you currently stand to where you aspire to be.

Have you ever felt like life's opportunities were slipping away? Do you find yourself stuck and unable to reach your full potential? Are you yearning for a vision that can turn your dreams into reality?

Our world is inherently binary, with two distinct states: those who choose growth, altruism, and creativity, and those who settle for survival mode, ego, and self-absorption. The former, creative amplifiers, comprise a mere 5 to 7 percent of the world's population, while the latter, subsisters, make up 15 to 20 percent.

However, the path from one extreme to the other may seem elusive, and we might lack a clear understanding of the steps required for this transformation. Each peak we conquer and each valley we rest in unlocks a new stage of development—the journey from being passion stuck in apathy to becoming passion struck and unstoppable.

To tap into your full potential, you must operate at the highest level—like the creative amplifiers. They have cultivated themselves cognitively, physically, ethically, spiritually, and emotionally, following the passion-struck framework continuum.

In the upcoming chapters, we will unravel the secrets of reaching this heightened state, enabling you to unleash your true potential and embrace the passion-struck journey. Get ready to embrace your transformation and become unstoppable in pursuing your dreams.

Sports as a Metaphor for This Journey

The journey of personal growth can be likened to participating in sports. As a Division 1A athlete, sports have always been an essential aspect of my life. And, as I look back on those experiences, there is tremendous value in examining the phases of an athlete's preparation (mind, body, spirit) in his or her sport. Those phases contribute to how well the athlete conquers the task at hand and whether they can achieve a higher level of performance.

During my interview with Sally Jenkins, a Hall of Fame sports columnist for the *Washington Post* and author of *The Right Call: What Sports Teach Us About Work and Life*, she delivered a powerful message about the profound impact coaches and athletes can have on our personal agency and decision-making.

Jenkins passionately emphasized, "We really understudy and utilize the guidance we can learn from coaches and athletes. Their decisional process, commitment, organization, and methodology are invaluable takeaways applicable to any endeavor, regardless of its perceived ordinariness."

Highlighting the remarkable achievements of Kurt Warner, Steph Curry, and Peyton Manning, Jenkins quoted Erik Spoelstra, the Miami Heat coach, who declared, "Everybody overestimates what you can get done in a day and underestimates what you can do in months and months of work."

Athletes and coaches excel in the art of incremental progress, dedicating themselves to consistent 1- to 2-percent improvements. They fearlessly confront their weaknesses and relentlessly push beyond plateaus. Take Michael Jordan, for instance, hitting the game winning basket over Cleveland's Craig Ehlo in Game 5 of the NBA playoffs May 7, 1989. His success was rooted in reaching a state researchers call "automaticity,"[187] where he had honed his shot-making skills through countless repetitions, making it a seamless and instinctive action in the heat of the moment. Similarly, Steph Curry's unwavering commitment to refining both his left and right foot, even training his non-dominant hand, exemplifies his relentless pursuit of excellence. These seemingly minor refinements accumulate over time, leading to extraordinary advancements that often go unnoticed by the casual observer.

Jenkins's fascination with the neurological processes of athletes unveils a profound truth. Athletes are not driven by mere intuition or fleeting bursts of inspiration; they rely on meticulously calculated methods that transcend the realm of the average spectator's comprehension.

"They're not acting on intuition. They're not acting on some fortunate jolt of inspiration in the moment. They are acting on methods and calculations much more than the average spectator would ever dream," she explained fervently.

Encouraging intentional decision-making, Jenkins urges us to categorize choices, recognizing the varying stakes and consequences involved. Just as in sports, where some decisions resemble first downs while others mimic fourth downs, understanding the significance of each decision empowers us to make impactful choices.

Like sports, whenever we enter a new chapter of self-development, we often take off at a sprint—excited to tackle a new challenge.

However, similar to life, there truly is a deeper level to achieving peak performance in sports. Working hard and being dedicated is just part of the formula for success, and it is so much more than just physical abilities. It requires deliberate improvement of body, brain, spirit, and emotion that is highly structured with increasing intensity that, on the surface, is not inherently enjoyable.

And, it is not just about training and clocking in the practice field hours. Similar to the toxic hustle culture, the grind doesn't bring success. Instead, achieving greatness goes far beyond that and is determined by your intentional daily actions.

As we conquer each development phase, that phase offers a unique perspective that appears complete from that viewpoint. Some athletes never move past the lower stages of performance. They lack the emotional and mental strength to move past that plateau, unaware that there's another one, above them, at a higher stage. So, in a sense, there is a center of gravity in sports, like life, that you must cross to achieve your end goal. For instance, runners often hit the eighteen-mile point or the wall at twenty-two miles in a marathon, and they can't go on.[188] The same can be said about the phases in life that we must transverse to reach our highest potential.

The path to achieving peak performance is not for the faint of heart and requires those seeking to become passion struck to traverse five development phases on their journey. Think of these as stages on the path to self-awareness, which are the growth levels that you step through to becoming passion struck.

Throughout the rest of this chapter, we will delve into the five crucial transition points that lead you from being a subsister to becoming a passion-struck creative amplifier. These points will offer valuable insights into your progression as you apply the passion-struck framework to your personal growth journey. They will help you understand where you currently stand on this transformative path.

Defining the Five Transition Points of the Passion-Struck Personal Growth Journey

The self-awareness journey is like venturing into an alleyway of exploration, uncovering your hidden potential. It's akin to a challenging mountain climb, with various transition points along the way. Many get stuck at the second or third stage, hindering their progress. But as an ambitious person you're meant to keep growing and conquering each phase with the determination to bring lasting change.

Let's delve into these transition points sequentially, so you can evaluate where you currently stand. Don't worry if you're at stage two or three; your ambition can take you far. Approximately 25 percent to 30 percent of the population is at the third stage, while 15 percent to 20 percent is at the fourth stage. The smallest percentage is at the fifth stage or beyond.

Some of us may be missing a critical developmental tool, or we might find ourselves trapped at a certain level due to an unseen psychological shadow. These hidden emotional energies and trained mental biases can lead to reactionary behavior. Alternatively, it could be a fear-based worldview that limits our vision. Importantly, there is no judgment attached to these levels; they merely serve as a guide to help us understand where we currently stand on our path of self-awareness and growth.

What are these five developmental stages? Let me explain them one by one.

1. The Subsister: Indifferent and self-centered, gripped by an overwhelming fear of change, settling for the comfort of the status quo.
2. The Imitator: Self-absorbed and conforming, driven by ego and the need to fit in, adhering strictly to societal norms.
3. The Vanquisher: Ambitious and relentless, constantly striving for personal success and determined to conquer obstacles on the path to greatness.

4. The Orchestrator: Balanced and visionary, possessing a managed ego and a genuine concern for the world, actively seeking systemic change and progress.

5. The Creative Amplifier: Conscious and humble, fully engaged with a world-centric perspective, resilient in the face of challenges, and empowered to realize their authentic self.

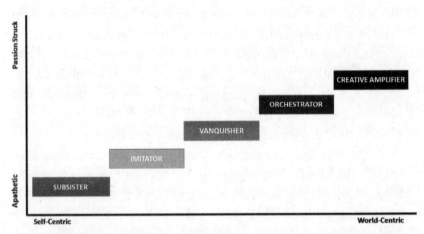

FIGURE 6: To move from being a subsister to being a creative amplifier requires a great deal of effort and concentration. It is learning to gradually change your viewpoint from a focus on self to solving problems for humanity. On the other axis, it is moving from being indifferent to the world around you and in survival mode to being passion struck and thriving in your desire to live an intentional life.

The Subsister: Indifferent and Self-Centered, with a Visceral Fear of Change

This stage of development reveals a harsh reality that often goes unacknowledged—the existence of those who simply subsist and operate in survival mode. It is a difficult truth to admit, as many individuals find themselves in this stage at some point in their lives, even if they are hesitant to recognize it. Life-altering events can plunge someone from a higher stage back to this initial stage, rendering them underdogs in their own lives.

In the subsister stage, individuals resemble pinballs in a noisy and distracting game, losing control to external forces. They live behind a façade, pretending to be someone they are not. Stressful events like trauma or loss can push them into survival mode, where they feel like victims and their basic needs go unfulfilled. In this stage, subsisters perceive themselves as victims of circumstances, their essential needs unmet. Their world revolves around self, making escape from this reality seem impossible. Survival instincts dominate, and a sense of control dwindles. Trapped here, existence overshadows thriving. Days are about getting by, consumed by immediate demands. Isolation and despair reign, pushing connections away. Apathy and complacency taint life, a result of feeling defeated. Nourishment, rest, and joy become distant echoes. Living turns reactive.

Breaking free from the subsister state involves self-awareness, confronting fears, seeking support, adopting a growth mindset, setting goals, and prioritizing self-care. Identify triggers, embrace vulnerability, and learn from setbacks. It's a process that requires persistence and patience, but with consistent effort and a positive outlook, one can move to a higher stage of personal growth.

Common characteristics of the subsister stage include:

- Affliction and self-doubt.
- An unhealthy victim mentality focus.
- Seeking instant satisfaction without considering long-term consequences for oneself or others.
- Actions driven by impulse or sudden emotions, rather than thoughtful deliberation.
- Manipulating situations for immediate self-interest.
- Living in a self-centered and egotistical mindset. Feeling fatigued, with no time to pursue excellence or focus on self-improvement.
- Exhibiting indifference and complacency with a fear of embracing vulnerability.

It is estimated that approximately 15 percent to 20 percent of people are in this stage.

The Imitator: Self-Absorbed and Conforming, Driven by Ego to Adhere to Social Norms

In Chapter 2, I discussed the human tendency to conform and seek belonging in social groups, which stems from our evolutionary history. This desire to fit in and imitate others often leads to a lack of personal growth and the adoption of invisible group norms. Individuals in this stage are heavily influenced by peers, family, and societal institutions, following social norms and seeking guidance from perceived leaders. They feel comfortable within the tribe's boundaries and may exhibit a traditionalist mindset, aligning themselves with the tribe's brand or ideology. Imitators are close-minded and conservative, valuing strong social relationships but often resistant to ideas outside their group's authority or hierarchy.

The problem with this imitative inclination is that it can lead to a set of invisible group norms that dictate daily behaviors. Individuals in this stage rely on logic and rationality, seeking guidance from experts or perceived leaders. During an eye-opening *Passion Struck* podcast episode, I had the privilege of engaging in a thought-provoking conversation with Brian Lowery, a distinguished Stanford professor and social psychologist, regarding his latest book, *Selfless: The Social Creation of "You."* In our conversation, I delved into the question of why we often become imitators, seeking to understand the underlying motivations.

Lowery explained, "We make decisions not just about how we interact with people, but also about who we interact with based on superficial cues. Our interactions are limited, and we tend to gravitate towards groups because of the strong tribal nature of human beings. It's a challenging aspect to overcome." Human behavior is deeply influenced by our inclination to think in terms of groups, which affects how we perceive and interact with the world around us.

Instead of embracing personal growth and pushing their boundaries, imitators choose to conform. Aligning themselves with groupthink feels comfortable, as if they belong to something greater than themselves. As we transition from survival mode, the next step in our progression is to collaborate and bond with others, with the hope of improving our situation.

Individuals in this second transition point are confident in their place in the world because it was bestowed upon them. However, they are deeply entrenched in archetypal notions of themselves and others' roles in society. Their worldview is shaped by others, providing them with a sense of comfort and alleviating feelings of isolation. Like the subsisters, the imitators are still concerned with self-orientation. They are incredibly concerned with social norms and making incremental improvements to existing problems "inside city walls." They do not strive to be original or forge their own identities, instead adopting the brand of the tribe to which they belong.

To break free from the imitator stage, a person must consciously challenge their reliance on group norms and hierarchical authority. They should actively seek diverse perspectives and experiences out-side their immediate social circle. Embracing discomfort and explor-ing unfamiliar ideas can help cultivate open-mindedness. Developing a strong sense of self and individuality is essential, allowing them to question traditional beliefs and forge their own identity. By embrac-ing personal growth, cultivating critical thinking, and daring to be original, individuals can break free from the imitator phase and prog-ress towards becoming passion-struck creative amplifiers.

Common characteristics of this imitator stage include:

- A cautious and meticulous approach to decision-making.
- Striving for win-win situations, prioritizing emotions over judgment.
- Enthusiastically emulating the actions, beliefs, and habits of those around them.
- Close-mindedness is common, making it challenging for them to adopt a broader global perspective.
- Retaining a sense of self-importance, contextualized within their tribe.
- Avoidance of risk or exploring new opportunities.

- Silent struggles to meet everyone's expectations, especially their own.
- Prioritize fitting in and conforming to the expectations of others over asserting their own unique identity and pursuing individual growth.
- Struggle to form genuine connections based on their own authentic selves.
- Ego-driven imitation stifles personal growth by fueling a constant need for external validation, conformity, and comparison.

It is estimated that approximately 20 percent to 25 percent of people belong to this stage.

The Vanquisher: Ambitious, Relentless, and Resolute in Pursuit of Greatness

In the transformative journey of self-discovery, the vanquisher emerges as a formidable force, driven by an insatiable desire to achieve their goals and etch an indelible mark on the world. This stage represents a profound evolution from earlier phases, as they shift from casual engagement to a conscious commitment to personal growth and the betterment of the broader system. These are the individuals who transcend mediocrity and strive for excellence in their chosen domains, be it through military service, academic pursuits, athletic prowess, corporate endeavors, or leadership roles.

What sets the vanquisher apart is their unwavering dedication and resolute focus on their objectives. Fearlessly pushing boundaries, they confront challenges head-on, demonstrating a remarkable capacity for resilience and adaptability. In their pursuit of success, they become the architects of action, reshaping their paths and redefining their brands along the way. They are fueled by an intrinsic sense of responsibility and mastery of cognitive abilities, enabling them to comprehend intricate systems and navigate complexities with strategic acumen.

A sense of integrity is woven into the fabric of their being, where honesty, duty, and loyalty serve as pillars of their value system. These principles guide their decisions and actions, inspiring those around them to elevate their own standards. Natural leaders, vanquishers exude confidence and take charge of situations, providing guidance and direction that unite diverse teams towards shared objectives. This innate ability to balance immediate priorities with a long-term strategic vision fosters collaboration and teamwork, propelling them and their associates towards a common goal.

However, within the vanquisher stage, certain adverse attributes emerge that can impede both personal growth and relationships. The unwavering pursuit of success and accomplishment can create a myopic focus, obscuring the consideration of others' well-being. Their resolute determination and assertiveness might inadvertently manifest as dominance and insensitivity, presenting challenges in understanding diverse viewpoints and alternative solutions. Additionally, their deep attachment to societal norms and status quo may lead to resistance against embracing originality and change. If unchecked, these inclinations can foster an environment of ego-driven competition, undermining genuine connections with others. As vanquishers tread their path towards becoming passion-struck individuals, they grapple with specific vulnerabilities that hinder their personal advancement. These include a lack of introspection, resistance to change, a narrow perspective fixated on personal ambitions, a strained equilibrium between work and life, dependence on external validation, perfectionistic tendencies, and a struggle to find contentment. These weaknesses trace back to their relentless pursuit of success, often sidelining introspection, adaptability, empathy, well-being, and the appreciation of the present moment.

In their quest to become passion-struck individuals, vanquishers must acknowledge and address these potential weaknesses. Introspection becomes paramount, enabling them to connect with their own motivations and cultivate a more profound understanding of themselves. Embracing change, even when it challenges their well-established routines, is crucial for continued growth and adaptation. Balancing personal ambitions with holistic well-being and nurturing authentic connections with others fosters a more wholesome perspective. Overcoming perfectionist tendencies and the need for external validation liberates them to find fulfillment from within. By embracing these aspects of personal development, the vanquisher's journey towards passion-struck greatness becomes even more profound and transformative.

As Albert Einstein cautioned, "Strive not to be a success, but rather to be of value."

Common characteristics of this vanquisher stage include:

- Firm belief in the rule of law and earned authority.
- Unyielding drive and an insatiable desire to achieve their goals.
- Hubris, characterized by abundant pride, self-assurance, and a sense of self-importance.
- Honesty, duty, and loyalty form the pillars of their value system.
- Difficulty embracing originality and innovation, favoring what has traditionally worked.
- Tendency to hold strong convictions and be dogmatic, hindering openness to alternative possibilities.
- Strong focus on social status and adherence to societal norms.
- Struggle with expressing emotions and empathizing with others' happiness.
- Longing for recognition and compliments to uphold high self-esteem.

Approximately 25 to 30 percent of individuals likely belong to this stage.

The Orchestrator: Balanced and Visionary, Driving Systemic Change with Genuine Concern for the World

Orchestrators, distinguished by their independent and non-conformist nature, embark on a profound journey of personal discovery and entrepreneurial exploration. Possessing a strong sense of self, they chart their path guided by an unwavering belief in individuality, rather than conforming to societal norms. Fueled by a deep desire for authenticity, they question the status quo and seek innovative solutions to life's challenges, refusing to be confined by conventional expectations.

Their independence fuels entrepreneurial pursuits as they identify opportunities aligned with their passions and values. Orchestrators thrive in environments promoting creative freedom and autonomy, leveraging unique perspectives to drive meaningful change. Prioritizing self-exploration, they engage in introspection to understand desires, strengths, and values, aligning actions with authenticity. While their independent nature sets them apart, orchestrators also possess a deep connection to the world, fueling a drive for systemic change and a better world.

As author, athlete, and veteran Steve Maraboli notes, "Incredible change happens in your life when you decide to take control of what you have power over instead of craving control over what you don't." Orchestrators understand this wisdom, and they actively embrace the elements within their control to steer their journey towards a purposeful and impactful life.

Orchestrators, while on their path to becoming passion struck, face negative traits that can hinder their personal growth. They can become excessively idealistic, rigid, and resistant to alternative perspectives. Their strong beliefs may lead to stubbornness and righteousness, limiting their ability to learn and adapt. Orchestrators' drive for change can make them impatient and ruthless, sometimes neglecting self-care. Unrealistic expectations can create a cycle of disappointment and self-criticism. Delegation may be challenging for them, leading to an overwhelming workload.

However, orchestrators possess the capacity for profound self-awareness and introspection, which empowers them to overcome these challenges. By cultivating humility, open-mindedness, and self-reflection, they can navigate through their weaknesses and continue their journey with a greater sense of fulfillment and purpose.

Common characteristics of the orchestrator stage include:

- Independent and non-conformist nature, driven by a personal vision and mission.
- Focus on systemic change, progress, and genuine concern for the well-being of others and the world.
- Ability to integrate personal actions with organizational goals and build innovative solutions.
- Value discussion, cooperation, equality, and empathy in relationships.
- Openness to vulnerability, constructive criticism, and continuous self-growth.
- Awareness of opportunities and threats, with a conscious engagement with the world.
- Idealistic, seeing the uniqueness and potential in every situation.
- Commitment to simplicity, essential qualities, and relationship-building.
- Tendency to be stubborn or inflexible in their ideas, which can lead to conflicts with those who prefer the status quo.
- Potential for self-centeredness, unrealistic expectations, and a ruthless pursuit of goals without considering the consequences.

Approximately 15 to 20 percent of the population likely resides in this stage.

The Creative Amplifier: Conscious, Authentic, Humble, and Engaged with a World-Centric Perspective

The fifth stage, ahh. Last, but not least, there are creative amplifiers. I realize that when some people think of a creator, they see it as synonymous with someone who is artistically skilled or a designer. But that is not what we are talking about here. Instead, we are diving into the essence of their being, which enables them to transcend the confines of convention and unleash an unstoppable torrent of innovation and profound meaning.

These extraordinary individuals embody the pinnacle of the passion-struck transformation. Their very presence radiates inspiration, igniting a fire in the hearts of those fortunate enough to witness their transformative journey. Building upon the solid foundation of the orchestrator stage, they ascend to unprecedented heights, tapping into their power to drive change that reverberates across the globe.

What sets the creative amplifiers apart is their boundless ability to harness the collective consciousness. They do not merely seek personal achievements; their vision extends far beyond the confines of individual success. In their presence, ego dissolves, replaced by a noble devotion to the greater good. Their energy is channeled towards selfless initiatives, emanating compassion and catalyzing profound shifts in the lives of others.

At the fifth stage, their worldview expands exponentially, embracing humanity as one harmonious whole. They revere themselves, their fellow beings, the vast global tapestry, and the boundless universe itself. Every decision they make resonates with an awareness of the intricate web of interconnectedness, transcending artificial boundaries and embracing the inherent unity of all life. Their choices radiate with a profound reverence for the tapestry of existence, transcending personal desires to uplift the collective.

The pursuit of becoming a creative amplifier is the voyage towards an extraordinary destiny. It beckons us to transcend our limitations, embarking on a quest to forge a world steeped in unity and egalitarian principles. It calls for a bold commitment to unleash our inner creativity, aligning it with the transformative forces that shape our collective destiny.

Let us dare to dream, to imagine, and to amplify our creative potential, for it is through this profound metamorphosis that we shall set ablaze the world with the brilliance of our authentic selves. As Pakistani female-education activist Malala Yousafzai notes, "When the whole world is silent, even one voice becomes powerful."

Characteristics of the creative amplifier stage include:

- Possess the ability to go beyond established norms and break free from conventional thinking.
- Unleash a torrent of creativity, constantly generating new and groundbreaking ideas.
- Transformative energy captivates others, inspiring them to embark on their own journeys of self-discovery and growth.
- Driven by a deep sense of interconnectedness, harnessing the power of unity for the betterment of all.
- Boldly confront challenges and adversity, bouncing back stronger and more determined than before.
- Envision a world that transcends individual success, focusing on uplifting and empowering others.
- Push the limits of what is possible, venturing into uncharted territories of thought and action.
- Channel their creative energy towards selfless initiatives, fostering positive transformation in society.
- Hold profound respect for the inherent worth and dignity of every individual, fostering inclusivity and equality.
- Embody their true selves, fearlessly expressing their unique perspectives and gifts, inspiring others to do the same.

Approximately 5 percent to 7 percent of the population likely resides in this stage.

Unleashing Your Creative Amplifier: Embracing Passion, Purpose, and Intentional Growth

To truly become creative amplifiers, individuals must set aside their egos, refrain from judgment, and cultivate a mindset of openness. This involves embracing the role of perspective harnessers and recognizing the interconnectedness of all human beings, regardless of their backgrounds or beliefs. It is a state of self-realization, as we acknowledge our shared motivations, fears, and desires.

Henry Ward Beecher, an anti-slavery clergyman, wisely observed, "We should not judge people by their peak of excellence, but by the distance they have traveled from the point where they started."

In my recent interview on the *Passion Struck* podcast, Robin Sharma eloquently underscores the differentiation between those who aspire to greatness and those who genuinely personify it. He accentuates that while many individuals yearn for the rewards and acclaim associated with being world-class, they often fall short by neglecting the essential commitment and meticulousness required. Consequently, they opt for mediocrity.

Sharma begins by pointing out, "Too many people are in the majority. They want the rewards of world-class, but they're not doing what world-class requires. They mail it in. They don't do their work with exquisite attention to detail to make everything beautiful."

Whether it's athletes striving to become world champions, business professionals dedicated to their craft, or individuals committed to their faith, family, and personal habits, Sharma sheds light on the unwavering dedication of the top 5 percent: "They are devoted to their families, their habits, and their mission of making the world a better place. Furthermore, they possess the resilience to get up every time they fall down."

Setbacks do not deter these individuals; rather, they fuel their resolute commitment to continual improvement. They understand that true greatness is not a destination but a lifelong journey, driven by unwavering devotion and a constant embrace of growth. Through their unwavering dedication to their chosen path, they exemplify the essence of extraordinary achievement.

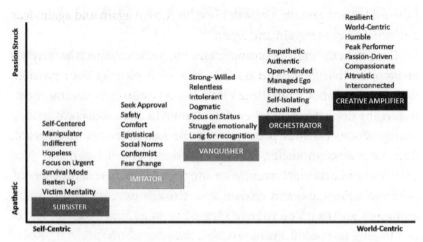

FIGURE 7: The five transition points with characteristics of each.

Becoming passion struck entails recognizing the significant impact our actions have on the world and making decisions that serve the greater good. This level of selflessness and broader perspective is only reached by a small percentage of the population. However, the goal of the passion-struck movement is to train millions of people to operate as world-centric creative amplifiers. As the great American author Mark Twain noted, "Twenty years from now, you will be more disappointed by the things that you didn't do than by the ones you did do. So throw off the bowlines. Sail away from the safe harbor. Catch the trade winds in your sails. Explore. Dream. Discover."[189]

Mark Twain's wise words remind us that we should prioritize taking action and pursuing our dreams to avoid future regrets.

Unleashing Your Passion: Embarking on a Transformative Journey Towards Becoming Passion Struck

Are you ready to embark on a transformative journey towards becoming passion struck? Imagine choosing growth over safety, just as Maslow wisely said: "One can choose to go back toward safety or forward toward growth. Growth must be chosen again and again; fear must be overcome again and again."

Throughout the upcoming chapters, we'll explore the physics of progress that guide you on this path of deploying your passion. Remember, it's not a one-time effort but a continuous commitment. It starts by decluttering your environment and consciously embracing change. Focus on your present reality and embrace transformation. Become a mission angler, identifying challenges that demand your attention and action. Nurture your mental and emotional well-being, confront your fears, and challenge social norms. Cultivate mindful awareness and examine your self-narrative, shedding toxic influences and freeing yourself for profound self-transformation.

Take that step back, chart your path towards growth and fulfillment. Embrace the process, cultivate resilience, and empower yourself to become passion struck. The transformation awaits, and the choice to embark on this extraordinary journey is yours. Don't wait— take action now!

Scan the QR code to take this short quiz to determine your own stage on your path to becoming passion struck.

CHAPTER 15

NEVER IGNORE THE PHYSICS
OF PROGRESS

*There is no passion to be found playing
small—in settling for a life that is less than
the one you are capable of living.*
—Nelson Mandela

have written extensively on the behavior and mindset shifts
required to become passion struck .[190] While there are many books
dedicated to exploring how you can discover your passion or purpose, there exists staggeringly little about the physics of progress—
how you deploy it. Why is this staggering? Well, simply put, putting
your passion into practice is the most challenging stage of your personal transformation, rendering it the most vital piece of the jigsaw
puzzle of becoming passion struck in your life and as a leader.[191]

Once you've found your passion or purpose, you must understand that there will be numerous roadblocks you'll need to overcome
to reach your final destination—that is where perseverance comes in.
The biggest of which is choosing to start. What may seem like a simple obstacle to overcome has been the undoing of many would-be
juggernauts. The unfortunate truth of the matter is that the most

incredible ideas in the world mean nothing without intentional focus and execution.

And yet, that's precisely where so many potential leaders fail, the very first hurdle. The reason? They ignored the most important law of physics—momentum.

Unlocking the Three Keys to an Extraordinary Life: Aspiration, Ambition, and Actions

In a transformative interview with renowned executive coach and bestselling author Marshall Goldsmith,[192] he shared profound insights about the three keys to living a truly extraordinary life. Goldsmith's words resonated powerfully:

> Aspiration, ambition, and actions—these three elements define a great life. Aspiration, the first key, compels us to ponder our purpose and the reason behind our existence on this earth. It extends far beyond simply showing up each day. Aspiration knows no finish line; it propels us to continually reach for something greater.
>
> The second key, ambition, aligns our aspirations with tangible achievements. Ambition drives us to set meaningful goals that contribute to our overarching aspirations. These goals provide the framework for our accomplishments, but they are not an endpoint in themselves. Rather, they serve as milestones on our journey towards fulfillment.
>
> However, it is in the third key, our actions, where the true essence of life resides. Our present actions— the choices we make, the steps we take—are what shape our reality. It is through our engagement in the day-to-day process of life itself that we manifest our aspirations and transform our ambitions into tangible outcomes.

Yet, amidst the vast game of life, many individuals find themselves lost in the action phase. They become consumed by the never-ending cycle of busyness, failing to align their actions with their aspirations and ambitions. In doing so, they lose sight of the greater purpose and potential that awaits them.

To lead an extraordinary life, it is imperative that we harmonize these three elements—aspiration, ambition, and actions. By ensuring their alignment, we tap into our innate capacity for greatness and fulfillment. We transcend the ordinary and embark on a journey of purpose, growth, and profound impact.

The First Step Is Making a Choice

It's important to understand that, when deploying your passion, you need to do whatever it takes to take the first step on your journey. The worst possible action you can take is none at all. One of the most powerful principles in physics is the law of momentum, which states that to change an object's equilibrium, you must first exert some force unto it. In the context of deploying your passion, it means making a start. I make no exaggeration by saying it's the single most critical thing you can do.

During our insightful interview, Robin Sharma beautifully encapsulated the essence of this concept: "The thousand-mile journey begins with a single step. It's easy to put icons like Kobe, Jordan, Ali, Mandela, Elon Musk, Oprah Winfrey, Serena Williams, and many others on a pedestal. One of the things a lot of people do, John, is they say, well, these people are just not like us. Or they say these people are cut from a different cloth. And the reality is, we all have gifts and natural talents. But the key is these people had an idea. And then they continually practiced. They stayed with the mission, day after day after day, until they went from being an amateur to a professional and a beginner to a master."

Think of it another way: Let's say you are driving a car, and it runs out of fuel. At this point, you have two options. First, you could sit in the car, put on your hazard lights, and hope that someone will come and help you (give up). Or you could choose the second option of opening the door, putting your shoulder against it, and beginning to push (take action). What you would notice is that the first yard is the hardest. Why? Because you have no momentum. But once you reach five, ten, one hundred yards down the road, suddenly you are rolling at a reasonable speed bound for the nearest gas station. The same is true of actively pursuing your purpose; the most challenging part of any journey of this nature is the first step. You need to remind yourself that you've got nothing to lose. You miss 100 percent of the shots you don't take.

Just look at the story of Jim McKelvey and Jack Dorsey. When they joined forces to explore the idea of creating the world's most accessible credit card processing company, it's not like there weren't any obstacles in the way. There were hundreds if not thousands of them. Neither of them had the answer to many of the issues that could have derailed Square in the early days. However, they made a start anyway. They tested ideas, scrapped what didn't work, pursued what did, and continued until they founded one of the biggest payment companies in the world. In my interview with Jim McKelvey, he put it this way:

> Taking that first step is really the hardest part. You're confronting one type of fear, which is the fear of incompetence. After that, you get a different type of fear, and that is the fear of survival: This isn't gonna work. This isn't working. I don't know what I'm doing, but this isn't working. It stays with you until you figure it out. That's the process. I have never found a shortcut. There's no guarantee of success.

You might well be wondering, what does that first move look like? In my mind, the first step should be (once you believe you've found your purpose) to test whether that hypothesis is correct or not, just as you would in a scientific environment. There is no right or wrong way to arrive at your final destination. There are no fixed roads or paths to be taken. The route you take will be continuously molded by your experiences, and pivoting is a natural progression of any entrepreneur's journey.

Remember, by continuously testing yourself, all you're doing is narrowing down the number of potential paths to success. Many things you may try might not work out. But that's fine. It still nudges you closer to your end goal. Each time you reach a dead end, just remember the words of Thomas Edison, who, at the time, was on his way to inventing the first commercially viable lightbulb: "I have not failed. I've just found ten thousand ways that won't work."

No, you might not write the best first article or run the best first race. But bear in mind that you will generally be the worst at anything you attempt for the first time. Just as in the case of the car, it's because you have no momentum. By accepting, or in fact, *anticipating* failure early on, you won't be put off your next attempt.

Using the example above, are you really going to stop trying to push the car because your first shove didn't work? No, of course not. With each attempt, you get the wheels to move a little more, and you learn that if you lean lower, you make more progress. Before you know it, you've gone from a helpless amateur to the best car pusher you know. That's because with repetition comes maturity, knowledge, and acquired wisdom. You'll obtain precisely none of these traits if you never make a start.

The Power of Inputs: Achieving Your Aspirations through Micro Wins

At the heart of our journey towards passion-struck living lies the understanding that momentum can drive us forward or leave us stranded. It's not mere motivation that propels us; it's genuine passion that continually fuels our actions and enables us to overcome our fears. This vital distinction between passion and motivation is the reason why many aspiring success stories lose momentum.

As an entrepreneur, I've experienced moments where I felt stuck and lost my forward momentum. Upon reflection, I realized that these times of stagnation arose from an imbalance in my approach. I had been focusing too much on the end results, the outputs, rather than the inputs that drive me toward my aspirations. What do I mean by that? Outputs are specific targets or goals, while inputs are the actions and decisions we make daily to achieve them. Choosing intentionally is the essence of this power. Small choices may seem insignificant, but they lead to remarkable outcomes when practiced consistently.

This understanding is rooted in the recognition of an incredible power we possess—the power of choice. Think of these intentional choices as micro wins—the small victories that create a big impact over time. We can choose to rise a little earlier tomorrow morning, prioritizing a workout over extra sleep. We can choose to nourish our bodies with clean, energy-boosting food. We can choose to go to work and exceed expectations, delivering more than what is asked of us. We can choose to return home and fully engage with our loved ones, listening and connecting with them. We can choose to spend a few moments before bed reading and expanding our knowledge.

These choices, explored extensively in Chapter 7, may appear small and seemingly insignificant at first. However, when practiced consistently over time, these moments of intentional choice yield remarkable outcomes. It is not the once-a-year endeavors that truly make a difference; rather, it is the daily choices we make, day in and day out, that shape our lives and pave the path to success.

By embracing the power of choice and recognizing the impact of our daily actions, we empower ourselves to create a meaningful and fulfilling life. Each intentional decision, regardless of its size, holds the potential to contribute to our growth and progress. For instance, during my time as a successful runner in high school and college, I learned a valuable lesson: outputs are unattainable unless we remain focused on the inputs.[193] No runner merely turns up at the Olympic trials expecting to run a 2:15 marathon or sub-four-minute mile. They've all trained relentlessly over the weeks, months, and years leading up to the race. Rather than obsessing over the time they need to hit or the position they need to finish, they have focused everything on their inputs, knowing that the outputs will subsequently take care of themselves.

I refer to these as micro wins—those small victories that are often overlooked because they seem too easy. However, if we observe the habits of exceptional athletes, we'll notice that they make every workout count, optimizing each session.

This emphasis on inputs is not limited to athletics. Consider the most successful running nation on planet Earth—Kenya. It's a lifestyle. Kenyan's national mantra of "train hard, win easy" epitomizes what it means to focus on the inputs (train hard) rather than the outputs (winning races). It is the same mantra that Mark Divine, Chris Cassidy, and Jesse Iwuji, who I discussed earlier, employ. Toby Tanser, author of the best-selling book *Train Hard, Win Easy: The Kenyan Way*,[194] coined the phrase after moving to Kenya to participate in the elite Kenyans' training sessions. He noted that they appeared to work harder than he did in training, to a level of near exhaustion. Then, when the race approached, they performed with ease.

This exemplifies how consistency becomes the catalyst for mastery. Each day presents an opportunity for incremental improvements in the areas that matter most to us. Over time, these seemingly insignificant steps generate tremendous momentum, often unnoticed in the moment. It may be months later when we suddenly realize that we have arrived at a completely new and transformative place in our journey. The focus on inputs applies to every aspect of life—relationships, wellness, and work. Your outputs are a sum of the inputs that came before them.

As we journey towards our aspirations, we must recognize that the path is not linear, nor is it one-size-fits-all. It's a commitment to consistently making intentional choices that propel us forward. Reverse-engineering the inputs needed to achieve our desired outcomes empowers us to chart a clear and purposeful path. Embrace the power of inputs and be prepared to adapt and refine them along the way. Your aspirations will guide your choices, and as you adjust your inputs, you'll witness the transformation taking shape. Your dedication to micro wins will bridge the gap between where you are now and where you aspire to be.

It is through the collective force of micro wins, fueled by passion, that we achieve our aspirations and embrace a life of fulfillment and purpose. Dare to dream, take intentional action, and celebrate each micro win as you journey towards passion-struck living—a life where you leave an indelible mark on the world.

Time Can Always Be Expanded

As explained, most individuals who manage to discover their passion fail to take action. The number one excuse? Yep, you guessed it. Time. How often have you heard someone say, "I would love to pursue X, but I just don't have the time." Many people believe this fallacy because they feel that time is a finite or fixed construct. However, I am of the opinion that time can be expanded. If you are willing to change your perspective, like I covered in Chapter 6 discussing Navy Seal and astronaut Chris Cassidy, you can literally expand time. Don't believe me? Let me give you an example.

I was a reasonably accomplished high school runner by the time I graduated. However, prior to the year we won the team state championship, I would often just go through the motions when I went for a run. I was progressing, but nowhere near as much as I had hoped. Looking back, I realize I was training for my teammates and not for me in many ways. When many of the high-profile athletes graduated, something changed. I started running for myself. I wanted to do everything to become the best runner I could be and be as flawless as I could become. I worked on my form, my breathing, and dedicated hours and hours to getting better at hill climbing for the cross-country season.

It was as if time had expanded as I aligned my actions, aspirations, and ambition. I acted with an urgency that made one hour feel more like five. Other times, thirty minutes on a run could feel like five. I was a young man on a mission. By embedding myself in every part of the process and looking for growth and progress, I was able to change my entire mindset. It made me realize that I could expand time when I truly was passionate about pursuing something.

Though on a completely different scale, my experience resembles Michael Jordan's. In case you were unaware, Jordan did not start life as a basketball prodigy. Far from it, in fact. As a high school athlete, he was more accomplished as a baseball player. When the varsity basketball team was announced his sophomore year, he found out that he had lost out to his much taller friend, Leroy Smith, a six-foot-seven forward. Embarrassed, hurt, and angry, Jordan threw everything he could into becoming a better basketball player. He would get up at 5 a.m. every day to squeeze in three hours of extra practice before school started. Within a year, he had earned his roster spot back. The rest, as they say, is history.

This incredible work ethic and expansion of time would last throughout the rest of his career. Even on game day, where players met up for a throw around at 10 a.m. or 11 a.m., he would start workouts with his personal trainer as early as 5 a.m. He was so eager to get started on many occasions that his personal trainer would arrive to find Jordan had already completed most of the workout.[195] It's the reason that, at age thirty-five, he managed to play 103 total games while averaging over thirty-nine minutes per game during the 1997–1998 season. In the twenty-two seasons that have followed, no player aged thirty-five or above has played as many minutes. Many think that nobody ever will. Jordan always found a way to expand time to meet his deep desire to become the best, and it's a practice that kept him at the top, even in the twilight of his career.

If Michael Jordan and I found a way to expand time, so can you, even if that means finding a mere extra hour each day to dedicate to learning a new skill or building a business. The point is, if you change your perspective and dedicate your very being to your passion, time will naturally expand for you. Pockets of slack will appear in your schedule that you didn't know existed. Suddenly, you can cram the equivalent of a whole day's work for your employer into the lunch hour you spend on your business.

The Power of Transformative Change

When pursuing your passion, it's not just about pouring your energy into the right actions or expanding time; it's about embracing intentional transformation. For example, if you want to lose weight by improving your diet and exercising, it's not just about showing up for workouts and eating fewer snacks. It's about fundamentally altering your identity and how you define yourself. It's transitioning from a night owl to an early bird and shifting from emotional eating to mindful consumption.

This is where many falter in unleashing their passion. They get stuck trying to take new actions without changing the habits and behaviors that have defined them until now. I experienced this as a CIO at Dell, where my self-identity was tied to my role. When I became the CEO of Genius Central, I had to undergo a monumental mindset shift to carry out my duties effectively. But the power lies within us to make these changes. The self-narrative in our minds is malleable. Just like Hilary Swank views herself as a storyteller of the human race, we have the power to redefine ourselves as we see fit.

Yet, many are held back from becoming passion-struck by their fear of leaving their comfort zones. They shy away from the optimal anxiety required for success and avoid sink-or-swim situations. The fear of failure becomes a barrier to fulfilling their purpose. Starting the journey is one thing, but without reimagining your self-narrative, you may never reach the end of your pursuit.

Embrace the power of transformation. Embody the person you need to become to live your passion fully. Shed the old skin of familiarity and venture into the realm of optimal anxiety. In this space, you'll discover the true depths of your potential and realize that the pursuit of your passion is a journey worth embarking on and seeing through to the end. The power is in your hands alone to redefine yourself and become passion-struck. So, take that leap of faith and embrace the transformation that awaits you.

Putting It All Together by Embracing Transformation: From Confinement to Catalyst

Nate Dukes, like many people, grew up in poverty in a small town. After graduating college, he and a friend took a failing business and turned it into something very successful over two years. It allowed him to become the entrepreneur he was on the inside, but it also touched on the party scene that he had developed in college. Dukes had access to more money than he had ever seen in his life. It wasn't a crazy amount of money, but it felt like the world to him as the poor kid growing up. He bought a great car, had a large apartment downtown with high-rise ceilings, and was in social settings that he had never had access to before. And he thought all this stuff was going to make him happy.

Then life started to catch up with his lifestyle and his decisions. He found himself going to casinos and gambling because he was chasing the next high. That is when things went from bad to worse. He started to embezzle money from his own business to feed a growing drug and gambling addiction. His co-business owner ultimately caught Dukes stealing from the company and forced him to terminate his ownership in the business. His misfortune didn't end there.

It was a humbling experience. Dukes became extremely depressed and was experiencing an intense form of anxiety, as he was still dealing with a drug and gambling addiction and could hardly hold down a job. At that point, he decided he wanted to escape everything, stole a car, and was on his way to Houston to visit a friend when he stopped outside Nashville and fell asleep in the stolen vehicle. He was awakened a few hours later by a loud knocking on his window and a police officer pulling him out of the vehicle.

Burdened by the weight of every decision he had ever made, it felt as if a ton of bricks rested upon his chest. The recurring thought echoed in his mind, an echo of what his business partner and others in his life had told him: "You'll never change." The consequences of his choices became evident as Nate found himself confined to the Cheatham County Jail for the following six months.

Within those confining walls, a profound realization struck him. The life he had been living was not the life he truly desired. The experience of incarceration, facing the consequences of felony theft and the ensuing probation, served as a powerful catalyst for change. It compelled him to reassess his path and make a decision that would redefine his future.

Nate understood that his journey toward becoming passion struck (see Figure 8) and a catalyst of transformation would require unwavering dedication, deep self-reflection, and a commitment to personal growth. He yearned to unlock his true purpose, to unearth the unique contribution he could make to the world. Each step he took on this journey would bring him closer to discovering the extraordinary possibilities that lay ahead.

	SUBSISTER	IMITATOR	VANQUISHER	ORCHESTRATOR	CREATIVE AMPLIFIER
MISSION ANGLER		X	X	X	X
BRAND REINVENTOR		X	X	X	X
MOSQUITO AUDITOR			X	X	X
FEAR CONFRONTER			X	X	X
PERSPECTIVE HARNESSER			X	X	X
ACTION CREATOR			X	X	X
ANXIETY OPTIMIZER				X	X
ORIGINALITY EMBRACER				X	X
BOUNDARY EXPANDER				X	X
OUTWARD INSPIRER					X
GARDENER LEADER					X
CONSCIOUS ENGAGER					X

FIGURE 8: Illustrative mapping of the passion-struck framework stages of development to the transition points on the passion-struck journey.

Upon completing his sentence, Nate seized the opportunity to return to his hometown in Ohio. This new chapter marked the beginning of a transformative journey, as he shared in our discussion. With unwavering determination, he embarked on the next steps, eager to shape a different future for himself:

> When I got home, I got obsessed with how do you change as a person. And, I started reading books, and I found a John Maxwell book that said, "If you want your world around you to change, you've got to be the one that changes first." And I became obsessed with this mantra and with personal development. I started to focus on how I become the best version of myself emotionally, mentally, spiritually. How do I become the best version financially? How do I become the best version physically?
>
> I committed a year to try to become the best version of myself. Because the truth was if I wanted to go back to the way I was living—taking advantage of people, hurting, stealing, drugs, gambling—I could always do that. I could always go back. But, what would happen to my life if I made the right choices using the right inputs? I found some mentors in these areas of my life, and then, several years removed from that, my life looked nothing like it used to.[196]

Dukes started his journey as a subsister. By facing the stark reality that was staring him in the face, he took steps to craft a new mission for his life and to discover a novel problem to solve (mission angler). With this newfound perspective, he embarked on the process of reinventing his life, implementing incremental changes to redefine his identity as a brand reinventor. From there, he started to perform a mosquito audit. Nate explains it like this:

> It's not until we start to let go of bad influences that we're open to receiving new ones. And so when I began to talk about this, people were saying, "Nate, are you telling me I have to walk away from some of my friends, I have to give up on people?" And for some of us? Yes, absolutely. It is the permission that you need to walk away from a toxic friendship, a toxic relationship, a toxic habit that is pulling you away from the direction and the purpose that God intends you to fulfill. It's doing more damage to you by sticking around and playing it safe. You are robbing yourself of the future that you deserve by staying in the same circle. And once we do that audit, now we've opened up ourselves to new connections, new relationships, and new people that can bring new ideas, adventures, and ways of living through a new mindset.

From here, Dukes started to confront his fears, changed his perspective, and began to take deliberate daily actions to change his life. It's important to understand that it is not information that changes anybody. It's how you apply the knowledge and the actions we take behind the information. But, if you are going to take action and have a desire to change your life, you need to know why and what you're changing your life to look like in the end. It's essential to have a clear vision for your life and alter your perspective of how you see things in the future. But, once you do, it's about knowing the daily inputs that take you there. Nate summarizes his journey:

> I know what my life looks like when I make the wrong decisions. What I don't know is what ten years from my life look like when I'm making the right decisions.

Ten years in the future, my life could look completely different as long as I stay on this path. See, who I was is not who I am now.

If you're looking to change, there's something beautiful about being at the bottom because you get this opportunity to now build your life back brick by brick. When I wanted to make some changes, I knew that I had to start to repair the relationship that I had with myself. So the most important relationship in my life is the one with God. But second to that, it's the relationship that I have with me. It's even more important than the relationship that I have with my wife. Because when I'm good with me, I'm a better husband. When I'm good with myself, I'm a better friend. When things are good with me, I'm a better leader. And so I had to invest in this relationship with myself.

It is our intentional choices at any given point in time that determine our destiny. I want you to think about your life right now:

- What city do you live in?
- What is the relationship you have?
- What career have you chosen?
- What is your physical and mental health?
- What is your spiritual health?

The answers to these questions are not based on one single decision but on multiple choices that led you to this point. And, if you start altering your inputs and confronting your fears, like Nate Dukes, you can change your destination.

But now comes the most challenging part. You have to multiply all of the choices that you take by "time." The harshest word any of us are going to hear is "waiting." That is why you have to be willing to commit to your journey over a long period. Figure 9 shows the typical path that is taken when looking at time versus results.

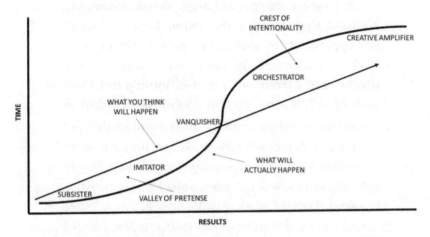

FIGURE 9: In the beginning, choosing to change requires a great deal of effort and the motivation to perform. Over time, it starts to magnify through conscious engagement, and the behavior becomes more automatic. Actions start stacking on each other, and the impact begins to magnify.

The passion-struck framework encompasses various stages that guide us towards living an intentional life. It begins with having a clear vision, followed by making informed decisions that align with our goals and values. Along the way, we must confront our fears and insecurities, finding the strength to overcome them.

Rebranding ourselves is another vital aspect of the journey, as we redefine our identity and align it with our passion and purpose. Time becomes a multiplier, allowing us to make progress and grow steadily over the long term. Surrounding ourselves with the right voices and influences positively impacts our mindset and beliefs, propelling us forward.

Changing our perspective is crucial, as it enables us to see opportunities where others might see obstacles. Finally, taking action is the key that unlocks the potential for transformation and propels us towards living a purposeful and intentional life.

When we embrace these stages of the passion-struck framework, we unlock our potential to create a life filled with meaning, fulfillment, and joy. It is through these intentional actions that we move closer to realizing our dreams and living a life that truly resonates with our authentic selves.

Unleashing Your Potential: The Alchemy of Ambition, Actions, and Aspiration in the Physics of Progress

Once you have unlocked the depths of your purpose, a new chapter in your life begins—a personal journey of experimentation and exploration. This is the time to test your hypotheses and identify the key inputs that will pave the way to your success. But the question lingers: What actions should you take to manifest your highest visions?

The answer lies in expanding your horizons beyond yourself and extending your influence to your communities. Embrace the interconnectedness of all life, for in these shared spaces, you possess the power to illuminate darkness with your light and touch the lives of strangers with your kindness. By engaging in inspiring endeavors and enriching the lives of others, you not only elevate yourself but also leave a lasting positive impact on those you encounter.

The journey towards an intentional life is not a solitary pursuit. Through incremental steps and unwavering commitment, you become a catalyst in the collective effort of building a brighter and better world. As you align your ambition with actions that empower and uplift, you bridge the gap between aspiration and reality. Your limited days should not be wasted, but used to intentionally create a life that resonates with purpose and meaning.

To become the future leader that the world needs, it's crucial to shift from a mindset of "fixed equilibrium" to "growth potential." Take stock of areas in your life that feel stagnant and identify your strengths and weaknesses both personally and professionally. Then, ask yourself: What would happen if I chose to expand beyond my current limitations? What steps can I take today to uncover new skills, talents, and connections that will facilitate my growth?

Embracing progress may feel uncertain and intimidating, but true innovation never arises from the mundane and status quo. You are in control of your life's alchemy, where ambition, actions, and aspiration blend to create transformative progress. Take the wheel and start paving new roads towards self-discovery, excellence, and fulfillment.

These insights are meant to illuminate the path of pursuing your purpose with clarity and conviction, empowering you to navigate life's course with ambition and aspiration as your guiding stars. As the old Chinese proverb wisely reminds us, "The best time to plant a tree was twenty years ago. The second-best time is now." It's never too late to take action and start creating the life you truly desire, where the alchemy of ambition, actions, and aspiration propels you towards an intentional and fulfilling life.

CHAPTER 16

PERFECT THE BEE-AND-TURTLE
EFFECT BY DREAMING BIG
AND PLANNING SMALL

Have patience. All things are difficult
before they become easy.
—Saadi

Studying passion-struck individuals has revealed a compelling pattern—fearless risk-taking. These trailblazers understand that thinking small won't change the world, and they are driven by the ambition to achieve their grandest goals. As I discussed in Chapter 7 while exploring the remarkable journey of Wendy Lawrence, becoming passion struck begins with granting yourself permission to dream boldly. However, dreaming big is just the first step; the real test lies in transforming those dreams into reality. It is in this transition from dreaming to delivering that true greatness is forged.

Earlier in my career, when I was a senior executive at Lowe's, my boss at the time, Steve Stone (who was Lowe's CIO),[197] gave me some excellent advice. In a one-on-one session, I remember to this day when he told me, "You know John, the vast majority of people completely miss envisaging the big picture and its strategic importance in life or their career because they lack patience."

What did he mean by that, you ask? He was referring to the fact that most people rarely look beyond the near future or the next couple of years and embrace their self-identity with renewed originality. It could be a professional athlete who fails to plan for life after sports. Or a pastor who concentrates on his weekly sermons but doesn't plan for her congregation's future growth. Or the CEO who places immense scrutiny on quarterly results while not contemplating emerging future competitive threats to the company's core products and their next chapters.

Stone posited that the best leaders picture what things may look like in the next five, eight, ten years, or longer into the future. He knew that through experience. During our time working together, a complete transformation of the way Lowe's approached customer experience and how it competed using data was his brainchild. Stone realized that creating change in a Fortune 500 organization, like Lowe's, doesn't happen on a dime; it takes incredible patience and persistence.

In our session, Stone told me that I am one of the few who possess the ability as a core and natural strength. He also advised that this ability could be a threat to others if not used correctly. He told me that I needed to learn how to harness its power. "The trick," he said, "is to lead people to the destination. Set reasonable goals and lay them out in bite-size, achievable chunks that you evaluate and refine. It's all about taking deliberate, intentional action. The more wins you have as they achieve these chunks, the more momentum, and eventually success, you will have achieving the bigger goal." This wisdom is just as valid in one's personal life as in a career.

Visionaries like Steve Stone epitomize the delicate equilibrium between swift, present actions and the patient pursuit of far-reaching objectives. By wholeheartedly embracing this bee-and-turtle effect, you possess the means to actualize your passion, ascend to expertise, and ultimately realize your fullest potential. This pivotal approach transforms your aspirations from mere dreams into tangible, impactful reality, etching an indelible mark on the canvas of the world around you.

To echo the timeless words of General David Petraeus, "I think leadership encompasses four critical tasks. Whether you're the commander in Iraq or Afghanistan, or the CEO of the Carlyle Group or KKR or Amazon, you have to get the big ideas right. You have to communicate those big ideas effectively through the breadth and depth of your organization. You have to oversee the implementation. And you have to determine how to refine the big ideas—and then do it all over again." This cyclical, deliberate action process is at the core of what I call the bee-and-turtle effect, a compass guiding you toward purposeful action and the realization of your loftiest dreams.

Combining Bees and Turtles to Change the World

Bees and turtles are diametrically different creatures, yet some of the greatest entrepreneurs, athletes, actors, and leaders borrow traits from both to create massive change and competitive advantage.

Bees, particularly worker honeybees, are widely known for being busy and productive throughout their days. Worker honeybees spend nearly their entire day, every day, outside,[198] making more than a hundred foraging trips per day.[199] They are laser-focused on the day's mission and work tirelessly to make their short-term goals a reality.

On the other hand, there is the turtle. Sea turtles are known for going on some of the longest migrations in the world. These migrations are critical, as they are often migrating between foraging and nesting grounds.[200] The journeys are quite long—sometimes thousands of miles—yet they keep this long-term objective in their minds as they grow and reproduce with unending patience.[201]

Let's say you want to elevate yourself from a rookie real estate agent into a millionaire property mogul within twenty years. On the surface, that transition feels so nebulous. But break it down into small achievable goals (like the bees), and suddenly you have a clear and unequivocal roadmap laid out before you.

As the Chinese philosopher Lao-Tzu famously postulated: "A journey of a thousand miles starts with a single step."

Thus, focus your initial energy on breaking your dream down into those steps. In this example, each step taken (such as saving up enough to buy your first investment property), would nudge you closer toward the end destination. With each completed step, your self-belief will grow; and once you're over halfway, you'll feel unstoppable. It's using the physics of progress to maximize your daily energy in an intentional way.

However, the journey won't always be plain sailing, and it takes the turtle's patience. Throughout this volume, I've delved into how there is going to be hardship, there is going to be failure, you are going to doubt yourself, you will feel like giving up, but that's all part of the journey and dark days it takes to reach your dream's endpoint.

If you don't have long-term goals, you run the risk of doing lots of little things every day—cleaning the house, sending emails, catching up on TV—without ever making a contribution to your future. That can leave you feeling restless and unfulfilled. It's the big-picture things that give life meaning.

Given this as a backdrop, it's useful to treat this chapter as a space to explore the lessons that I have learned from a passion-struck leader who perhaps has the most significant dream there is: to save humanity from itself.

Don't Be Afraid to Dream Big Like the Turtle

Elon Musk is such a unique and talented entrepreneur for countless reasons, and I have genuinely relished our interactions. Among his remarkable traits, his acute sense of maximizing daily output and unyielding patience towards astonishingly high long-term goals stand out. Famously disdainful of excessive meetings,[202] Musk chooses to immerse himself in technical and engineering tasks, squeezing the most from every day. During Tesla's Model 3 sedan ramp-up, he slept on the factory floor,[203] tackling production challenges and outworking even his employees.

Yet, it's not just about today for Musk; he keeps his sights firmly set on tomorrow. Dreams of a mission to Mars and multiplanetary societies drive him, and he perseveres with unwavering patience, working on short-term goals that inch closer to his audacious aspirations.

In a conversation with TED talk curator Chris Anderson, Musk passionately revealed the core of his life's purpose: "There have to be reasons that get you up in the morning and make you want to live. Why do you want to live? What's the point? What inspires you? What do you love about the future? If the future does not include being out there among the stars and being a multi-planet species, I find that incredibly depressing."[204]

His grand vision transcends conventional boundaries, seeking to revolutionize humanity's state with space travel and renewable living. Critics may question its feasibility, but Musk insists it fuels his passion and purpose, driving him forward with an unwavering sense of mission. With unyielding determination, little by little, Musk advances towards his extraordinary ambition, proving that a powerful blend of daily output and enduring patience can unlock even the most audacious dreams.

Understanding How the Bee-and-Turtle Effect Enabled SpaceX to Win the "Race Back to Space"

A decade ago, when the commercial space program was born, few experts gave the fledgling startup, SpaceX, little if any hope of taking on the Boeing behemoth in the "race to return to space." However, with the first launch of a privately owned, manned spacecraft, Elon Musk and SpaceX changed history forever and took a giant leap towards a mission to Mars. It is a perfect illustration of the bee-and-turtle effect and a defining moment for Musk.

During one of my discussions with former NASA astronaut Captain Wendy Lawrence, she told a fascinating story about Elon Musk and SpaceX that rarely gets much attention. It all started in 2006 at the onset of the Commercial Orbital Transportation Services (COTS) program.[205] Musk forever changed history by using the bee-and-turtle effect to win the race back to space. As Lawrence revealed,

> When it was clear from President Bush that the shuttle was going to be retired, NASA set up a division to go figure out commercial spaceflight and provide commercial companies the opportunity to provide services to NASA. The commercial program leaders had the foresight to structure the statement of work so that companies could bid on delivering cargo if they wanted to. And, they could also bid to develop the spacecraft to carry crew members back and forth from the ISS.

And that is precisely the approach Elon Musk took—*he did them both simultaneously.*

SpaceX made a decision to design the Dragon spacecraft so that it not only could be used to carry cargo, but SpaceX also modified some of the systems for crewed flight. SpaceX looked at capsule design capability and determined that it could develop an overall outside design for capsule profiles that would allow it to modify it for the crew. That is why SpaceX is so much further along than Boeing. SpaceX decided to do the entire scope of work upfront so Dragon can be used for both functions without a significant number of changes. It was ingenious.

Using the power of the bee-and-turtle effect, Musk created the long-term goal of crewed flight while also focusing on maximizing daily output along the way. By doing so, when it came to the task of flying astronauts, SpaceX created an edge. Because it focused on daily micro steps, it's been flying cargo and supplies to the space station since 2012, giving it much practice (over 266 flights as of August

2023[206]) in launching spacecraft to orbit and having them meet up and dock with the station.

SpaceX today is widely recognized as the world's most successful private space company and is eclipsing the "sure bet" Boeing with significantly less funding. As Musk explains: "What I am trying to do is to make a significant difference in spaceflight and help make spaceflight accessible to almost anyone."

The company combined the bees' short-term goals and agile work ethic (cargo delivery) and coupled it with the slower long-term approach of the turtle (crewed exploration). As a result, Musk is almost single-handedly leading the charge to land humans on the moon and later Mars through SpaceX.

Understanding the Vital Importance of Achievable Goals

Earlier, I mentioned my mentor's wisdom in breaking down gargantuan goals into smaller bite-size chunks. Musk doesn't just believe in the bee-and-turtle effect, he lives and breathes it.

Take his overarching aim of transforming the human race into an interplanetary species, for example. What may look like sizeable projects in their own right—Tesla, SpaceX, SolarCity, The Boring Company, Neuralink, and Starlink—are all, in fact, the corner pieces of his much larger jigsaw puzzle of taking us to Mars.

Musk takes each of those smaller component parts and splits them down even further into time-sensitive goals. Each company has long-range objectives that are worked back into ten-year, five-year, and one-year targets. For example, Musk has insisted that SpaceX won't go public via an IPO until it is regularly flying to Mars.[207] That remains at least twenty years off, if not more. But that goal already has clear steps attached to it. The first of which was taken by landing the first reusable rocket (one-year target). The next step is the first unmanned mission to Mars by 2024 (five-year target),[208] followed by taking the first manned mission to Mars before 2030 (ten-year target).[209]

He famously takes the same approach to his personal life, with his days broken down into five-minute chunks.[210] Not only does this approach to time help to achieve his primary objective of the day, week, or month, it's also the secret behind his renowned productivity. Breaking your targets down into smaller time-sensitive ambitions will not only help you achieve them, it will help you to arrive at your end goal *faster*.

By breaking down his day into five-minute intervals, he uses Parkinson's law to his advantage. Parkinson's law stipulates that work expands to fill the time available for its completion.[211] That's why you find yourself filing your taxes a few days before the deadline every year, despite the fact you had twelve months to do so. By only giving himself a few minutes for each task, he accelerates his progress towards his goals. Instead of taking an hour for lunch, he takes five minutes. Catching up on emails? Five minutes. Unless there's an urgent issue, his involvement in business meetings rarely exceeds five minutes, and they are limited to four to six key individuals.[212]

Does that mean that everything he does is a five-minute task? Of course not. Does he ever fail to meet his daily, weekly, or even yearly objectives despite his relentless near-superhuman efforts? Of course, he does. Musk realizes that failures and near misses are just part and parcel of the journey. Like many other passion-struck leaders, he actually spends a great deal of his time seeking out failure as opposed to avoiding it.

Failure Is Part of the Journey for Those Who Are Passion Struck

Many people give up at the first sign of failure. But to be truly successful, you must embrace failure. My friend and peer, the now-deceased Steve Shirley, would always say in our staff meetings (and it drove the aforementioned Stone nuts): "We need to fail fast and fail often. For it is from these small failures that we learn, adjust, and improve."

In other words, failure is where the real lessons are learned, and the real improvements are made. Musk shares the same attitude towards failure as my peer did. Throughout SpaceX's existence, there have been multiple problems and failures. From missed platforms,[213] exploding boosters, and failed landings, the road toward economical spaceflight has been a rocky one, to say the least. But Musk accepted early on that failure was part of making progress. In fact, he conceived the SpaceX venture after witnessing a disastrous rocket engine test event, as co-founder Jim Cantrell explains:

> [Rocketeer] John Garvey had taken him for a tour of all his friends' homes in the fall of 2001. They even took him out for a rocket engine test and they blew the rocket up, right there on the test stand. Elon was not deterred by all of this. He suddenly realized that, hey, if you guys with pocket change can build rockets in your garage, then what can we do with real money and Silicon Valley-style leadership? That's where Elon really got his inspiration. He had like a religious conversion at this rocket test.[214]

Back in 2016, SpaceX failed to land a Falcon 9 rocket on a barge, striking the robotic ship in the Atlantic Ocean, eventually exploding. Musk's response? "We didn't expect this one to work (very hot re-entry), but the next flight has a great chance."

Just let that sink in for a moment. SpaceX, which on average, burns through $57 million per launch,[215] deliberately set up a mission that was almost certain to fail. And it did so willingly. Musk and his co-founders realize that you literally *have* to fail before you can succeed. Theorizing can only get you so far. Eventually, you need to give something a try, even if it's almost certain to fail, as Musk explains in an interview about dealing with early failure at SpaceX:

> There's a ton of failures along the way, that is for sure. For SpaceX, the first three launches failed. And we were just barely able to scrape together enough parts

to make the fourth launch. If that fourth launch would have failed, we would have been dead. I tried very hard to find the expertise for SpaceX. I tried hard to find a great chief engineer for the rocket, but the good chief engineers wouldn't join, and the bad ones, there is no point in hiring them. So, I ended up being chief engineer for the rocket. So, if I could have found somebody better, then we would have had maybe less than three failures.[216]

You can then—literally, in the case of SpaceX—pick apart the wreckage and ascertain what went wrong and assess the adjustments that need to be made for the next attempt. I mentioned this same observation when describing Thomas Edison and his pursuit of the lightbulb. However, underestimate the power of that momentum at your peril. Carving up life goals into their component parts dramatically affects your mindset.

If you're mulling over pursuing a new idea, I encourage you try it out. Test your hypothesis and don't be afraid to fail. Instead, expect to fail, and fail often, so that you can subsequently adapt and evolve. Don't frame mistakes and missteps as failures, but as lessons. You rarely achieve any qualification in life (such as a degree) without first attending lessons. So why would you expect to complete the qualification of attaining your goal without first taking those vital opportunities to learn?

I'm not going to sugarcoat it for you; if you have some big dreams, there are going to be severe bumps along the road. The bigger the vision, the harder it is to achieve it. Every successful person in life has been knocked back at some point. Remember, these setbacks represent just a few small, but necessary, steps that you need to take on your much bigger journey. So, embrace them, and come back stronger.

Passion-Struck Leaders Build Support Networks Just Like Bees in a Hive

Success is never achieved alone. Without the help of those around you, it's going to be very difficult to achieve your aspirations. Without a support network that Elon Musk could rely on, it's a genuine possibility that neither Tesla nor SpaceX would be here today.

After personally netting $22 million and $165 million from the sale of Zip2 and X.com respectively, he invested everything he had into both Tesla and SpaceX. Each business was running smoothly until the financial crash of 2008 put both of his companies on the line. To compound matters, during the latter half of the same year, Musk went through a costly divorce from his first wife, Justine.

He responded by pouring everything he had left in cash reserves into the businesses to keep them afloat. At the peak of his personal and company-wide crisis, he had so little money to his name that he had to ask close friends and family for money to buy the most basic of living essentials.[217] He could have opted for voluntary liquidation of the companies and returned most of that money to investors, which many would have deemed as smart at the time considering the losses everyone was incurring on the stock market. But he didn't. He risked it all by placing a bet on himself to get each company out of the mess in which they found themselves. His relationships, his reputation, his own wealth, and the wealth of others was all on the line.

Today we can safely say it was a gamble that paid off. But it takes a specific type of person to take those kinds of risks; to be so laser-focused on the mission that everything else pales into significance. Those types of people are passion-struck leaders.

Nevertheless, even passion-struck leaders who are willing to risk it all need the support network provided by close friends and family. If he had tried to go it alone, there's almost no doubt that neither company would exist today, and who knows what effect it would have had on him as a person. It was with the encouragement and emotional and financial support of his closest friends, colleagues, and mentors that he managed to soldier on.

When it comes to your own aspirations, those in your close prox-imity can pick you up during the darkest moments and carry you for-ward when you feel like giving up. With that in mind, it's important not to operate in a bubble. Talk to those you care about most about your journey, heed their advice, and use them as a sounding board for your ideas. The emotional aspect of going on a journey towards achieving your dream is often underplayed. For passion-struck lead-ers, their goal becomes their very being, and without anyone to share those trials and tribulations with, the road can become incredibly lonely and challenging.

Trials and tribulations can also become pivotal to your motiva-tion, which will undoubtedly wax and wane with your setbacks and accomplishments, which nicely dovetails with my next point.

Like a Turtle, Motivation Doesn't Always Come Easy, Even for Passion-Struck Leaders

Achieving your dream is a long process. For most, it takes a lifetime of work to get there. In the U.S., the average person lives until 78.69 years of age.[218] Over the 28,742 days we're on this planet, do you think we are unwaveringly motivated to work on our dream every single day? No, of course not. But by taking the right steps to understand what motivates us, we can begin to find out what drives us forward and separate those items about which we don't care. It comes down to mastery of your purpose, which is a journey, not a race.

In the case of Musk, it's his passion to transform the human race into an interplanetary species that drives him forward every day. In other words, his motivation is endlessly maintained because he feels he owes a responsibility to the human race. He's able to achieve what others can only dream of because he wakes up every day motivated to take one step closer to achieving his aim, no matter the obstacles.

When setting out on the mission of making electric motoring accessible for all via the first affordable mass-market Tesla, he ran into several production issues that cost $700 million in losses.[219]

Undeterred, Musk, despite having a net worth of $19.2 billion, spent every night of the Model 3 production crisis sleeping on the factory floor, under his desk, or on the office couch to work through the problems. At one point, he even wore the same clothes for five consecutive days.[220] This is what it means to be unerringly motivated. Leaders of this ilk spend every day obsessing about how to fix problems that prevent the overarching goal from being achieved. It keeps them up at night (literally in the case of Musk), and they are willing to go above and beyond their peers in the commitment to solving the problem.

How many leaders within the electric car divisions within Toyota, General Motors, Ford, and Chrysler are motivated enough to stay up all night thinking about how to fix their electric car manufacturing bottlenecks? I'm betting that the number is below a handful, which is why Tesla may likely leave them behind.

But even passion-struck leaders such as Musk sometimes need help with their motivation. In the early days, it was his brother Kimbal that helped to drive him forward. They bounced off each other and took shifts when coding their first online business called Zip2.[221] Both he and his brother—when starting the company—didn't even rent somewhere to live. They used the office as living accommodation. Without proper bathroom facilities, Musk had to shower at the local YMCA,[222] and while the website was up during the day, Elon and Kimbal would spend all night adding code. They would spend seven days a week in the tiny office space, taking turns sleeping on the couch. By pushing each other on, they sold their business within a couple of years to Compaq for $305 million, personally netting $22 million and $15 million respectively.

Therefore, if you know that you're going to sometimes struggle with motivation, try and find someone you trust to hold you accountable. Take the time to learn about what drives you. Figure out what's going to help you get the best out of yourself and how you will carry on when the going gets tough. Motivation often deserts you when you need it the most, so strategize how you're going to retain it for an extended period. For passion-struck leader Steve Jobs, continually reminding himself about his own mortality (even before his cancer diagnosis) was enough to drive him forward each and every day: "Remembering that I'll be dead soon is the most important tool I've ever encountered."

As Jobs did on a daily basis, try to project yourself ten, twenty (or even thirty) years into the future, and ask yourself, "What will I regret not having done?" You will struggle to muster up the motivation to accomplish goals set for each day, each month, and each year without the incentive provided by the bigger objective at the end of the road.

Big Dreams Require Big Commitment—But They're Never Impossible to Achieve

For passion-struck leaders such as Elon Musk, their dreams consume them whole. In many ways, they define themselves by their dreams. They become part of their very being. Without them, they wouldn't be able to muster the endless motivation to achieve their ambitions.

In the case of Musk, his dream is bigger than perhaps any other: to single-handedly save the human race from itself by changing the way we live and venturing to planets other than our own. For a dream of this size, he needs the support of others, incredible levels of motivation, and a willingness to embrace failure. But most importantly, he achieves success by breaking down his dream into a roadmap of small and easily achievable incremental steps.

Referring back to Lao-Tzu (who is quoted at the beginning of this chapter), a journey of a thousand miles consists of 2,640,000 steps for the average person. If each of those steps takes you five minutes to achieve (as per Musk's schedule), you'll complete twelve steps in an hour, 288 steps each day, and 105,120 steps toward your target each year. Within just twenty-five years, you'll have arrived at your destination. By reframing your goals in this way, you can increasingly build momentum, shortening the timeframe it takes for you to reach your target.

While your dream might not have the scale of Elon Musk's, it's wise to learn lessons from the example he has set. Break overarching goals down into smaller, more achievable chunks. Do not be daunted by failure; instead, seek it out. Find out what drives you from within your very core and use the utopian vision of your future to keep pushing yourself forward. Never put limits on your dreams. Lean on those around you when you need to instead of trying to go it alone.

Everyone's dreams are different. But our innate ability to accomplish them is the same.

Applying the Bee-and-Turtle Effect in Our Own Lives to Support Our Long-Term Goals

This balance of efficiency by day and long-term planning by night is critical for world-changing success, yet many struggle to strike this balance. For the next generation of future leaders with ambitious goals, lack of patience can rear its ugly head. It's easy to see twenty- and thirty-somethings with millions of followers or on the cover of magazines and think: "Why haven't I been as successful at this point in my life?" It can be extremely frustrating, especially if you have achieved substantial success in your early life.

On the other hand, some of us may be patient, but may not have the urgency to maximize our daily output. Whether from fear, indecision, or something else, the calendar keeps advancing while we are stuck in our own heads.

These are real challenges. But your lack of patience or lack of efficiency is not a death sentence for your dreams and high goals. You can shift the paradigm—so long as you shift your thinking and work on these psychological shortcomings.

Ultimately, much of this comes down to having a process in place to help you analyze your progress and provide you with the motivation and clarity to keep going. If the lack of patience is frustrating, you work hard on perspective. It helps to read the biographies of some of your heroes, as it will likely show you that the road to success was longer and more perilous than most people think. Meanwhile, keep executing and being efficient on a day-to-day basis. The perspective will help you be more patient as you continue to make things happen every day.

If you have patience but struggle to be productive on a daily basis, I encourage you to take small steps towards your short-term goals. Action is everything, even if you are taking a tiny step towards your long-term objectives. You want to get in the habit of taking action— even in the face of massive uncertainty. You may fail at times, but also, through failure, you are building your hustle muscles. Acting will become second nature to you. Combining your action-first mentality with the power of patience, you will be significantly closer to that long-term goal.

In the pursuit of purpose, it becomes crucial to discern what truly warrants our unwavering commitment. Professor Art Markman, an esteemed psychologist at the University of Texas at Austin and author of *Smart Change*, offers a compelling approach: "Project yourself deep into the future and ask: What will I regret not having done?" By envisioning the potential regrets that may haunt us later in life, we can effectively work backward, charting a path that circumvents such remorse. This forward-thinking methodology serves as a powerful compass for orchestrating a life that aligns with our deepest aspirations and values.[223]

By considering the long-term consequences of your choices, you can make informed decisions today that align with your aspirations. Let this forward-thinking approach be the compass that directs your path, ensuring that each step you take is purposeful and aligned with your desired future.

The Cycle of Progress—Applying the Bee-and-Turtle Effect to Create Deliberate Action

While I was a senior manager at Arthur Andersen, I was trained on the company methodology called Method 1,[224] which Andersen pioneered into a step-by-step method to handling large-scale IT projects. Method 1 evolved over the years into a framework meant to assist its users in deploying complex enterprise resource planning (ERP) systems by providing a common language for questioning potential clients about what needs to be done and which kinds of software and hardware they require. It also offered strict guidelines for managing a project.

However, the engagements I was leading were much smaller in size, and I needed a more agile approach (prior to the Agile Manifesto's roll-out[225]) of simplifying the overbearing framework. By taking the core tenants of Method 1 and using a simplified process on projects, I found that we were able to iterate and deliver them at a much faster pace. It was all about building the momentum of progress focused on continuous improvement. That is because, without a continual cycle of building momentum and placing your focus and energy on the right things, you will run into entropy over time.

My team and I reached a pivotal moment where our strategies, when implemented by willing clients, yielded extraordinary results. The impact on their businesses became profound, leading to substantial increases in income. The success of our practice soared to unprecedented heights. Behind our remarkable achievements lies a profound reason—a six-step process that has the power to permanently transform businesses. Surprisingly, this methodology is far simpler than one might anticipate. With each successful application of this approach across diverse projects, our triumphs became overwhelming. Our journey was marked by an extensive collection of testimonials and success stories, where individuals who embraced this methodology experienced astonishing business growth. Countless entrepreneurs and small business owners witnessed their ventures skyrocket, expanding by 200 percent, 300 percent, even 400 percent within a mere year to eighteen months. However, fate took an unimaginable turn when Arthur Andersen, driven by its own greed, fell victim to its largest client: Enron.

I embarked on a transformative journey, breathing new life into my career by harnessing the power of the methodology I had developed. As my professional path unfolded within esteemed Fortune 500 companies, I remained steadfast in employing this process. Through deliberate actions, learning from failures and embracing the wisdom they offer, and a commitment to continuous improvement, I harnessed the methodology's potential across a myriad of domains. From driving organizational enhancements to spearheading data center establishment, implementing large-scale IT projects, navigating budget cuts, transforming sales, and fostering marketing innovation—this approach proved effective in every realm. The remarkable outcomes that ensued propelled my career to new heights.

Along this remarkable voyage, I discovered that the methodology also found a place in my personal life. It became the ultimate manifestation of the "bee-and-turtle effect," enabling me to unravel grand ideas into actionable steps that yielded consistent results over time. With a formalized process for deliberate action, prioritization, revision, and intentional achievement of long-term objectives, I established an enduring cycle of progress. In essence, I forged an unending loop of advancement, perpetually propelling myself forward.

It's simple. It's six steps that you apply within the passion-struck framework. You will be shocked at how much you can accomplish.

The six simple steps are: analyze, prioritize, ignite, execute, measure, and renew.

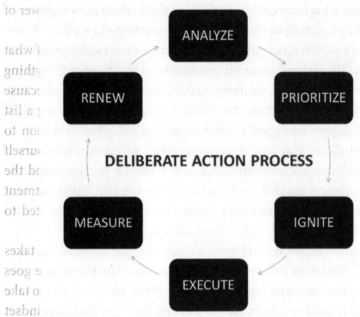

FIGURE 10: The Six-Step Deliberate Action Process that creates a cycle of progress.

Let's start with the first step, analyzing. This is a step that most people omit when they're creating any kind of outcome or what they're going to do next. During goal setting, you need to start by analyzing where you are (in a personal setting or where your team is now, in a business setting). One of the biggest challenges that I see is that, prior to outcomes being created or goals being set, there's rarely any type of analysis where you can see where things currently stand, what you should do, or what you shouldn't do.

Then comes the next step in the process, which is prioritization. This is a major element that most companies and individuals leave out. The key here is not to do this exercise once or twice during the year but repeatedly. Throughout my career, the challenge I found is that people want to get everything done all at once and right away. They dream big and want it now. And they typically start with a gigantic to-do list and try and get the tasks all done as fast as they can randomly. When you conduct this type of prioritization over and over again, here's what happens. You and your team create a superpower of prioritization, getting the right thing done at the right time.

In the first two steps, you have laid out an understanding of what you should do and prioritized in what order. This changes everything because the next step is igniting. And it's a step all by itself. Because here's what igniting means. When you ignite, you are creating a list of tasks that you can commit to and are backed by the emotion to implement them. You have to ignite the enthusiasm within yourself and those you are leading to commit to a long-term vision and the incremental steps along the way to achieving it. See, the commitment level is usually, "We committed to a project" or "We committed to working every day."

When people get ignited with enthusiasm and devotion, it takes away the frustration of not understanding the goals. The same goes for you in your personal life. You need to ignite your inner self to take action and to undertake the daily incremental behavior and mindset shifts to get you to where you want to go.

After igniting, the next crucial step is execution. However, what often happens in both businesses and our personal lives is that we mindlessly jump into action. We get an idea and hastily execute it without clear expectations or a solid plan. This step is pivotal because it not only marks the beginning of most passion journeys but also where many of them come to an end. That is because when you start on a task without clear expectations and a plan, and you haven't prioritized, the task is unclear to your overall end game.

But when you analyze, prioritize, and ignite the work you need to do, the setup is completely in place. It doesn't matter how incredibly you can swing for a baseball. If the head of that bat is a few degrees off, the ball's going to go in a different direction than you want. So, you can execute a swing perfectly, but if the setup isn't there, you're not going to get the result you want. And, because you've set up execution in an understandable way, the prioritization has been done, you've analyzed what's going to work, and you're now set up to succeed. When you start to execute, you feel real results. You feel progress and that forward motion. You feel things happening. You feel the momentum. And isn't that what we're all in this for?

And once you've executed and completed the tasks, you have to measure your progress. Measurement systems are often the least favorite subject for two different kinds of people: actuators and subsisters. Measurement systems seem old-fashioned and burdensome to the actuator, a quagmire of policies and procedures that will only slow you down. To the subsisters, established methods are the only thing between themselves and self-destruction. In other words, if it isn't broken, they don't fix it.

Measurement is critical because it accelerates the passion journey. It gets you into momentum and shows you that you can verify your perspective that you are creating results.

This leads me to Marc Benioff, the co-founder and CEO of Salesforce. I have mentioned Marc throughout the book. He is, in fact, the first leader I met that genuinely defined to me what it meant to be passion struck, and in many ways, he is the inspiration for this book and my long-term study of leadership.

As I mentioned in the opening chapter, I had the privilege of meeting Marc at Oracle, and our paths crossed again during the early stages of Salesforce's development. A few years later, I had the opportunity to travel with him around the world as he passionately advocated for a future without on-premises software, inspiring thousands of people. During one of our conversations in France, I eagerly asked him to share with me his secret to success and how he keeps his company aligned with its purpose. He murmured an acronym to me that, at first, I thought sounded like *vroom*, the sound a car makes. I asked him to repeat it, and in a louder tone, he said, "V2MOM." I thought to myself, what on earth does that mean?

Marc explained that it stands for vision and values (V2) combined with methods, obstacles, and measures (MOM).[226] It's a shorthand for a central organizational system, which he claims is "the biggest secret of Salesforce.com's success." The most important aspect of V2MOM is measurement because, as he said, "the measures specified the actual result we aimed to achieve."

After completing the first five steps of the process through weekly or bi-weekly iterations, it's time to move on to the next crucial step: renewal. This step involves taking the data, progress, and results you've obtained and revisiting the backlog of tasks that still need to be completed. It's a continuous cycle of analysis, prioritization, ignition, execution, and result measurement. To visualize your progress, you can utilize the agile principle of a burndown chart. This chart represents the outstanding work (in hours) on the vertical axis and time (in days) on the horizontal axis. It allows you to track and monitor your progress visually. And once you follow a consistent process, you have a management system in place to clearly understand what you're capable of achieving. You start to really know what is possible, and it gives you the momentum to keep on going.

The Most Important Lesson Is to Grasp the Best of Both the Bee and the Turtle

Leveraging the bee-and-turtle effect can help you to seize the day while staying patient. It satisfies your desire to see progress on a day-by-day basis while keeping the long game close to your chest. The key to using the bee-and-turtle effect is that the same structure can work for any individual or organization and every phase of its life cycle. It can just as quickly help to clarify a business plan for a startup or a Fortune 500 transformation as to outline an individual's passion journey.

You can also use this concept to think through your personal or overall organizational goals. It provides you with a cycle of progress that, if used in conjunction with the passion-struck framework, will enable you to keep the main thing the main thing in your life.

Passion-struck leaders like Elon Musk, Marc Benioff, and Steve Stone intuitively recognize the power of both productivity and patience. But even if you are missing one side of the equation, the good news is that you can improve. You can be more like the bee or the turtle.

By focusing on this fact and shifting your mindset, breakthrough results will undoubtedly happen as you make your long-term objectives a reality.

Don't settle for idling through life, only to later regret your choices on your deathbed. You can do whatever you set your mind to. That ability is buried somewhere within us all.

Passion-struck leaders have utilized that ability to achieve mind-boggling feats. Those who break through master the bee-and-turtle effect.

The question is, will you?

Scan the QR code for more insights and resources on the Deliberate Action Process.

CHAPTER 17

UNLEASH INTENTIONALITY—
IGNITE YOUR PATH TO MEANING
AND FULFILLMENT

What is defeat in life? It is not merely making a
mistake; defeat means giving up on yourself in
the midst of difficulty. What is true success in life?
True success means winning in your battle with
yourself. Those who persist in the pursuit of their
dreams, no matter what the hurdles, are winners
in life, for they have won over their weaknesses.
—Daisaku Ikeda

In the preceding chapters of this book, I delved into the pervasive grip of a transactional mindset within our society. It's a mindset that infiltrates our pursuit of success and colors our perception of self-love. We're bombarded relentlessly with the notion that our worth hinges upon a ceaseless chase for accomplishments, material gains, and an insatiable hunger for more. This paradigm shackles us in an unending loop of seeking external approval to define our self-value, convincing us that our love and acceptance are contingent on meeting expectations and outshining others.

Our quest for success becomes entwined with an insatiable hunger for validation, while self-love teeters precariously on the precipice of external achievements. Yet, the truth remains stark: this transactional approach to self-love and success is fundamentally flawed, a misleading path that veers us away from authentic fulfillment and self-embrace.

Enter the captivating *Passion Struck* podcast interview with Kristina Mand-Lakhiani, Mindvalley's co-founder, writer, speaker, and philanthropist. With luminous insight, she casts a radiant light on the critical importance of transcending this constrained mindset, reshaping our understanding of success and self-worth. Her perspective challenges the widely accepted belief that love and approval are rewards earned through ceaseless achievements and validation. In shaking free from this confining outlook, we unveil the true intentional route to fulfillment, igniting profound action towards a life imbued with passion and purpose.

From a young age, we are taught to view love as a transactional currency. We internalize the idea that in order to earn love and validation, we must consistently do the "right" things and meet society's expectations. Mand-Lakhiani eloquently captures this sentiment when she states, "We learn to use love as currency in a very transactional way. And to earn that currency, we need to do the right things. And when we do the wrong things, we lose the currency." This flawed perspective creates a relentless pursuit of success and perfection, where our sense of self-worth becomes tightly intertwined with external accomplishments and the approval of others.

As life unfolds, we inadvertently absorb the external clamor for validation, internalizing the belief that our worth is dictated solely by accomplishments. Mand-Lakhiani exposes the trap where our aspirations become entangled with a relentless pursuit of validation and love: "We think that the only way I can be lovable and worthy is if I do the right things; if I keep accomplishing; if I keep being a good boy, good girl. It's amazing when people are ambitious, but our ambitions should not be fueled by our need to feel our worth and our need for love. Because once they are fueled by these two things, it's a dead end."

While ambition is a noble drive, it takes a treacherous turn when steered solely by the quest for external validation and love. Herein lies the downfall—a cul-de-sac where success loses its essence, and genuine fulfillment remains elusive.

A paradigm shift is imperative, urging us to redefine success and self-worth. Rather than seeking external validation through accolades, let us forge an intentional path in alignment with our authentic selves. Release the compulsion to prove your worth through accomplishments; instead, nurture an inner wellspring of contentment. Embrace your unique journey, liberating your self-worth from the expectations of others.

In the pursuit of a passion-struck life, genuine success is found in embracing your true self, fostering meaningful connections, and living a life driven by love, compassion, and purpose. By acknowledging and embracing our inherent worthiness, cultivating self-acceptance, and committing to an authentic path, we can break free from the never-ending cycle of seeking external validation.

Now is the time to take bold action and embark on an intentional transformative journey toward a passion-struck life, where purpose, fulfillment, and genuine happiness abound.

Unleashing the Power Within: Stephen King's Journey to a Passion-Struck Life

Stephen King's story provides a powerful example of how breaking free from the confines of transactional love and redefining success can lead to a passion-struck life. Today King's literary works are responsible for some of the highest grossing films of all time,[227] such as *Carrie, The Shining, The Shawshank Redemption, The Green Mile,* and *It*. But not many people realize the struggles he faced when starting his career. His first novel, *Carrie*, was rejected not once, but thirty times before it was finally accepted and published, leaving him feeling discouraged and questioning his worth as a writer.

Imagine for a second that King gave up after that first rejection. Where do you think he would be today? He could have easily succumbed to the trap of seeking external validation and tying his self-worth solely to the acceptance and approval of others. He could have allowed the rejections to define him and control his intentional pursuit of success. But would he have achieved the remarkable feat of selling more than 350 million copies of his various novels with a net worth of half a billion dollars? I highly doubt it. King has admitted himself that there were many times he thought about quitting, but his dogged tenacity launched a career that would see him become one of the most successful authors of all time.

King's key was turning inward to find meaning and fulfillment in the act of writing itself. He embraced his unique voice and focused on the creative process, not just the end result. By redefining success on his terms, he unleashed his true potential. His passion, dedication, and commitment to his craft drove him, not just external markers of achievement. He delved into the depths of his imagination, creating stories that resonated with millions. His journey exemplifies the power of shifting away from a transactional mindset to an intentional one. King found liberation by realizing his worthiness as a writer wasn't dictated by publishers or rejections. Instead, it was rooted in his love for storytelling and dedication to honing his craft.

By embracing his authentic self and cultivating a deep sense of fulfillment through his creative endeavors, King not only achieved tremendous success but also lives a passion-struck life. His work continues to inspire and captivate readers worldwide because it is infused with his genuine passion and love for storytelling.

The story of Stephen King serves as a powerful reminder that true success and fulfillment come from within. When we break free from the confines of transactional love, redefine success on our own terms, and align our actions with our authentic selves, we can unlock the door to a passion-struck life filled with purpose, creativity, and genuine happiness.

As I reflect on King's journey, I am reminded of moments in my own life where I refused to settle and instead pursued a path aligned with my authentic identity.

Embracing Authenticity: Redefining Success on My Own Terms

My transformative journey began at the Naval Academy Preparatory School and was solidified during the rigorous Plebe Summer. This experience ignited a profound realization within me—an understanding that true success is not merely a reflection of external validation but an alignment of actions, aspirations, and ambition with my authentic self.

This realization continued to shape my mindset during training exercises at Camp Lejeune and Fort Bragg. Despite the discomfort of enduring fleas, ants, flies, and ticks crawling over me for hours on end, I remained steadfast in my commitment to live a purpose-driven life. The physical strain of forced marches, with the weight of forty-five pounds on my back and every fiber of my being screaming for rest, only fueled my determination to push beyond perceived limitations and redefine my own measure of achievement.

This resolute mindset persisted during my training with the Navy SEALs, where I faced bone-chilling waters, towering waves, and formidable currents. No matter the obstacles, I refused to let external factors define my success. My focus shifted to personal growth, resilience, and the unwavering pursuit of my objectives, regardless of the challenges that lay before me.

Even as I stood watch for hours on end on various naval vessels, enduring grueling days at sea that stretched into eighteen to twenty hours, punctuated by mere moments of rest, I remained committed to redefining success on my own terms. The choice between eating or sleeping became inconsequential compared to the fulfillment I found in fulfilling my responsibilities, leading with integrity, and embracing the unique journey I had charted for myself.

Similar to Stephen King's unyielding determination, my experiences reinforced the importance of staying true to oneself and embracing purpose. I learned that fulfillment emerges from aligning personal values, passions, and purpose with deliberate action. It is through this conscious choice that we navigate challenges with unwavering determination, create our unique paths to fulfillment, and ultimately live a passion-struck life that aligns with our authentic selves.

Embracing Perseverance on the Path to Success

In a captivating *Passion Struck* podcast interview, David Rubenstein, a renowned entrepreneur, author, philanthropist, and co-founder of the Carlyle Group, shared profound advice for aligning actions, aspirations, and ambitions. He emphasized the vital role of perseverance and the firm belief that "anything is possible," drawing from his own inspiring journey of overcoming obstacles and rising from a modest background.

For Rubenstein, perseverance is the cornerstone of creating an intentional life—a powerful force that propels individuals forward, even in the face of adversity. He reflected on the fundamental questions that drive us each day: "Why do you want to live? What's the point? What inspires you? What do you love about the future?" These questions catalyzed his purpose-driven life, centered on making meaningful contributions to society.

Addressing the issue of inadequacy, Rubenstein conveyed a compelling message: "But don't feel that you're a second-class or third-class citizen because of your background... You can develop these skills." He reminded listeners that the key to looking back with pride on our accomplishments lies in finding something that makes our lives meaningful.

Moreover, Rubenstein emphasized that genuine success transcends mere external achievements. As he put it, "The trick is to lead people to the destination… It's all about taking deliberate, intentional action." In the pursuit of an intentional life, Rubenstein's belief that "anything is possible" serves as a guiding principle, propelling us forward with unwavering dedication.

Consider the significance of Olympic gold medals. They hold immense value because they symbolize the dedication and countless hours of training that athletes put in to surpass their competitors. Each victory is a testament to their unwavering commitment and their ability to overcome adversity and embrace the pain and difficulty that come with the pursuit of greatness. If success were handed out arbitrarily, it would hold no meaning for anyone.

Theodore Roosevelt summed it up well: "Nothing in the world is worth having or worth doing unless it means effort, pain, difficulty…. I have never in my life envied a human being who led an easy life. I have envied a great many people who led difficult lives and led them well."[228]

It is in those who lead difficult lives and navigate them well that we find inspiration. Talent may provide a head start, but it is perseverance that ultimately leads to Olympic gold medals and mastery in any field. The ability to push through challenges, even when faced with exhaustion and unfavorable circumstances, is what sets the truly passionate apart.

Angela Duckworth's book *Grit: The Power of Passion and Perseverance* reinforces the importance of passion and unwavering determination in achieving long-term success. Whether in sports, business, or academia, individuals who consistently demonstrate grit are more likely to reach their goals. True grit allows us to stay focused, committed, and resilient in the face of obstacles, ensuring that we continue moving forward on our journey to becoming passion struck.

By embracing our true selves, persevering through challenges, and nurturing our passion, we can redefine success on our own terms. The stories of Oprah Winfrey, Stephen King, Mark Divine, and countless others remind us that it is the combination of purpose, perseverance, and unwavering intentional action that leads to extraordinary achievements.

Unleashing Intentionality: The Power to Transform Your Life

Can intentionality be developed?

Absolutely! It's time to break free from the shackles of fear and uncertainty and tap into the courage within you. Imagine the empowerment that comes from acting despite those daunting emotions. It's time to take charge of your destiny and turn your dreams into reality. The great news is that intentionality, much like a muscle, can be strengthened through practice and perseverance.

Are you ready to exercise your courage? Start by taking small but boundary-expanding actions that propel you beyond your comfort zone. Each step forward reduces fear and fuels your confidence. Even in the face of overwhelming challenges, embrace the strength to be vulnerable, hopeful, patient, and to believe in a brighter tomorrow that can bring positive change.

In my own journey, I have witnessed my own development of intentionality. From my high school running career to the rigorous training at the Naval Academy, I experienced the transformation of my willpower, character, and "never-say-die" attitude. The challenges I faced during those times made subsequent obstacles seem like a breeze. This is proof that intentionality and deliberate action can be honed and strengthened over time.

Bearing that in mind, here are the critical four steps to support your quest to develop your intentionality and grit.

Four Steps for Developing and Nurturing Intentionality

This chapter began with a discussion about our tendency to seek validation for love and acceptance. But there is another path—an intentional path. By embracing intentionality, we can break free from these traps and redefine our own sense of self-worth. In this section, we will explore four powerful steps that can guide us on the journey towards building intentionality, reclaiming our inner power, and living a life aligned with our true purpose.

1. Practice Deliberate Action

Most individuals rarely stray out of the things that bring fear into their lives. They don't take any risks that could rock the boat of their so-called "stable" lives; they don't go the extra mile, content instead with simply "staying in their lane." But all it takes is a cursory glance back through history to realize that those who achieve greatness put it all on the line, going to extraordinary lengths to achieve their goal.

Before collecting twenty-three gold medals, three silver medals, and two bronze medals at the Olympics,[229] Michael Phelps dedicated his very being to swimming. As a teenager, Phelps went five years without taking a day off. Christmases, Thanksgivings, and birthdays all became irrelevant to the most decorated swimmer of all time. His motivation for swimming for 1,800 days straight? "I couldn't stand the thought of losing…. I wanted to do something that no one had ever done before." By spending more time in water each day than most people do at their job,[230] Phelps was able to do just that.

What will it take for you to extract effort of this nature from yourself? Take intentional and deliberate actions towards your goals. As I discussed in the last chapter, break down your objectives into smaller, manageable steps and consistently work towards them. Stay focused and committed, even when faced with obstacles. It is through consistent action that you build momentum and create lasting change.

For instance, if you're a keen fun runner who's never run a race longer than ten kilometers, enter a marathon. You already know that it's going to require extraordinary resolve to make the leap from racing just over six miles to a little over twenty-six, so you have no other option but to commit and make a start with your new training regimen. Each day that passes will see you striving to go further in your training, drawing on reserves you didn't know you had to ensure you reach your goal.

2. Embrace the Power of Purpose

In our pursuit of intentionality, it is crucial to recognize that the goal or purpose we are striving for is bigger than ourselves. Shifting our perspective from self-centered motivations to a broader sense of purpose unleashes a profound source of motivation and commitment. When we understand that our actions and decisions can have a positive impact on others or contribute to a greater cause, our intentionality becomes fueled by a deeper drive.

A powerful example of this principle is embodied in the journey of Stephen King. In 1973, King barely had a penny to his name. He lived in a small trailer, and duct tape held his Buick together. He taught English at Hampton Academy, but during the summer (when the money dried up), he worked in an industrial laundry facility while moonlighting as a janitor and a gas pump attendant. He didn't even own his own typewriter; he had to borrow the Olivetti that his wife had from high school.

Every night he could, he locked himself in the laundry room. With the typewriter wedged between the washer and the dryer, King began to write his stories while his wife cooked dinner and looked after their toddler and newborn baby. He even turned down a new position that came with a significant pay raise because he wouldn't have any time left to write. It proved to be a wise decision. Less than a year later, *Carrie* had hit the bookshelves, and both he and his family were out of that trailer.

King's burning passion for dragging his family out of abject poverty gave him the purpose he needed to lock himself away every night and achieve his goal, even though he got knocked back so many times in the process.

If you have a goal, think about the deeper purpose that lies behind your objective. Many of you may have the simple aim to "earn more money." But what are the driving forces behind that desire? Do you want to increase the amount you earn so that your partner doesn't have to work two jobs? Do you want to build a fund for your kids' college education? When there's more than just your own aspirations on the line, you find a way to keep moving forward, no matter the setbacks you may face.

Building intentionality requires aligning ourselves with a purpose greater than ourselves. By understanding the impact our actions can have on others or the contribution we can make to a cause, we ignite a powerful force within us. Like Stephen King, when our purpose extends beyond personal fulfillment, we find the resilience to overcome obstacles and embody true intentionality in our pursuit of a brighter future.

3. Foster Collaboration and Connection

The road to success is never easy, but it becomes impossible if you don't enlist the help of others. When trying to achieve extremely ambitious goals, it's the people you surround yourself with that help you get there. Like-minded people fight in your corner when you're running low on energy and drive you on when you think about quitting.

Steve Jobs, for instance, was a visionary leader, but without the help and constant support of Steve Wozniak, Apple would never have gotten off the ground. Jobs came up with the product ideas; Wozniak executed them. In the early years, Wozniak was a constant fixture in that fabled small garage in Los Altos,[231] down in the trenches, dedicating his life to the vision Jobs had created.

Having these kinds of people in your life is crucial. Recognize that you are not alone on this journey. Seek out individuals who share your vision or are working towards similar goals. Collaborate with them, exchange ideas, and support one another. No one has ever achieved greatness alone, and passion-struck leaders like Jobs recognize this early on in their journey.

4. Banish "Can't" From Your Vocabulary

I have mentioned this concept repeatedly throughout the book because it is so important it deserves repeating. Setbacks happen to us all. They are an inescapable fact of life. But what separates the resilient from those who give up is their ability to accept failures for what they are, learn lessons, and reposition moving forward. Those who fail at the first hurdle often shrug their shoulders, saying, "I can't do it; it's too difficult." I heard the same doubting voices in my head telling me, "I can't make it through this race; I can't make it through Plebe Summer; I can't make it through this forced march or complete this project," but I refused to listen. I replaced those old patterns of thought to a new mindset of positivity that said: "I *can* find a way through this."

I remember well how my old peer Steve Szilagyi always responded with "Tremendous!" when asked how his day was going. Not because things were always so great, but because he'd realized that his attitude controlled much of who he was as well as his outlook. Rote responses like "It's okay," or "Another day in paradise," or "Not so great" did nothing to improve his overall perspective and bearing, while "Tremendous!" gave him the energy boost to change the way he went through his day. Just as he did, you can adjust your mindset when approaching difficult tasks. In other words, remove the word "can't" from your vocabulary.

Professor Carol Dweck detailed the advantages of reframing your mindset in the wake of a setback in her book *Mindset: The New Psychology of Success*. Dweck explains that the natural reaction to a roadblock or an obstacle is to have a fixed mindset. We tend to think we will never be able to get past it; we believe we cannot better ourselves and overcome the obstacles to success. However, Dweck asserts that by developing a growth mindset, we can turn our failures into opportunities for improvement.

To quote Michael Phelps once more, "I don't like to lose. If I fail, I ask myself, 'What can I do to make sure this doesn't happen again?'" In other words, he doesn't let himself get down in the dumps about losing a race; instead, he looks at it as an opportunity to get even better. Embracing this mindset builds resilience. Just because achieving your objective became even tougher, it doesn't mean you can't do it. It just means it will taste all the sweeter when you get there.

One way to start building this resilience is by reframing your mindset towards a specific task. Let's say you really dislike taking out the trash. Despite the fact you know it has to be done every week, something about having to empty all the trash cans in your house before taking them out to the dumpster out front irks you. How can you reframe your mindset to enjoy this task? Find a way to look forward to taking out the trash instead of dreading it as a chore. It's the old "glass half full" way of looking at things. Think about the more-toned muscles you'll have from heaving the heavy trash bags, or about how you're making a valuable contribution to your household. Changing how you view tasks you would rather avoid builds resilience. Changing perception deletes the "I can't" from your mindset.

The Road to Success Is Tough, But Never Give Up

Now it's your turn. It's time to unleash your intentionality and make bold strides towards the life you desire. Just as physical exercise shapes our bodies, intentional and deliberate action molds our minds and shapes our character.

Just think of the story about Chris Gardner (played by Will Smith in the movie *The Pursuit of Happyness*), a man who lost his home, his car, and almost his last dollar in his bid to land a job at stock brokerage firm Dean Witter Reynolds through an unpaid internship. How easy would it have been instead to take a job flipping burgers to pay his rent? Gardner made the choice to tough it out, despite being homeless for *a whole year*. A few years later, through sheer grit and determination, he built his own brokerage business and eventually sold it for a multimillion-dollar fee. His story exemplifies the power of grit and intentional action.

No more settling for mediocrity. Seize the reins of your life and steer it towards purpose and fulfillment. Answer the call to action, recognizing that the power to shape your destiny lies within you. Embrace the challenges that come your way, understanding that they serve as stepping stones on your path to greatness.

With unwavering commitment and deliberate action, you can unleash your intentionality and create an extraordinary life. Remain steadfast in your commitment, fueling your progress with the audacity to dream big. Each moment is an opportunity for growth and transformation.

As Emperor Hadrian once said during the rebuilding of fire-damaged Rome, "Brick by brick, my fellow citizens, brick by brick." Similarly, building deliberate action and nurturing intentionality requires consistent effort and determination. Lay the first brick of your transformative journey, and don't allow anything or anyone to hinder your progress.

The choice is yours, and the power lies within you to shape your destiny. Ignite your intentionality, unlock your purpose, and witness the extraordinary unfold. Embrace the challenges that come your way, knowing they are catalysts for growth. It's time to unleash your intentionality and embark on the path to becoming passion struck. Your destiny awaits.

CHAPTER 18

CONCLUSION—STEP INTO YOUR SHARP EDGES EVERY DAY

I have learned over the years that when one's mind is made up, this diminishes fear; knowing what must be done does away with fear.
—Rosa Parks[232]

We have made it to the end of the road, where the true essence of becoming passion struck awaits. Throughout this book, my goal has been to fully immerse you in what it takes to become passion struck and how you can intentionally deploy these behavior and mindset shifts in your life. Whether you are a recent college graduate embarking on your first job or a seasoned professional seeking to lead with greater impact, understanding how to become passion struck can profoundly transform your journey, regardless of your background or past failures.

At this point, you may find yourself thinking, "Yes, becoming a passion-struck trailblazer sounds amazing, but can I truly achieve that level of impact? Do I have what it takes to follow in the footsteps of awe-inspiring individuals like Jeff Bezos, Dwayne Johnson, Oprah Winfrey, General Stan McChrystal, or Astronaut Wendy Lawrence?

They seem larger than life, while I am just one person without their resources or expertise."

It's important not to let the presence of these remarkable individuals intimidate you. While they have left an indelible mark on the world, the path to becoming passion struck is not as overwhelming as it may appear. The qualities and characteristics discussed in this book are not prerequisites that you must possess in their entirety. Rather, they serve as guiding principles and aspirations on the ongoing journey of finding significance and purpose.

During my captivating interview with my friend Seth Godin,[233] entrepreneur, best-selling author, and speaker, we engaged in a soulful discussion that led us into the intricate world of a beehive—an allegory for the journey toward significance.

In the feral beehive, a tale of resilience, courage, and unwavering purpose unfolds—a phenomenon known as the "time increase,"[234] coined by Jacqueline Freeman. It narrates the extraordinary journey of bees striving to restore their hive's former glory.

Within a mere three weeks, the bees gather abundant pollen to replenish the missing honey, and a new queen egg is laid—a rare occurrence. Guided by the maidens' signal, over twelve thousand bees take flight from their hive, forming a breathtaking swarm that settles upon a distant tree a hundred feet away.

This symphony of growth resonates deeply with those who witness it, leaving an indelible mark of awe-inspiring courage. Seth describes it as "the song of increasing," a leap into the unknown that remains etched in the memories of those who hear it.

However, their journey does not end there. Perched upon the tree, these brave creatures face a profound test of survival. With a mere seventy-two hours to find a new home, the threat of rain or disturbance looms, posing a menacing challenge to their very existence. They huddle together, forming a tight-knit ball, maintaining a crucial body temperature of ninety-eight degrees—a testament to their commitment to safety.

Drawing a parallel, Seth points out, "Too many humans have been singing that song for too long, hunkering down, avoiding all inputs, just trying to get through life. But we're not bees."

Just as bees emerge from the depths of despair, we, too, have the opportunity to break free from the suffocating confines of safety. We are not meant to hunker down, avoid risks, and settle for mere survival. Deep within our hearts, a yearning arises—an innate desire to be part of something greater, to have a purpose, and to make a meaningful impact. We long to chart our own path and leave our mark on the endeavors we undertake. We aspire to be passion struck.

Go Forth and Ignite a Revolution of Meaning and Purpose

As we conclude this transformative journey together, remember that the ball is in your court. It doesn't matter where you come from or what you have accomplished thus far. Past failures are merely stepping stones on the path to greatness. The lessons and insights offered in this book are meant to be applied to your own life, empowering you to become passion struck.

Becoming passion struck is a continuous process of growth and refinement. It requires perseverance, self-belief, and the willingness to battle for your dreams. As Hall of Fame volleyball player Kerri Walsh Jennings said, "Breathe, believe, and battle. My former coach, Troy Tanner, told us that before each match. Breathe—be in the moment. Believe—have faith that you can rise above it. Battle—you gotta be prepared to go for as long as it takes."[235]

Together, we can challenge the status quo and create a culture of significance that is not just a nice-to-have but an absolute necessity. Imagine the ripple effect of genuine significance, where individual sparks ignite a wildfire of motivation, loyalty, and exceptional performance personally and professionally.

Embrace the power of significance.

It's time to ignite a revolution of meaning and purpose, where every heartbeat counts, and every soul shines brightly. By embracing the path of becoming passion struck, you transcend boundaries and limitations, creating a future where passion reigns and purpose prevails.

Let the lessons of this journey guide you as you embark on your own path of significance. Apply these insights to your life and take intentional action. The time for transformation is now. Together, let us reshape the world and weave an extraordinary tapestry of significance and fulfillment.

By challenging the status quo and embracing the power of significance, we become agents of change, inspiring others to join us on this journey. As we do, we create a world where every voice is valued, every contribution matters, and every individual finds their true purpose.

So, breathe, believe, and battle for your dreams. Embrace the most fulfilling, rewarding, and inspiring way to live your life—being passion struck. Together, let us make every heartbeat count, and let our souls shine brightly in this magnificent symphony of meaning. The revolution starts with you.

I can't wait to see what you accomplish.

Make a choice. Work hard. Step into your sharp edges with significance.

RESOURCES: WHAT'S NEXT ON YOUR PASSION-STRUCK ADVENTURE?

I trust that *Passion Struck* has sparked numerous ideas on how to embrace an intentional life. As we reach the end of this book, remember that it signals the start of your transformative journey towards becoming passion struck. To aid you in seamlessly integrating and sustaining the principles you've learned, I've thoughtfully prepared a collection of powerful growth tools. These invaluable resources are offered to you completely free of charge, empowering you on your quest to discover passion and purpose. Let these tools be your compass as you navigate the path of intentional living.

The Passion Struck Discussion Guide
I've crafted a comprehensive discussion guide tailored for book clubs, work teams, faith and spirituality groups, workshops, accountability circles, and similar gatherings. This guide is designed to facilitate in-depth conversations and enhance your exploration of the book's concepts.

The Passion Struck Challenge
You'll receive a stream of content-rich, immensely practical coaching, videos, and mentoring modules. I've created these world-class resources to empower you to stay committed to operating at the peak

of your abilities and maximize your victories. As you embrace your passion and become passion struck, you'll continuously elevate your genius and exemplify the true elements of living with purpose and intentionality.

Passion Struck Quiz

Discover where you stand in your journey towards becoming passion struck by taking our quiz. This insightful assessment will analyze your position along the five transition points that lead to a passion-filled life. Gain valuable insights into your progress and uncover the path towards living with purpose and intentionality.

The Passion Struck Guided Meditation

To support you in achieving a state of deep focus, enhanced creativity, elevated performance, and profound tranquility throughout your day, I have meticulously crafted a collection of distinctive guided morning meditations. These sessions are designed to empower you to awaken as your best self—a leader, achiever, and creator. I trust you will find great value and enjoyment in them.

Newsletter

Enroll now for my widely acclaimed, complimentary weekly newsletter at passionstruck.com and unlock a world of inspiration.

To get full access to all of these valuable resources being made available to you at zero cost scan the QR code below.

Join the conversation by following @john_r_miles on…

Instagram
Facebook
Twitter
YouTube
LinkedIn
Goodreads
TikTok

Email me about your own experiences, insights, and questions through my site, passionstruck.com.

I look forward to hearing from you about this fascinating subject: the practice of living intentionally.

—John Miles

APPENDIX 1: SUGGESTIONS FOR FURTHER READING

Each week on the *Passion Struck* podcast, I delve into the mindset and philosophy of the world's most insightful individuals. In pursuit of becoming passion struck, numerous extraordinary books have been written to aid your journey. To assist you further, I have personally curated a list of these books, which you can access by scanning the QR code below.

APPENDIX 2:
LISTEN TO PASSION STRUCK WITH JOHN R. MILES

Passion Struck is your guide to creating an intentional life filled with purpose and meaning. Through insightful conversations with experts and thought leaders, we explore the mindset and philosophy of remarkable individuals who have harnessed the power of intentionality to achieve extraordinary success.

In this podcast, we not only uncover practical strategies to enhance your performance in various aspects of life but also delve into the science of human behavior change. By understanding the underlying motivations that drive our actions, we can make intentional choices that align with our goals and values.

With engaging and enjoyable content, we strive to empower you with the knowledge and tools to navigate life's challenges and transform your aspirations into reality. Join us on this journey of discovery and transformation as we unlock the secrets to living a passion-filled, intentional life. New episodes are released every Tuesday, Thursday, and Friday, so you can continuously fuel your pursuit of an intentional and purpose-driven existence.

APPENDIX 3:
PASSION STRUCK
CORE BELIEF SYSTEM

In the journey of self-discovery and personal growth, we often find ourselves searching for a guiding light—a philosophy that resonates deeply and provides a roadmap to navigate the complexities of life. At its essence, the Passion Struck Core Belief System is not just a philosophy; it's a way of life that centers around the power of passion and purpose. Born from the shared experiences and wisdom of diverse minds, this belief system offers a unique lens through which to view the world and engage with it. You can access the core belief system by scanning the QR code below.

ENDNOTES

1   Mark Travers, "The Student Debt Crisis Is Crushing Entrepreneurship,"
     Forbes, October 17, 2019, https://www.forbes.com/sites/
     traversmark/2019/10/17/the-student-debt-crisis-is-crushing-ent
     repreneurship/?sh=3dba760f7610.

2   "Social Cycle Theory," The Lucian of Samosata Project,
     January 14, 2014, http://lucianofsamosata.info/wiki/
     doku.php?id=vico%3Asocial-cycle-theory.

3   Federal Reserve Bank of St. Louis and the Board of Governors of
     the Federal Reserve System, ed., "Economic Mobility: Research &
     Ideas on Strengthening Families, Communities & the Economy,"
     Federal Reserve Bank of St. Louis, 2016, https://www.stlouisfed.
     org/community-development/publications/economic-mobility.

4   Steve Denning, "Why U.S. Entrepreneurship Is Dying," *Forbes*, May 27,
     2016, https://www.forbes.com/sites/stevedenning/2016/05/27/why-us-
     entrepreneurship-is-dying/?sh=186cd10c7d74.

5   "Is the American Dream Alive or Dead? It Depends on
     Where You Look," Economic Innovation Group, https://
     eig.org/distressed-communities/dcieop/.

6   "Ewing Marion Kauffman Foundation," Ewing Marion
     Kauffman Foundation, 2023, https://www.kauffman.org/.

7   Robert Fairlie, "National Report on Early-Stage Entrepreneurship in the
     United States (2021)," Ewing Marion Kauffman Foundation, March 1,
     2022, https://www.kauffman.org/entrepreneurship/reports/early-stage-
     entrepreneurship-
     national-2021/.

8   Ewing Marion Kauffman Foundation, "2017 The Kauffman Index:
     Startup Activity: National Trends," Ewing Marion Kauffman Foundation,
     https://www.kauffman.org/wp-content/uploads/2019/09/2017_
     Kauffman_Index_Startup_Activity_National_Report_Final.pdf.

9   Judy Rider, "Do We Really Live in a Golden Era of Startups?" Crunchbase
     News, August 23, 2017, https://news.crunchbase.com/startups/

really-live-golden-
era-startups/.

[10] Ian Hathaway and Robert E. Litan, "Declining Business Dynamism in the United States: A Look at States and Metros," The Brookings Institution, May 5, 2014, https://www.brookings.edu/articles/declining-business-dynamism-in-the-united-states-a-look-at-states-and-metros/.

[11] "Private Sector Employee Distribution by Firm Size U.S. 2021," Statista, October 12, 2022, https://www.statista.com/statistics/235529/employment-by-firm-size-in-us/.

[12] Patrick Kesler, "Is the American Dream Alive or Dead?" Economic Innovation Group, https://eig.org/distressed-communities/dcieop/.

[13] Patricia Cohen, "A Bigger Economic Pie, But a Smaller Slice for Half of the U.S.," New York Times, December 6, 2016, https://www.nytimes.com/2016/12/06/business/economy/a-bigger-economic-pie-but-a-smaller-slice-for-half-of-the-us.html.

[14] Ryan Pendell, "The World's $7.8 Trillion Workplace Problem," Gallup, June 14, 2022, https://www.gallup.com/workplace/393497/world-trillion-workplace-problem.aspx.

[15] Amy Adkins, "Millennials: The Job-Hopping Generation," Gallup, https://www.gallup.com/workplace/231587/millennials-job-hopping-generation.aspx#:~:text=Gallup%20has%20found%20that%20only,do%20damage%20to%20their%20company.

[16] Mark Manson, "Screw Finding Your Passion," Mark Manson, https://markmanson.net/screw-finding-your-passion.

[17] Mark Manson, "Articles," Mark Manson, February 21, 2023, https://markmanson.net/articles.

[18] Mark Manson, "5 Mindsets That Create Success," Mark Manson, February 8, 2023, https://markmanson.net/5-mindsets-that-create-success.

[19] "Long working hours increasing deaths from heart disease and stroke: WHO, ILO," Joint News Release, World Health Organization, May 17, 2021, https://www.who.int/news/item/17-05-2021-long-working-hours-increasing-deaths-from-heart-disease-and-stroke-who-ilo.

[20] JoAnna Daemmrich and Tom Bowman. "125 Kids Now Suspected as Exam Scandal Grows 6 Already Convicted of Cheating," Baltimore Sun, September 29, 2021, https://www.baltimoresun.com/news/bs-xpm-1993-09-14-1993257033-story.html.

[21] Tom Bowman, "Stalled by a Scandal, Admiral Is Reassigned," Baltimore Sun, September 29, 2021, https://www.baltimoresun.com/news/bs-xpm-1994-07-28-1994209034-story.html.

[22] John R. Miles and Katy Milkman, Ph.D., "Creating Lasting Behavior Change for Good," podcast, Passion Struck, https://passionstruck.com/katy-milkman-behavior-change-for-good/.

23 Jim Lucas, "What is the second law of thermodynamics?" Live Science, February 7, 2022, https://www.livescience. com/50941-second-law-thermodynamics.html.

24 William Damon, *The Path to Purpose: How Young People Find Their Calling in Life* (New York: Free Press, 2009), https://parentotheca. com/2021/02/24/the-path-to-purpose-william-damon-book-summary/.

25 John R. Miles and Hal Hershfield, "How You Embrace Your Future Self Today," podcast, *Passion Struck*, https://passionstruck. com/hal-hershfield-embrace-your-future-self-today/.

26 Jeremy Sutton, Ph.D., "18 Best Growth Mindset Activities, Worksheets, and Questions," PositivePsychology.com, October 27, 2021, https://positivepsychology.com/growth-mindset/.

27 Klaus Schwab, "The Global Competitiveness Report 2019," World Economic Forum, https://www3.weforum.org/docs/WEF_TheGlobalCompetitiveness Report2019.pdf.

28 "Jobs lost, jobs gained; What the future of work will mean for jobs, skills, and wages," McKinsey Global Institute, November 28, 2017, https:// www.mckinsey.com/featured-insights/future-of-work/jobs-lost-jobs- gained-what-the-future-of-work-will-mean-for-jobs-skills-and-wages.

29 Bold Business, "Square Founder Jim McKelvey Discusses the Characteristics that Make a Leader BOLD!!!" YouTube video, February 27, 2019, https://www.youtube.com/watch?v=jjI9BMmp-HY.

30 "Jim McKelvey," Wikipedia, https://en.wikipedia.org/wiki/Jim_McKelvey.

31 "Jim McKelvey," Wikipedia, https://en.wikipedia.org/wiki/Jim_McKelvey.

32 John R. Miles, "Bold Leader Spotlight: Jim McKelvey, Founder of Square, LaunchCode, and Invisibly," Bold Business, March 1, 2019, https://www. boldbusiness.com/human-achievement/bold-leader-spotlight-jim- mckelvey- founder-square-invisibly/.

33 "Jim McKelvey, Wikipedia, https://en.wikipedia.org/wiki/Jim_McKelvey.

34 "Square Revenue: Annual, Quarterly, and Historic," Zippia, updated July 21, 2023, https://www.zippia.com/square-careers-10755/revenue/.

35 "Jim McKelvey," Wikipedia, https://en.wikipedia.org/wiki/Jim_McKelvey.

36 "Home – Third Degree Glass Factory," Third Degree Glass Factory, updated April 27, 2023, https://thirddegreeglassfactory.com/.

37 "Cultivation Capital – A Venture Capital Firm," Cultivation Capital, 2023, https://cultivationcapital.com/.

38 "LaunchCode," LaunchCode, 2023, https://www.launchcode.org/.

39 "Jim McKelvey," Wikipedia, https://en.wikipedia.org/wiki/Jim_McKelvey.

40 "Jim McKelvey," Wikipedia, https://en.wikipedia.org/wiki/Jim_McKelvey.

41 E.B. Boyd, "How Jack Dorsey's Square Is Accidentally Disrupting The Entire Payments Industry," *Fast Company*, May 23, 2011, https://www.

fastcompany.com/1754859/how-jack-dorseys-square-accidentally-disrupting-entire-payments-industry.

42 C.J. Prince, "Square's Jim Mckelvey: Innovation Is The Only True Hedge Against Crisis," *Chief Executive*, April 17, 2020, https://chiefexecutive.net/squares-jim-mckelvey-small-businesses-need-more-help/.

43 James Clear, "First Principles: Elon Musk on the Power of Thinking for Yourself," James Clear, https://jamesclear.com/first-principles.

44 Michael E. Price, Ph.D., "Human Herding: How People are Like Guppies," *Psychology Today*, June 25, 2013, https://www.psychologytoday.com/us/blog/darwin-eternity/201306/human-herding-how-people-are-guppies.

45 Dan Schawbel, "14 Things Every Successful Person Has In Common," *Forbes*, October 12, 2022, https://www.forbes.com/sites/danschawbel/2013/12/17/14-things-every-successful-person-has-in-common/?sh=40f065f53c74.

46 Eleanor Roosevelt, quote, Goodreads, https://www.goodreads.com/quotes/3823-you-gain-strength-courage-and-confidence-by-every-experience-in.

47 Travis Clark, "The Rock Topped Forbes' List of the Highest-Paid Actors in the World, Which Also Includes 5 from the Marvel Cinematic Universe," Business Insider, August 21, 2019, https://www.businessinsider.com/the-rock-tops-list-of-highest-paid-actors-in-world-2019-8?r=US&IR=T.

48 "Warren Sapp," Wikipedia, February 18, 2023, https://en.wikipedia.org/wiki/Warren_Sapp.

49 The Rock, "Seven Bucks Moment: Dwayne 'The Rock' Johnson," YouTube video, December 6, 2016, https://www.youtube.com/watch?v=RjATMi9yNd0.

50 "Live Legendary – Horse Soldier Bourbon Whiskey," Horse Soldier Bourbon Whiskey, 2022, https://horsesoldierbourbon.com/.

51 *12 Strong*, directed by Nicolai Fuglsig (Warner Bros., 2018), https://www.amazon.com/12-Strong-Michael-Shannon/dp/B0791T5DTV.

52 9/11 Memorial Staff, "'Horse Soldier' Statue Dedicated in Liberty Park," 9/11 Memorial & Museum, https://www.911memorial.org/connect/blog/horse-soldier-statue-dedicated-liberty-park.

53 The Mirror, "David Gray Interview – Draw The Line," YouTube video, September 18, 2009, https://www.youtube.com/watch?v=JLQ13oLpNfo.

54 Matt Weinberger and Taylor Nicole Rogers, "The Rise of Marc Benioff, the Bombastic Owner of Time Magazine Who Just Became Salesforce's Sole CEO, Has an $8 Billion Fortune, and Owns a 5-Acre Compound in Hawaii," Business Insider, updated February 5, 2020, https://www.businessinsider.com/the-rise-of-salesforce-ceo-marc-benioff-2016-3?r=US&IR=T#carlye-adler-wrote-in-fortune-they-

sailed-to-the-mediterranean-on-ellisons-yacht-visited-japan-during-
cherry-blossom-season-spent-thanksgiving-together-and-ev.

55 Dan Sullivan and Dr. Benjamin Hardy, *The Gap and The Gain: The High Achievers' Guide to Happiness, Confidence, and Success* (Carlsbad, CA: Hay House Business, 2021), https://www.penguinrandomhouse.com/books/679143/the-gap-and-the-gain-by-dan-sullivan/.

56 John R. Miles and Dr. Benjamin Hardy, "The Psychology of Your Future Self," podcast, *Passion Struck*, https://passionstruck.com/dr-benjamin-hardy-7-ways-to-be-your-future-self/.

57 The Growth Faculty, "Katy Milkman: How to Change Despite Those Obstacles Inside You," The Growth Faculty, August 31, 2022, https://www.thegrowthfaculty.com/blog/howtochange#:~:text=A%20great%20place%20to%20start,for%20behaviour%20change%20more%20appealing.

58 Pete Blackburn, "Dwayne 'The Rock' Johnson discusses his battle with depression, mental-health issues," CBS Sports, April 2, 2018, https://www.cbssports.com/wwe/news/dwayne-the-rock-johnson-discusses-his-battle-with-depression-mental-health-issues/.

59 "Fighting the World's Deadliest Animal," CDC, updated August 15, 2019, https://www.cdc.gov/globalhealth/stories/2019/world-deadliest-animal.html.

60 "Fighting the World's Deadliest Animal," CDC, updated August 15, 2019, https://www.cdc.gov/globalhealth/stories/2019/world-deadliest-animal.html.

61 Bill Gates, "The deadliest animal in the world," GatesNotes, April 25, 2014, https://www.gatesnotes.com/Most-Lethal-Animal-Mosquito-Week.

62 "Vector-borne diseases," World Health Organization, March 2, 2020, https://www.who.int/news-room/fact-sheets/detail/vector-borne-diseases.

63 John R. Miles and Matt Higgins, "How to Burn the Boats and Just Figure It Out," podcast, *Passion Struck*, https://passionstruck.com/matt-higgins-on-how-to-burn-the-boats/.

64 Carolina Herrando and Efthymios Constantinides, "Emotional Contagion: A Brief Overview and Future Directions," Frontiers, July 16, 2021, https://www.frontiersin.org/articles/10.3389/fpsyg.2021.712606/full.

65 "Thaddeus Bullard – Football – Florida Gators," Florida Gators, https://floridagators.com/sports/football/roster/thaddeus-bullard/7909.

66 Brian Steele, "Ex-Gator Bullard, Blaze enter arena playoffs," *Gainesville Sun*, June 30, 2007, https://www.gainesville.com/story/news/2007/06/30/ex-gator-bullard-blaze-enter-arena-playoffs/31529788007/.

67 "Forbes Names World's Most Powerful Women," Bet, https://www.bet.com/photo-gallery/12yx8y/forbes-names-world-s-most-powerful-women/tuw99b.

68 Peter Jones, "How Oprah Winfrey Overcame Failure," The Job
    Network, https://community.thejobnetwork.com/how-oprah-
    winfrey-overcame-failure/#:~:text=She%20was%20set%20
    up%20for,of%20hard%2Dnosed%20reporting%20required.

69 Kristin Deiss, "Dances with Defeat: How Oprah Winfrey
    Overcame Failure," Stir the Sage, September 21, 2020, https://
    stirthesage.com/how-oprah-winfrey-overcame-failure/.

70 Oprah Winfrey, "What Oprah Knows for Sure About a Difficult Climb,"
    Oprah.com, 2013, https://www.oprah.com/spirit/what-oprah-knows-for-
    sure-
    about-a-difficult-climb.

71 John R. Miles and Dr. Ethan Kross, "The Hidden Power of Our Inner
    Voice," podcast, *Passion Struck*, https://passionstruck.com/ethan-kross-
    power-of-our-
    inner-voice/.

72 Douglas Main, "Becoming King: Why So Few Male Lions
    Survive to Adulthood," Live Science, November 27, 2013, https://
    www.livescience.com/41572-male-lion-survival.html.

73 "Survival of private sector establishments by opening year," U.S. Bureau of
    Labor Statistics, https://www.bls.gov/bdm/us_age_naics_00_table7.txt.

74 John R. Miles, "How Lowe's Created the First Interconnected Shopping
    Experience," John R. Miles, February 29, 2020, https://johnrmiles.
    com/creating-the-first-interconnected-shopping-experience/.

75 James Melton, "Home Depot plans to spend $5.4 billion to sharpen its
    omnichannel strategy, Digital Commerce 360, December 8, 2017, https://
    www.digitalcommerce360.com/2017/12/08/home-depot-spend-5-4-billion-
    sharpen-omnichannel-strategy/.

76 Alyssa Roenigk, "Veteran and hopeful Paralympian Ennis on the power of
    sports," ESPN, June 30, 2017, https://www.espn.com/olympics/story/_/page/
    espnwbodyennis/mountaineer-wounded-warrior-kirstie-ennis-long-
    road-recovery-body-2017.

77 Alyssa Roenigk, "Veteran and hopeful Paralympian Ennis on the power of
    sports," ESPN, June 30, 2017, https://www.espn.com/olympics/story/_
    /page/espnwbodyennis/mountaineer-wounded-warrior-
    kirstie-ennis-long-road-recovery-body-2017.

78 Adam Zagoria, "Roger Federer Say It's 'Obvious' Rafael Nadal, Novak
    Djokovic 'Will Win More' Grand Slam Titles Than Him," *Forbes*, January
    16, 2020, https://www.forbes.com/sites/adamzagoria/2020/01/16/
    roger-federer-say-its-obvious-rafael-nadal-novak-djokovic-will-
    win-more-grand-slam-titles-than-him/?sh=5b72853f42cb.

79 Stephanie Denning, "Hilary Swank And Her Nine-
    Year Overnight Success," *Forbes*, June 30, 2018, https://

www.forbes.com/sites/stephaniedenning/2018/06/30/
hilary-swank-and-her-nine-year-overnight-success/?sh=45332c5e4bcf.

80 Thomas R. Covington, "Three-Dimensional Evaluation of
Mandibular Changes Associated with Herbst Treatment in Growing
Class II Patients," Carolina Digital Repository, UNC, https://cdr.
lib.unc.edu/concern/parent/9z903007m/file_sets/fb4948624.

81 Thomas R. Covington, "Three-Dimensional Evaluation of
Mandibular Changes Associated with Herbst Treatment in Growing
Class II Patients," Carolina Digital Repository, UNC, https://cdr.
lib.unc.edu/concern/parent/9z903007m/file_sets/fb4948624.

82 "Srebrenica massacre," Wikipedia, https://
en.wikipedia.org/wiki/Srebrenica_massacre.

83 John R. Miles, Marianne W. Lewis, and Wendy K. Smith, "The Power
of Both/And Thinking," podcast, *Passion Struck*, https://passionstruck.
com/marianne-lewis-and-wendy-smith-both-and-thinking/.

84 "James G. March, Professor of Business, Education, and Humanities, Dies
at 90," Stanford Graduate School of Business, October 29, 2018, https://
www.gsb.stanford.edu/newsroom/school-news/james-g-march-professor-
business-
education-humanities-dies-90.

85 Christopher Cassidy, Wikipedia, https://en.wikipedia.org/wiki/
Christopher_
Cassidy#:~:text=Cassidy%20graduated%20from%20BUD%2FS,member%
20of%20the%20Navy%20SEALs.

86 "National Medal of Honor Museum Foundation President and
CEO Chris Cassidy, Retired U.S. Navy SEAL, Releases Statement of
Remembrance Ahead of Memorial Day," National Medal of Honor
Museum, May 26, 2022, https://mohmuseum.org/memorialday2022/.

87 Stavros Atlamazoglou, "Navy SEAL Doctor Speaks about the Peculiar
Dangers of Hell Week," Sandboxx, June 23, 2022, https://www.sandboxx.
us/blog/navy-seal-doctor-speaks-about-the-peculiar-dangers-of-hell-
week/#:~:text=Basic%20Underwater%20Demolition%2FSEAL%20
(BUD,pipelines%20in%20the%20U.S.%20military.

88 Stavros Atlamazoglou, "Navy SEAL Doctor Speaks about the Peculiar
Dangers of Hell Week," Sandboxx, June 23, 2022, https://www.sandboxx.
us/blog/navy-seal-doctor-speaks-about-the-peculiar-dangers-of-hell-
week/#:~:text=Basic%20Underwater%20Demolition%2FSEAL%20
(BUD,pipelines%20in%20the%20U.S.%20military.

89 Tony Reichhardt, "The Spacewalk That Almost Killed Him," Air & Space
Magazine, *Smithsonian Magazine*, May 2014, https://www.smithsonianmag.
com/air-space-magazine/spacewalk-almost-killed-him-180950135/.

90 John R. Miles and Chris Cassidy, "The Importance in Life of Being Present," podcast, *Passion Struck*, https://passionstruck.com/vital-importance-in-life-of-being-present/.

91 "Home," Joint Interagency Task Force South, https://www.jiatfs.southcom.mil/.

92 Evan Munsing and Christopher J. Lamb, "Joint Interagency Task Force-South: The Best Known, Least Understood Interagency Success," Institute for National Strategic Studies, June 2011, https://ndupress.ndu.edu/portals/68/documents/stratperspective/inss/strategic-perspectives-5.pdf.

93 "Mercury Seven," Wikipedia, https://en.wikipedia.org/wiki/Mercury_Seven.

94 John R. Miles and Wendy Lawrence, "Permit Yourself to Dream the Dream," podcast, *Passion Struck*, https://passionstruck.com/how-to-dream-the-dream-you-want/.

95 Mark Cuban, "Success and Motivation, Part 2," Blog Maverick: The Mark Cuban Weblog, April 25, 2004, https://blogmaverick.com/2004/04/25/success-and-motivation-part-2/.

96 "Mark Cuban," Wikipedia, https://en.wikipedia.org/wiki/Mark_Cuban.

97 John R. Miles and Mark Divine, "How to Create a Life of Excellence," podcast, *Passion Struck*, https://passionstruck.com/mark-divine-living-a-life-of-excellence/.

98 "Mark Divine," Wikipedia, https://en.wikipedia.org/wiki/Mark_Divine.

99 Joey Hadden, "'Top Gun' and 'Top Gun: Maverick' are based on a super-elite US Navy training program, and fighter pilots say the films are pretty spot on," Insider, February 2, 2020, https://www.insider.com/real-story-behind-top-gun-maverick-2019-12.

100 Shonda Rhimes, "My year of saying yes to everything," TED video, February 17, 2016, https://www.ted.com/talks/shonda_rhimes_my_year_of_saying_yes_to_everything.

101 Shonda Rhimes, *Year of Yes* (New York: Marysue Rucci Books, 2016), https://www.simonandschuster.com/books/Year-of-Yes/Shonda-Rhimes/9781476777122.

102 Mihaly Csikszentmihalyi, *Flow: The Psychology of Optimal Experience* (New York: Harper Perennial Modern Classics, 2008), https://www.goodreads.com/book/show/66354.Flow.

103 "Pareto principle," Wikipedia, https://en.wikipedia.org/wiki/Pareto_principle.

104 "10 Inspiring Quotes by Eleanor Roosevelt," Virtues for Life, https://www.virtuesforlife.com/10-inspiring-quotes-by-eleanor-roosevelt/.

105 Robert M. Yerkes and John D. Dodson, "The Relation of Strength of Stimulus to Rapidity of Habit-Formation," *Journal of Comparative Neurology and Psychology* 18 (1908): 459-482, http://psychclassics.yorku.ca/Yerkes/Law/.

106 "Jesse Iwuji Racing," Jesse Iwuji Racing, 2023, https://www.jesseiwuji.com/.

107 John R. Miles and Jesse Iwuji, "Creating an Unstoppable Life," podcast, *Passion Struck*, https://passionstruck.com/creating-an-unstoppable-life-jesse-iwuji/.

108 "Groupon," Wikipedia, https://en.wikipedia.org/wiki/Groupon.

109 Alice Truong, "Groupon is still the fastest company to reach a billion-dollar valuation," Quartz, May 5, 2015, https://qz.com/398090/groupon-still-the-fastest-company-to-reach-a-unicorn-billion-dollar-valuation.

110 Shane Parrish, "Eight Things I Learned from Peter Thiel's Zero To One," Farnam Street, September 2014, https://fs.blog/2014/09/peter-thiel-zero-to-one/.

111 "History of Amazon," Wikipedia, https://en.wikipedia.org/wiki/History_of_Amazon.

112 "History of Amazon," Wikipedia, https://en.wikipedia.org/wiki/History_of_Amazon.

113 Shana Lebowitz and Weng Cheong, "Here's the mindset that helped Jeff Bezos expand Amazon from an online bookstore to a $1.7 trillion 'everything store,'" Business Insider, updated February 2, 2021, https://www.businessinsider.com/how-amazon-decided-to-sell-books-2018-4.

114 Tom Popomaronis, "Jeff Bezos: Amazon turned into 'the everything store' thanks to an email to 1,000 random people," CNBC, updated October 9, 2020, https://www.cnbc.com/2020/10/08/jeff-bezos-amazon-turned-into-the-everything-store-because-of-an-email-i-sent-in-1997.html.

115 Natalie Fratto, "3 ways to measure your adaptability – and how to improve it," TED video, May 1, 2022, https://www.ted.com/talks/natalie_fratto_3_ways_to_measure_your_adaptability_and_how_to_improve_it?utm_campaign=tedspread&utm_medium=referral&utm_source=tedcomshare.

116 Sarah DiGiulio, "In good company: Why we need other people to be happy," NBC News: Better, January 9, 2018, https://www.nbcnews.com/better/health/good-company-why-we-need-other-people-be-happy-ncna836106.

117 Seesmic, "John Miles CIO of Dell explains how Seesmic is used with Chatter at Dell," YouTube video, April 11, 2011, https://www.youtube.com/watch?v=-q6Quh9nKio.

118 Matt Weinberger, "This is why Steve Jobs got fired from Apple – and how he came back to save the company," Business Insider, July 31, 2017, https://www.businessinsider.com/steve-jobs-apple-fired-returned-2017-7#things-came-to-a-head-in-1985-under-jobs-guidance-apple-had-released-the-lisa-the-first-ever-computer-with-a-graphical-user-interface-gui-it-was-a-technical-marvel-but-a-total-flop-sales-wise-his-follow-up-project-the-macintosh-sold-better-but-still-not-well-enough-to-make-a-sizable-dent-in-ibms-control-of-the-pc-market-5.

119 "Steve Jobs," Wikipedia, https://en.wikipedia.org/wiki/Steve_Jobs#Apple_(1976%E2%80%931985).

[120] "Steve Jobs," Wikipedia, https://en.wikipedia.org/wiki/Steve_Jobs#Apple_ (1976%E2%80%931985)

[121] Matt Weinberger, "This is why Steve Jobs got fired from Apple – and how he came back to save the company," Business Insider, July 31, 2017, https://www.businessinsider.com/steve-jobs-apple-fired-returned-2017-7#jobs-would-go-on-to-form-next-a-company-creating-what-he-hyped-as-the-next-evolution-of-the-pc-while-the-machines-were-technically-impressive-the-prices-were-high-and-sales-were-slow-8.

[122] Matt Weinberger, "This is why Steve Jobs got fired from Apple – and how he came back to save the company," Business Insider, July 31, 2017, https://www.businessinsider.com/steve-jobs-apple-fired-returned-2017-7#so-when-modern-tech-execs-like-ex-uber-ceo-travis-kalanick-say-that-theyre-steve-jobs-ing-it-and-plan-to-return-to-companies-from-which-they-were-fired-just-know-that-its-harder-than-it-might-seem-18.

[123] "Steve Jobs," Wikipedia, https://en.wikipedia.org/wiki/Steve_Jobs#Apple_ (1976%E2%80%931985).

[124] Shawn Knight, "Original iPod first went on sale 12 years ago with 5GB of storage capable of holding 1,000 songs," TechSpot, November 11, 2013, https://www.techspot.com/news/54647-original-ipod-first-went-on-sale-12-years-ago-with-5gb-of-storage-capable-of-holding-1000-songs.html.

[125] Andy Langer, "Is Steve Jobs the God of Music?" Esquire, September 10, 2014, https://www.esquire.com/news-politics/a11177/steve-jobs-esquire-interview-0703/.

[126] Andy Langer, "Is Steve Jobs the God of Music?" Esquire, September 10, 2014, https://www.esquire.com/news-politics/a11177/steve-jobs-esquire-interview-0703/.

[127] Seth Mnookin, "Universal's CEO Once Called iPod Users Thieves. Now He's Giving Songs Away," WIRED, November 27, 2007, https://www.wired.com/2007/11/mf-morris/.

[128] "US – Lenlease," Lendlease, https://www.lendlease.com/us/.

[129] "Proverbs 6:13," Bible Study Tools, https://www.biblestudytools.com/commentaries/gills-exposition-of-the-bible/proverbs-6-13.html.

[130] "Susan Wojcicki," Forbes, updated June 1, 2023, https://www.forbes.com/profile/susan-wojcicki/?sh=5e2a22b43ae3.

[131] "Susan Wojcicki," Wikipedia, https://en.wikipedia.org/wiki/Susan_Wojcicki.

[132] "Susan Wojcicki Leadership Style," StudySmarter, https://www.studysmarter.us/explanations/business-studies/business-case-studies/susan-wojcicki-leadership-style/.

[133] Kit Smith, "57 Fascinating and Incredible YouTube Statistics," Brandwatch, February 21, 2020, https://www.brandwatch.com/blog/youtube-stats/.

[134] Daniel Strauss, "Here's why one analyst thinks YouTube could be worth $300 billion as a standalone company, making it more valuable than AT&T, Exxon Mobil, and Bank of America," Business Insider, October 29,

2019, https://markets.businessinsider.com/news/stocks/youtube-value-as-separate-company-is-300-billion-analyst-says-2019-10-1028641059.

135 Courtney Connley, "YouTube CEO Susan Wojcicki: Here's what to say when men are talking over you at a meeting," CNBC, August 20, 2019, https://www.cnbc.com/2019/08/20/susan-wojcicki-what-to-say-when-men-are-talking-over-you-at-a-meeting.html.

136 Courtney Connley, "YouTube CEO Susan Wojcicki: Here's what to say when men are talking over you at a meeting," CNBC, August 20, 2019, https://www.cnbc.com/2019/08/20/susan-wojcicki-what-to-say-when-men-are-talking-over-you-at-a-meeting.html.

137 Courtney Connley, "YouTube CEO Susan Wojcicki: Here's what to say when men are talking over you at a meeting," CNBC, August 20, 2019, https://www.cnbc.com/2019/08/20/susan-wojcicki-what-to-say-when-men-are-talking-over-you-at-a-meeting.html.

138 "Susan Wojcicki Leadership Style," StudySmarter, https://www.studysmarter.us/explanations/business-studies/business-case-studies/susan-wojcicki-leadership-style/.

139 IntelligentHQ, "Seven Quotes By Susan Wojcicki, Google's Money Fairy," IntelligentHQ, https://www.intelligenthq.com/seven-quotes-by-susan-wojcicki/.

140 "Derek Jeter," Wikipedia, https://en.wikipedia.org/wiki/Derek_Jeter.

141 Joe Giglio, "Derek Jeter's Former Teammates Discuss His Leadership, Legacy and More," Bleacher Report, April 1, 2014, https://bleacherreport.com/articles/2012761-derek-jeters-former-teammates-discuss-his-leadership-legacy-and-more.

142 Ellen McGirt, "Bono: I Will Follow," Fortune, March 24, 2016, https://fortune.com/longform/bono-u2-one/.

143 "Let's work to end extreme poverty and preventable disease," ONE Campaign, https://www.one.org/us/.

144 Marina Hyde, "Bono: the celebrity who just keeps giving," The Guardian, September 23, 2010, https://www.theguardian.com/lifeandstyle/lostinshowbiz/2010/sep/23/bono-one-millennium-development-goals.

145 Alan McPherson, "U2's Activism: From Innocence to Experience," The Globalist, July 25, 2015, https://www.theglobalist.com/u2-activism-music-social-cause/.

146 Alan McPherson, "U2's Activism: From Innocence to Experience," The Globalist, July 25, 2015, https://www.theglobalist.com/u2-activism-music-social-cause/.

147 Wikipedia Contributors, "Presidency of Franklin D. Roosevelt: Presidency (1933-1945)," in Focus On: 100 Most Popular 20th-century American Politicians, https://books.google.com/books?id=EM5CDwAAQBAJ&pg=PA2011-

IA28&lpg=PA2011-IA28&dq=%22the+president+stayed+in+charge+of+
his+administration…by+drawing+fully+on+his+formal+and+informal+
powers+as+Chief+Executive;+by+raising+goals,+creating+momentum,+
inspiring+a+personal+loyalty,+getting+the+best+out+of+people.%22&source=
bl&ots=RB33MzcLX8&sig=ACfU3U33P8uQuAoR-4VzffIdzh5QB5pJxw&
hl=en&sa=X&ved=2ahUKEwi12KPu5s_7AhWVFFkFHfHQDi4Q6AF6BAg
GEAM#v=onepage&q=%22the%20president%20stayed%20in%20charge%
20of%20his%20administration…by%20drawing%20fully%20on%20his%
20formal%20and%20informal%20powers%20as%20Chief%20Executive%
3B%20by%20raising%20goals%2C%20creating%20momentum%2C%20
inspiring%20a%20personal%20loyalty%2C%20getting%20the%20best%20
out%20of%20people.%22&f=false.

[148] Heather R. Huhman, "Micromanagement Is Murder: So Stop Killing Your Employees," *Entrepreneur*, December 19, 2016, https://www.entrepreneur.com/leadership/micromanagement-is-murder-so-stop-killing-your-employees/
286333.

[149] "Larry D. Stone," Wilkes County Hall of Fame, 2017, https://wilkes countyhalloffame.org/hall-of-fame/2017-inductees/larry-stone.

[150] Michael Ray, "Stanley McChrystal," Britannica, https://www.britannica.com/biography/Stanley-McChrystal.

[151] "Stanley A. McChrystal," Wikipedia, https://en.wikipedia.org/wiki/Stanley_A._McChrystal.

[152] "Stanley A. McChrystal," Wikipedia, https://en.wikipedia.org/wiki/Stanley_A._McChrystal.

[153] Marilyn Haigh, "Retired Gen. Stanley McChrystal's advice to leaders: Be more humble," CNBC, October 30, 2018, https://www.cnbc.com/2018/10/30/retired-gen-stanley-mcchrystals-advice-to-leaders-be-more-humble.html.

[154] "Keith Krach," U.S. Department of State, https://2017-2021.state.gov/biographies/keith-krach/index.html.

[155] "About Overview," Keith Krach, https://keithkrach.com/about-overview/.

[156] "Keith Krach," U.S. Department of State, https://www.state.gov/biographies/keith-krach/

[157] John R. Miles, "Bold Leader Spotlight: Keith Krach, Transformational Leader," Bold Business, December 19, 2018, https://www.boldbusiness.com/human-achievement/bold-leader-spotlight-keith-krach-docusign-chairman/.

[158] Heather R. Morgan, "Entrepreneur Keith Krach Reveals His Secret Sauce for Creating Billion Dollar Companies," *Forbes*, February 25, 2019, https://www.forbes.com/sites/heathermorgan/2019/02/25/entrepreneur-keith-krach-reveals-his-secret-for-creating-billion-dollar-companies/?sh=78178d2c7476.

159 Keith Krach, "The Ariba Legacy Built-to-Last," Keith Krach, June 22, 2017, https://keithkrach.com/keith-articles/the-ariba-legacy-built-to-last/.

160 Keith Krach, "Turning Your Weaknesses into Strengths," Medium, March 21, 2019, https://medium.com/@KeithKrach/turning-your-weaknesses-into-strengths-904188a45bb1.

161 Heather R. Morgan, "Entrepreneur Keith Krach Reveals His Secret Sauce for Creating Billion Dollar Companies," Forbes, February 25, 2019, https://www.forbes.com/sites/heathermorgan/2019/02/25/entrepreneur-keith-krach-reveals-his-secret-for-creating-billion-dollar-companies/?sh=4347d1777476.

162 Keith Krach, "How Do You Make Your Weaknesses Your Strengths? Building High-Performance Teams," Forbes, September 19, 2018, https://www.forbes.com/sites/keithkrach/2018/09/19/how-to-make-weakness-your-strength-building-high-performance-teams/?sh=1db87b222f13.

163 Colette Bennett, "Elon Musk Admits He Was Late to Understand One Thing About Twitter," The Street, April 3, 2023, https://www.thestreet.com/technology/elon-musk-admits-he-was-late-to-understand-one-thing-about-twitter.

164 Marilyn Haigh, "Retired Gen. Stanley McChrystal's advice to leaders: Be more humble," CNBC, October 30, 2018, https://www.cnbc.com/2018/10/30/retired-gen-stanley-mcchrystals-advice-to-leaders-be-more-humble.html.

165 "The 7 Habits of Highly Effective People," FranklinCovey, https://www.franklincovey.com/the-7-habits/.

166 Melody Barnes & Paul Schmitz, "Community Engagement Matters (Now More Than Ever)," Stanford Social Innovation Review, Spring 2016, https://ssir.org/articles/entry/community_engagement_matters_now_more_than_ever.

167 "Immediate Return vs. Delayed Return Societies," P2P Foundation Wiki, https://wiki.p2pfoundation.net/Immediate_Return_vs._Delayed_Return_Societies.

168 John R. Miles and Gloria Mark, "The Art of Attention: Cultivating Focus in the Digital Age," podcast, Passion Struck, https://passionstruck.com/gloria-mark-the-power-of-attention/.

169 "Bluma Zeigarnik," Wikipedia, https://en.wikipedia.org/wiki/Bluma_Zeigarnik.

170 Sam Tabahriti, "Tim Cook says he monitors his Screen Time reports 'pretty religiously' – but doesn't say how long he spends using his iPhone," Business Insider, April 7, 2023, https://www.businessinsider.com/tim-cook-monitors-apple-iphone-screen-time-reports-pretty-religiously-2023-4#:~:text=Tim%20Cook%20told%20GQ%20magazine,his%20own%20Screen%20Time%20reports.

[171] Tim Cook, "Apple CEO Tim Cook: I use my phone too much," interview by Laurie Segall, CNN Business, June 2018, https://www.cnn.com/videos/business/2018/09/27/apple-ceo-tim-cook-smartphone-addiction.cnn-business.

[172] John R. Miles and Isa Watson, "Why Life Beyond Likes Is Finding Authentic Joy," podcast, *Passion Struck*, https://passionstruck.com/isa-watson-on-why-life-beyond-likes/.

[173] Boris Kotchoubey, "Human Consciousness: Where Is It From and What Is It For," *Frontiers in Psychology*, April 23, 2018, https://www.frontiersin.org/articles/10.3389/fpsyg.2018.00567/full.

[174] "Nikola Ilankovic," ResearchGate, https://www.researchgate.net/profile/Nikola-Ilankovic-2.

[175] Christopher James Davia, "Minds, Brains & Catalysis: A theory of cognition grounded in metabolism," ResearchGate, July 2014, https://www.researchgate.net/publication/264004162_Minds_Brains_Catalysis_A_theory_of_cognition_grounded_in_metabolism.

[176] Sue Patton Thoele, *The Courage to Be Yourself: A Woman's Guide to Emotional Strength and Self-Esteem* (Newburyport, MA: Conari Press, 2001), https://books.google.com/books?id=3XefEAAAQBAJ&pg=PT22&lpg=PT22&dq=Sue+Thoele+%E2%80%9DEmotional+dependence+is+the+opposite+of+emotional+strength.+It+means+needing+to+have+others+to+survive,+wanting+others+to+%E2%80%9Cdo+it+for+us,%E2%80%9D+and+depending+on+others+to+give+us+our+self-image,+make+our+decisions,+and+take+care+of+us+financially.+When+we+are+emotionally+dependent,+we+look+to+others+for+our+happiness,+our+concept+of+%E2%80%9Cself,%E2%80%9D+and+our+emotional+well-being.+Such+vulnerability+necessitates+a+search+for+and+dependence+on+outer+support+for+a+sense+of+our+own+worth.%E2%80%9D&source=bl&ots=IAeui7xV6F&sig=ACfU3U3tvKh_kv02RA7CRp79DrbX40zQRw&hl=en&sa=X&ved=2ahUKEwjdmfH8y8j-AhWjlGoFHVIiD-EQ6AF6BAgkEAM#v=onepage&q=Sue%20Thoele%20%E2%80%9DEmotional%20dependence%20is%20the%20opposite%20of%20emotional%20strength.%20It%20means%20needing%20to%20have%20others%20to%20survive%2C%20wanting%20others%20to%20%E2%80%9Cdo%20it%20for%20us%2C%E2%80%9D%20and%20depending%20on%20others%20to%20give%20us%20our%20self-image%2C%20make%20our%20decisions%2C%20and%20take%20care%20of%20us%20financially.%20When%20we%20are%20emotionally%20dependent%2C%20we%20look%20to%20others%20for%20our%20happiness%2C%20our%20concept%20of%20%E2%80%9Cself%2C%E2%80%9D%20and%20our%20emotional%20well-being.%20Such%20vulnerability%20necessitates%20a%20search%20for%20and%20dependence%20on%20outer%20support%20for%20a%20sense%20of%20our%20own%20worth.%E2%80%9D&f=false.

177 "Historical rankings of presidents of the United States," Wikipedia, https://en.wikipedia.org/wiki/Historical_rankings_of_presidents_of_the_United_States.

178 Biography.com Editors and Tyler Piccotti, "Abraham Lincoln," Biography.com, updated July 13, 2023, https://www.biography.com/political-figures/abraham-lincoln.

179 Eerdmans, "Abraham Lincoln's 'Doctrine of Necessity,'" Eerdword, July 1, 2017, https://eerdword.com/abraham-lincolns-doctrine-of-necessity/.

180 Tom Heyden, "The 10 greatest controversies of Winston Churchill's career," BBC News Magazine, January 26, 2015, https://www.bbc.com/news/magazine-29701767#sa-link_location=story-body&intlink_from_url=https%3A%2F%2Fwww.bbc.com%2Fnews%2Fmagazine-30934629&intlink_ts=1588275591558-sa.

181 John Simpson, "Winston Churchill: How a flawed man became a great leader," BBC News Magazine, January 23, 2015, https://www.bbc.com/news/magazine-30934629.

182 Kim Andreello, "How To Increase Employee Engagement," Rocketrip, March 19, 2021, https://rocketrip.com/employee-engagement/.

183 Rob Fletcher, "Winston Churchill was a bricklayer," At Your Best, Rob Fletcher's Blog, February 8, 2010, http://quixoteconsulting.com/Blog/2010/02/08/winston-churchill-was-a-bricklayer/.

184 Herbert G. Nicholas, "Winston Churchill: Leadership during World War II," Britannica, https://www.britannica.com/biography/Winston-Churchill/Leadership-during-World-War-II.

185 Austin Carr, "Solving Problems The Square Way," Fast Company, January 23, 2013, https://www.fastcompany.com/3004037/solving-problems-square-way.

186 Zameena Mejia, "Steve Jobs nearly kept Apple from inventing its most successful product: the iPhone," CNBC, updated September 12, 2018, https://www.cnbc.com/2018/08/03/apple-hit-1-trillion-but-steve-jobs-nearly-prevented-the-iphone.html.

187 Kendra Cherry, MSEd, "What Is Automaticity?" Verywell Mind, updated February 10, 2022, https://www.verywellmind.com/what-is-automaticity-2795018.

188 "What is the hardest mile of a marathon?" Ready.Set.Marathon., https://readysetmarathon.com/what-is-the-hardest-mile-of-a-marathon/.

189 Mark Twain, quote, Quote Investigator, https://quoteinvestigator.com/2011/09/29/you-did/.

190 John R. Miles, "Looking in the Mirror Is Vital to An Entrepreneur's Success," Entrepreneur's Handbook, October 5, 2020, https://entrepreneurshandbook.co/looking-in-the-mirror-is-vital-to-an-entrepreneurs-success-bafd221457ce.

191 John R. Miles, "Passion Struck: Practice Transformational Leadership," John R. Miles, January 14, 2020, https://johnrmiles.com/passion-struck-how-this-transformational-leadership-style-results-in-massive-success/.

192 John R. Miles and Marshall Goldsmith, "How You Create the Earned Life," podcast, *Passion Struck*, https://passionstruck.com/marshall-goldsmith-create-your-earned-life/.

193 John R. Miles, "Life Lessons Learned From Running," John R. Miles, January 18, 2020, https://johnrmiles.com/life-lessons-learned-from-running/.

194 "Toby Tanser," Linkedin, https://www.linkedin.com/in/toby-tanser/.

195 Ryne Nelson, "Inside Michael Jordan's Game-Day Routine During 'The Last Dance,'" *Slam*, May 20, 2020, https://www.slamonline.com/the-magazine/michael-jordan-gameday-routine/.

196 John R. Miles and Nate Dukes, "You'll Never Change Syndrome," podcast, *Passion Struck*, https://passionstruck.com/nate-dukes-you-will-never-change-syndrome/.

197 "Microstrategy Recognizes CIO of Lowe's Companies with Individual Excellence Award," Lowe's, January 24, 2007, https://corporate.lowes.com/newsroom/press-releases/microstrategy-recognizes-cio-lowes-companies-individual-excellence-award-01-24-07.

198 Forrest Wickman, "Minding Their Own Beeswax: How busy are bees, really?" *Slate*, June 19, 2012, https://slate.com/technology/2012/06/busy-as-a-bee-are-bees-really-busy.html.

199 C. Ronald Ribbands, *The Behaviour and Social Life of Honeybees* (Mineola, NY: Dover Publications, 1964), https://books.google.com/books/about/The_behaviour_and_social_life_of_honeybe.html?id=S40pAQAAMAAJ.

200 "Sea Turtle Migration," SEE Turtles, https://www.seeturtles.org/sea-turtle-migration.

201 "Sea Turtle Migration," SEE Turtles, https://www.seeturtles.org/sea-turtle-migration.

202 Taylor Locke, "Productivity tips from Elon Musk, Jeff Bezos and Steve Jobs," CNBC, updated November 24, 2020, https://www.cnbc.com/2019/09/11/productivity-tips-from-elon-musk-jeff-bezos-steve-jobs-and-more.html.

203 Mark Matousek, "Elon Musk said he slept on the floor of Tesla's factory because he wanted to suffer more than any other employee during Model 3 'production hell,'" Business Insider, July 12, 2018, https://www.businessinsider.com/elon-musk-said-he-slept-on-tesla-factory-floor-to-maximize-suffering-2018-7.

204 Nic Kocher, "Use Elon Musk's 12 Principles to Knock Out Your Biggest Creative Projects," Entrepreneur's Handbook, October 14, 2019, https://entrepreneurshandbook.co/use-elon-musks-12-principles-to-knock-out-your-biggest-creative-projects-9c4ccf851996.

205 "Commercial Orbital Transportation Services," NASA, https://www.nasa.gov/commercial-orbital-transportation-services-cots.

206 "SpaceX Stats," SpaceX, https://www.spacexstats.xyz/#launchhistory-per-year.

207 Michael Sheetz, "Elon Musk's sudden plan to take Tesla private complicates any possible SpaceX IPO," CNBC, updated August 10, 2018, https://www.cnbc.com/2018/08/09/musk-reportedly-no-longer-considering-spacex-ipo-plans.html.

208 Brett Tingley, "These 2 private companies aim to beat SpaceX to Mars with 2024 flight," Space.com, July 19, 2022, https://www.space.com/relativity-space-private-mars-mission-launching-2024.

209 Rina Torchinsky, "Elon Musk hints at a crewed mission to Mars in 2029," NPR, March 17, 2022, https://www.npr.org/2022/03/17/1087167893/elon-musk-mars-2029.

210 Aine Cain, "Bill Gates and Elon Musk share a daily scheduling habit that helps them tackle their busy routtimes," Business Insider, February 6, 2018, https://www.businessinsider.com/bill-gates-elon-musk-scheduling-habit-2017-8.

211 Joel Falconer, "How to Use Parkinson's Law to Get More Done in Less Time," LifeHack, updated March 17, 2023, https://www.lifehack.org/articles/featured/how-to-use-parkinsons-law-to-your-advantage.html.

212 Justin Bariso, Inc, "Elon Musk tries to avoid having meetings at Tesla – and encourages people to leave if they're not adding any value," Business Insider, updated March 10, 2020, https://www.businessinsider.com/elon-musk-3-rules-running-better-meetings-like-having-less-2019-8?r=US&IR=T.

213 Will Martin, "Video shows SpaceX rocket booster narrowly missing its platform and hitting the sea after 'the most difficult launch ever,'" Business Insider, June 25, 2019, https://www.businessinsider.com/video-spacex-rocket-crashes-into-sea-and-explodes-2019-6?r=US&IR=T.

214 Amit Katwala, "What's driving Elon Musk?" WIRED, September 8, 2018, https://www.wired.co.uk/article/whats-driving-elon-musk.

215 Andrew Chaikin, "Is SpaceX Changing the Rocket Equation?" Air & Space Magazine, Smithsonian Magazine, January 2012, https://www.smithsonianmag.com/air-space-magazine/is-spacex-changing-the-rocket-equation-132285884/.

216 Michael Simmons, "Elon Musk On His Biggest Failure," YouTube video, November 24, 2020, https://www.youtube.com/watch?v=3Pll3AjT3aQ.

217 Amit Katwala, "What's driving Elon Musk?" WIRED, September 8, 2018, https://www.wired.co.uk/article/whats-driving-elon-musk.

218 Max Roser, Esteban Ortiz-Ospina, and Hannah Ritchie, "Life Expectancy," Our World in Data, updated October 2019, https://ourworldindata.org/life-expectancy.

219 Faiz Siddigui, "Tesla lost $700 million in the first quarter with Model 3 problems," *Washington Post*, April 24, 2019, https://www.washingtonpost.com/technology/2019/04/24/tesla-lost-million-first-quarter-model-problems/.

220 Mark Matousek, "Elon Musk said he slept on the floor of Tesla's factory because he wanted to suffer more than any other employee during Model 3 'production hell,'" Business Insider, July 12, 2018, https://www.businessinsider.com/elon-musk-said-he-slept-on-tesla-factory-floor-to-maximize-suffering-2018-7?r=US&IR=T.

221 "Zip2," Wikipedia, https://en.wikipedia.org/wiki/Zip2.

222 Tom Huddleston Jr., "Elon Musk slept on his office couch and 'showered at the YMCA' while starting his first company," CNBC, June 19, 2018, https://www.cnbc.com/2018/06/19/how-elon-musk-founded-zip2-with-his-brother-kimbal.html.

223 Rebecca Webber, "Reinvent Yourself," *Psychology Today*, updated June 9, 2016, https://www.psychologytoday.com/us/articles/201405/reinvent-yourself.

224 Glenn Rifkin, "Andersen Consulting's Culture of 'Clones,'" *New York Times*, September 6, 1992, https://www.nytimes.com/1992/09/06/business/andersen-consulting-s-culture-of-clones.html.

225 "Manifesto for Agile Software Development," Manifesto for Agile Software Development, https://agilemanifesto.org/.

226 Rebecca Webber, "Reinvent Yourself," *Psychology Today*, updated June 9, 2016, https://www.psychologytoday.com/us/articles/201405/reinvent-yourself.

227 Ana Peres, "Highest-Grossing Stephen King Movies, Ranked by Box Office," MovieWeb, February 9, 2023, https://movieweb.com/top-stephen-king-movies-box-office/.

228 Theodore Roosevelt, quote, Goodreads, https://www.goodreads.com/quotes/312751-nothing-in-the-world-is-worth-having-or-worth-doing.

229 Rahul Venkat, "Michael Phelps: The man who dominated the Olympic pool like no other," Olympics, updated on June 27, 2023, https://olympics.com/en/news/michael-phelps-olympic-medals-record-how-many-gold-swimmer-world-record.

230 Catherine Clifford, "Olympic hero Michael Phelps says the secret to his success is one most people overlook," CNBC, February 14, 2017, https://www.cnbc.com/2017/02/14/olympic-hero-michael-phelps-says-this-is-the-secret-to-his-success.html.

231 Catherine Clifford, "Olympic hero Michael Phelps says the secret to his success is one most people overlook," CNBC, February 14, 2017, https://www.cnbc.com/2017/02/14/olympic-hero-michael-phelps-says-this-is-the-secret-to-his-success.html.

232 Rosa Parks, quote, BrainyQuote, https://www.brainyquote.com/quotes/rosa_parks_390344.

233 John R. Miles and Seth Godin, "How You Create the Song of Significance," podcast, *Passion Struck*, https://passionstruck.com/seth-godin-the-song-of-significance/.

234 Jacqueline Freeman, "Home - Spirit Bee," Spirit Bee, https://www.spiritbee.com/.

235 Kerri Walsh, quote, A-Z Quotes, https://www.azquotes.com/quote/873347.

ACKNOWLEDGMENTS

This book represents the culmination of an extraordinary fusion of ideas, extensive research findings, and meaningful collaborations. Along this transformative journey, my heart overflows with love and deep gratitude for the multitude of individuals who have been an unending source of inspiration, profoundly shaping my thoughts and directly contributing to the profound research explored within these pages.

While the list of deserving individuals surpasses the confines of this section, let us spotlight a select few whose impact has been immeasurable. First and foremost, my deepest thanks go to the enthusiastic and supportive librarians, booksellers, readers, and podcast listeners. Your engagement and encouragement have been invaluable. Special mention to those readers and listeners who reached out with questions, ideas, and resources, as your insights shaped this book in invaluable ways.

Passion Struck owes its very existence to the brilliant and unwavering Jill Marsal, my literary agent extraordinaire, and the incredibly discerning, patient, and empathetic Debra Englander, my editor at Post Hill Press, who championed this work from the outset. My heartfelt appreciation also extends to Madeline Sturgeon, Tiffany Alexander, and Ashlyn Inman from Post Hill Press, whose unwavering support and patience during countless hours of rewriting and editing have been invaluable. A special shout-out goes to Farrukh Bala for capturing my vision and breathing life into the book through his masterful cover design.

To all the readers who navigated through the unpolished versions of this manuscript, I am deeply grateful for your sharp insights, gentle feedback, and unwavering encouragement. Your contributions have transformed *Passion Struck* into its finest form, and I am thankful for each and every one of you.

I extend my sincere gratitude to Steve Allen, Jay Lombard, Dawna Stone, Nir Bashan, Dara Kurtz, Mark Borgner, Rob King, Dan O'Shea, John Doolittle, Tom Riley, and Matt Higgins for their unwavering friendship, mentorship, and support. Matt, in particular, I thank you for graciously penning the foreword, adding immeasurable value to this work.

The remarkable individuals I had the privilege to write about, quote, and interview have left an indelible mark on this book. My heartfelt thanks go to: Adam Grant, Aidan McCullen, Angela Duckworth, Art Markman, Benjamin Hardy, Bono, Bob Pennington, Brian Lowery, CAPT Chris Cassidy, CAPT Wendy Lawrence, Carol Dweck, Chris Gardner, Claude Silver, CDR Bill Fitzsimmons, Dandapani, Dan Schawbel, Dan Sullivan, Dara Kurtz, David Rubenstein, Derek Jeter, Elon Musk, Emily Morse, Ethan Kross, Gary Vaynerchuk, General David Petraeus, General Stan McChrystal, Gloria Mark, Gretchen Rubin, Hal Hershfield, Hilary Swank, Isa Watson, Jack Dorsey, Jay Skibinski, Jeff Bezos, Jeremy Utley, Jesse Iwuji, Jim Collins, Jim McKelvey, John Koko, Jonah Berger, Keith Krach, Kerri Walsh Jennings, Kirstie Ennis, Katy Milkman, Larry Page, Larry Stone, Lydia Fenet, Marc Benioff, Marianne Lewis, Mark Manson, Martin Seligman, Michael Dell, Michael Jordan, Michael Phelps, Michelle Segar, Natalie Fratto, Nate Dukes, Nikola Ilankovic, Novak Djokovic, Oprah Winfrey, Perry Klebahn, Rob Schaefer, Robin Sharma, Scott Neil, Seth Godin, Shonda Rhimes, Steven Kotler, Steve Maraboli, Steve Stone, Steve Szilagyi, Sue Thoele, Susan Wojcicki, Terri Cole, Thaddeus Bullard, Tim Cook, Toby Tanser, VADM Sandy Stosz, Wayne Hameloth, Wendy Smith, and William Damon. Your insights and wisdom have enriched this work beyond measure.

To all who have played a role, big or small, in bringing this book to fruition, I offer my heartfelt appreciation. Your support has been the driving force behind this labor of love.

In my journey, I owe an immense debt of gratitude to a remarkable group of individuals who have left an indelible mark on my work and content, including: Admiral James Stavridis, Admiral William McRaven, Andrew Huberman, Annie Duke, Ari Wallach, Arthur Brooks, Ayelet Fishbach, BJ Fogg, Bob Waldinger, Brene Brown, Cassie Holmes, Cathy Heller, Chip Heath, Colin O'Brady, Dacher Keltner, Dan Heath, Daniel Pink, D.J. Vanas, David Goggins, David Vago, David Yaden, Dolly Chugh, Dorie Clark, Douglas Rushkoff, Dr. Amy Shah, Dr. Kara Fitzgerald, Dr. Mark Hyman, Dr. Neeta Bhushan, Dr. Peter Diamandis, Dr. Will Cole, Emily Morse, Gay Hendricks, Gabby Bernstein, Gabor Mate, Hilary Billings, James Clear, Jay Shetty, Jay Van Bavel, Jeff Eggers, Jeff Struecker, Jeffrey Walker, Jen Bricker-Bauer, John List, Jordan Harbinger, Jordyn Feingold, Juliet Funt, Kris Carr, Lewis Howes, Lisa Honig, Marisa Franco, Mark Fortier, Matthew Walker, Max Bazerman, Mel Robbins, Michael Abrashoff, Michael Watkins, Nate Zinnser, Rachel Hollis, Ryan Holiday, Scott Barry Kauffman, Simon Sinek, Steven Konkoly, Susan Cain, Susan David, Tom Bileyeu, and Tony Robbins.

To my family, including my supportive parents, Jack and Betty, Aunt Pat, and Uncle Perry, I offer extraordinary gratitude for being my biggest cheerleaders, role models, and exemplars of living a passion-struck life. To Carolyn and Patrick, my remarkable siblings, I am filled with a profound appreciation for your unwavering support, accountability, and acceptance of my uniqueness. Your love means everything to me.

And to my loving partner, Cori Brodsky, I am forever grateful for you patiently listening to me talk about *Passion Struck* every day for over four years and never wavering in your support. Your love and encouragement have been my anchor throughout this journey. There is no one I admire more than you.

ABOUT THE AUTHOR

John R. Miles, a leading authority in intentional behavior change, personal growth, and mattering, is a beacon of inspiration and transformation. As a celebrated leader, captivating keynote speaker, and the host of the award-winning podcast "Passion Struck with John R. Miles," he's on a mission to help individuals unlock their untapped potential, challenge the status quo, and embark on a journey toward profound meaning and purpose. Recognized as one of the top thinkers in personal mastery and a Premier 100 Leader, his influence extends far and wide. His podcast consistently ranks among the world's top 100 shows, offering practical insights for those who aspire to live a life of significance. With over two decades of corporate and military leadership experience, he's the trusted advisor sought after by some of the world's most prominent companies and visionary startups. His leadership has been instrumental in generating billions in sales and advising multiple unicorn startups. Yet, beneath these remarkable achievements, John's true passion lies in guiding individuals to live a passion-struck life in every facet. His story, akin to his podcast, is an inspiring journey toward significance. John lives in Tampa, FL, and he's a proud parent to two accomplished adults.